Finding **Joy** in Teaching Students
of Diverse Backgrounds

Finding Joy
in Teaching Students
of **Diverse Backgrounds**

Culturally Responsive and Socially Just

Practices in U.S. Classrooms

SONIA NIETO

HEINEMANN
Portsmouth, NH

Heinemann
361 Hanover Street
Portsmouth, NH 03801–3912
www.heinemann.com

Offices and agents throughout the world

Library of Congress Cataloging-in-Publication Data
Nieto, Sonia.
    Finding joy in teaching students of diverse backgrounds : culturally responsive and socially just practices in U.S. classrooms / Sonia Nieto.
        pages cm
    Includes bibliographical references and index.
    ISBN 978-0-325-02715-9
1. Multicultural education—United States. 2. Minorities—Education—United States. I. Title.
    LC1099.3.N542 2013
    370.1170973—dc23   2013022679

Editor: Holly Kim Price
Production: Hilary Zusman
Cover and interior designs: Suzanne Heiser
Cover image: © Ocean/Corbis
Typesetter: Valerie Levy, Drawing Board Studios
Manufacturing: Steve Bernier

Printed in the United States of America on acid-free paper
21   20   VP   07   08   09

CONTENTS

Acknowledgments xi
Introduction xiii
Thriving Teachers, Diversity, and Change xiii
The Interviews xiv

PART I Recognizing the Current Context of Public Education

CHAPTER 1 Surviving in Today's Schools: Taking Stock of Where We Are 3

Federal Policy and the Marketization of Schooling 5

Sociopolitical Issues in Schools and Society 9
Societal Barriers 9
School Conditions 11
The Ideological Barrier 12

Students and Teachers in U.S. Public Schools 13
Teachers: Between a Rock and a Hard Place 14
Students in U.S. Public Schools: Change and Diversity 15

■ ***Conclusion:*** Context Always Influences Teaching 17

CHAPTER 2 Professional Development: Preparing for the Real World 19

Learning to Teach Students of Diverse Backgrounds 20

Teaching from a Social Justice Perspective 20
Defining Social Justice in Education 21
The Political Nature of Social Justice Teaching 21
Social Justice Pedagogy 22

Professional Development 23
Teacher Preparation Programs 24
Inservice Professional Development 25
Mentoring and Induction Programs 26
Teacher Collaboration 26

The Problem of Assessing Teacher Quality 27

■ ***Conclusion:*** What Does Professional Development Mean to Teachers? 29

PART II Profiles of Thriving Teachers

CHAPTER 3 It's *Whom* You Teach, Not Just What You Teach   33

Starting Where Kids Are At   34

Bringing Your Identity into the Classroom   35

Two Models of Caring   36
Angeles Pérez   36
Angeles's Approach   38
Roger Wallace   40
Roger's Approach   42

■ *Conclusion:* Teaching Is an Act of Love   44

CHAPTER 4 "If I Haven't Taught Them How to Be Good People, That's Failure":
Teachers' Perspectives on the Moral Dimensions of Teaching   47

Instilling Values of Empathy and Responsibility   48
Carmen Tisdale   48
Adam Heenan   49
Amber Bechard   51

Culturally Responsive Pedagogy   53
Carmen Tisdale   53
Amber Bechard   56
Adam Heenan   57

■ *Conclusion:* Teaching Is an Ethical Endeavor   59

CHAPTER 5 The Quest for Knowledge: Teacher Learning In and Out of the Classroom   60

Learning as a Lifelong Journey   61

John Nguyen   63
Self-Initiated Learning   64
Creating Curriculum Through Learning   64
Passing on a Passion for Learning   65

Alicia López   66
On-the-Job Learning   67
Learning Through Professional Organizations   69
Learning from and About Students   71

■ *Conclusion:* Teachers Thrive When They Keep Learning   73

CHAPTER 6 "I Hope I Can Become *That* Teacher":

Teaching to Honor Language and Culture 75

What's in a Name? Emergent Bilingual Students 76

Emergent Bilingual Students in the United States 77

The Loyola Marymount University Teachers 77

Replicating or Rewriting Their Autobiography 78

Making a Difference for Emergent Bilingual Students 80

Affirming Family and Community Resources 86

Disillusionment with the Current State of Public Education 88

■ **Conclusion:** Teaching Is Honoring Students' Identities and Believing

in Their Futures 90

CHAPTER 7 Teaching to Nurture Students' Dreams 92

Yolanda Harris 92

María Ramírez Acevedo 94

John Gunderson 96

Common Values in Diverse Settings 97

A Life of Service 97

Connecting with Students Through Shared Identities and Experiences 98

Questioning Conventions 102

■ **Conclusion:** Teaching Is Challenging the Status Quo 104

CHAPTER 8 Teaching as Social Justice and Advocacy 106

Social Justice Education: Different Contexts, Diverse Strategies 107

Stories of Social Justice Teachers 109

Geoffrey Winikur 109

María Federico Brummer 110

Hyung Nam 113

Social Justice in Practice 115

Social Justice and Curriculum 115

Social Justice and Pedagogy 117

Social Justice and Relationships 119

Social Justice and Courage 121

■ **Conclusion:** Teaching Is Advocacy 122

PART III Lessons Learned

CHAPTER 9 Teaching Students of Diverse Backgrounds: What Does It Take? 125

Teaching Is an Act of Love 126

Teaching Is an Ethical Endeavor 127

Teachers Thrive When They Keep Learning 128

Teaching Is Honoring Students' Identities and Believing in Their Futures 130

Teaching Is Challenging the Status Quo 132

Teaching Is Advocacy 134

■ *Conclusion:* Teachers Make a Difference 136

**CHAPTER 10 From Dispositions to Actions: Becoming Culturally
Responsive Teachers 137**

Enacting Values in the Classroom 138

Engaging in Critical Self-Reflection 139

Valuing Language and Culture 140

Insisting on High-Quality, Excellent Work from All Students 141

Honoring Families 142

Exemplifying a Commitment to Lifelong Learning 143

■ *Conclusion:* Living the Values of Social Justice 144

CHAPTER 11 From Surviving to Thriving: The Role of Hope in Teaching 145

What Does It Mean to Thrive? 146

Thriving Despite Anxiety, Insecurity, and Frustration 146

Diverse Perspectives on Thriving 147

Thriving as Learning and Renewal 148

Bringing Feeling Back into the Teaching Profession 148

Four Pieces of Advice 150

Learn About Yourself 150

Learn About Your Students 151

Cultivate Allies 152

Have a Life 154

Final Thoughts 155

Additional Resources 157

References 163

Index 173

ACKNOWLEDGMENTS

No book is written entirely by just one person, even if that person's name appears as the sole author. This truth is especially evident in a book that includes many collaborators. First, of course, I want to thank the teachers whose words are the backbone of this book. To a person, they were gracious and generous in telling their stories. Their motivations for beginning a life of teaching, their commitment to and love for their students of diverse backgrounds, and the fulfillment they find in teaching illuminate the book. I hope that my rendering of their stories has done them justice.

As you will see in reading their stories, there is no template for a thriving teacher. On the contrary, like their students, teachers are different from one another in many ways, including their identities, experiences, reasons for becoming teachers, and future plans. They organize their classrooms in different ways, and their approaches to teaching and even their teaching philosophies differ. What distinguishes them as a group is the realization that what they do every day matters.

I am indebted not only to those who recommended these fabulous teachers and the teachers themselves but also to those who helped transcribe some of the interviews: Andrea Callanan, from western Massachusetts, and Julia Martinelli, a resident of South Africa who I found when I was a visiting scholar at Witwatersrand University, in Johannesburg. Both spent many hours in what can be a tedious chore, but both told me that, although not teachers, they were inspired by the teachers' stories.

Besides the teachers who are featured in the book, numerous other teachers have provoked my learning and imagination over the years. These include many of the teachers with whom I've had the distinct privilege to work, as well as nationally known teachers who grace the pages of such publications as *Teaching Tolerance*, *Rethinking Schools* and many scholarly books and textbooks. Some of the following are in the first category, and some are in the second, while a few inhabit both the worlds of teaching and the academy. Most have taught in K–12 classrooms and some have written stirringly and cogently about both their triumphs and their frustrations. All of them have inspired me. They include Patty Bode, Kristen French, Jason Irizarry, John Raible, Mary Ginley, Bill Dunn, Mary Cowhey, Jennifer Welborn, Kerri Warfield, Junia Yearwood, Nina Tepper, Maury Bohan, Yahaira Marquez, Wilma Ortiz, Laila Di Silvio, Stephen Gordon, Beth Adel, Karen Gelzinis, Melinda Pellerin-Duck, Sonie Felix, Seth Peterson, Katina Papson, Judith Baker, Ayla Gavins, Claudia Bell, Anne Lundberg, Berta Berriz, Lizette Roman, David Ruiz, Elaine Stinson, Bob Amses, Sandra Jenoure, Ambrizeth Lima, Linda Christenson, Bob Peterson, Bill Bigelow, Wayne Au, Greg Michie, Ernest Morrell, Jeff Duncan-Andrade, Bill Ayers, Deborah Meier, Herb Kohl, Bob Fecho, Gerald Campano, among others too numerous to mention. I feel honored to have worked with all of them, either when they were classroom teachers or when they became academics, administrators, or full-time writers.

A word of thanks also goes out to David and Yvonne Freeman who first approached me about writing a book for Heinemann a number of years ago. I am grateful for their patience as they waited for me to have the time to interview, analyze, and write the book. Working with Holly Price, my editor at Heinemann, has been a joy, and Hilary Zusman and Sarah Fournier were tremendously helpful in the production process.

My silent partners in this endeavor are ever-present: my husband, Angel, our daughters Alicia, Marisa, and Jazmyne (our granddaughter/daughter), and our eleven other grandchildren, all of whom inspire me every day. My sister Lydia, a former teacher and currently a poet and writer, is one of my first and constant hero/mentors.

Writing a book about teachers is a daunting task. While not wanting to romanticize or misrepresent the work they do, I confess that I have a built-in bias for good teachers. They exemplify the best of our nation, our hopes and dreams for the future, and the belief that, in the end, as Dr. Martin Luther King, Jr. said, in paraphrasing the words of abolitionist Theodore Parker more than 150 years ago, "The arc of the moral universe is long, but it bends toward justice." As a teacher, teacher educator, mother, and grandmother, my hope is that this is indeed the case.

INTRODUCTION

Our society has undergone extraordinary changes in the past several decades, none more dramatic than the enormous increase in the diversity of our population. *What* teachers teach, *how* they teach, and *who* they teach have changed in innumerable ways. Teaching is, and has always been, hard work, but given the current demands of accountability and the accompanying deprofessionalization, it is more challenging than ever. Nevertheless, under conditions and in a context of respect and support, teaching is also tremendously rewarding and even life-changing, for both teachers and students.

These simple truths are what this book is about. In spite of their tremendous enthusiasm and commitment when they begin, many teachers are unprepared for the demands of teaching, particularly teaching students of diverse backgrounds in schools that are overlooked and under-resourced. It is no surprise that moments of joy and success may be hard to find. These teachers often end up exhausted and disillusioned and, in increasing numbers, leave the profession.

Thriving Teachers, Diversity, and Change

This book, however, is about teachers who thrive. They work in a variety of contexts: urban, suburban, and rural schools; elementary and secondary schools; struggling schools and successful schools. Some work with supportive colleagues and administrators; others, with colleagues and administrators who are less so. All of them feel the relentless pressures associated with inequality, standardization, and constant references to the "achievement gap." In spite of the difficult school and societal contexts in which they may work, these teachers find joy in teaching. All teach students of diverse backgrounds and they are good at it; they find their jobs fulfilling, even though on some days, like all teachers, they struggle. These teachers are not merely survivors; they are thriving in the profession and in their classrooms, and they make a difference in the lives of their students.

What is it that helps teachers thrive in the classroom, especially teachers who work in challenging situations? The question has intrigued me for some time, not only because of my own experience as a classroom teacher, but also because for many years, first at Brooklyn College and later at the University of Massachusetts, I taught aspiring and practicing teachers. Before becoming a teacher educator, I was first a middle school and then an elementary school teacher. Close family members—my husband, daughter, and sister—have also chosen this profession. I have had the great privilege of working with teachers for many years as mentor, colleague, teacher, and friend, and I am always inspired by those who retain the energy, enthusiasm, and commitment to their craft, their subject matter, and, of course, their students. But given the conditions in the profession today, many are leaving. I am saddened by those who leave because many of them were also caring and talented teachers, and it makes me wonder what we can do, as a society and a profession, to help the most talented teachers remain.

Don't think that thriving teachers are uniformly ecstatic every time they step foot in their class-room. They may not be consistently energetic and they are not Pollyannas unaware of the tremendous challenges in the profession. Several of the teachers I interviewed made it clear that they go through ups and downs just like all teachers, like people in all walks of life. María Ramirez could have been speaking for all thriving teachers when she said:

> *A thriving teacher is somebody who's there for the long haul, who believes in what she's doing, who is competent, who is effective with the children, and who loves the children she's teaching.*

Yet, on some days, even these teachers have their doubts and may question their effectiveness and stay-ing power. Nevertheless, as a group and in general, thriving teachers are hopeful people who are both pragmatic and visionary.

About the book's title: why "finding joy"? While there are certainly many teachers who love teaching students of diverse backgrounds, the title acknowledges that not all teachers, for a number of reasons, are joyful about doing so. They may know little about the students' backgrounds or harbor misconceptions about them. They may have had little experience with people different from themselves. They may be severely tested by the students. They may be afraid to teach in a particular neighborhood. Nevertheless, all teachers *can* find joy in teaching students of diverse backgrounds. It takes humility, a willingness to learn, an openness to acknowledging and valuing the tremendous assets of students of diverse backgrounds, and a commitment to public education.

The Interviews

Given my desire to find teachers who find joy in teaching students of diverse backgrounds, whenever I traveled to a conference, university, or school district to give a presentation, I would ask my host to recommend such a teacher. It didn't matter whether they were veteran teachers (Roger Wallace, for ex-ample, who had been teaching for more than thirty-seven years in Amherst, Massachusetts) or novice teachers (Angeles Pérez, in her second year of teaching in Dallas, Texas) or whether they taught kinder-garten or high school or any level in between. In a couple of instances, I interviewed teachers I knew and had worked with. This is how I came to interview Roger Wallace from my hometown and known as an exemplary teacher. Also, because I frequently hear testimonials from neighbors and her students and fellow teachers about what a great teacher she is, I included my daughter, Alicia Lopez, a teacher for seventeen years in our hometown middle school.

In all, I interviewed twenty-two teachers. I conducted a two-hour group interview with nine of them, graduate students in bilingual education at Loyola Marymount University. Dr. Magaly Lavadenz, director of the program, said she couldn't recommend just one because "they're all fabulous!" (They are featured in Chapter 6.) I conducted each individual interview (anywhere from one to three hours) in a hotel lobby, a restaurant, or a university or school classroom. I was inspired by these teachers' humility, stamina, and enthusiasm, and I am indebted to them for allowing me to tell their stories.

Interviews are an effective, close-up way of gaining a personal perspective. The teachers were able to reflect on their philosophy and practice, something they rarely have the time to do otherwise. They also had the chance to talk about what's important to them and why. Nonetheless, no research method is perfect. An interview reflects the perceptions and experiences of just one person. The people with whom a teacher interacts each day—students, colleagues, family members—might describe him or her quite differently. Interviews are also subjective. They are limited by what the interviewee chooses to disclose; no one wants everybody to know *everything*; everyone is likely to omit the most challenging, difficult, or embarrassing experiences. Still, most of the teachers were remarkably honest, sometimes putting themselves in a negative light in an effort to be totally open.

I used interviews primarily because teachers' voices are largely missing from current conversations and debates on public education. I knew they would share their stories of success and frustration, and these were the stories I wanted to hear. Gillian Maimon (2009) powerfully captures the significance of stories in today's sociopolitical context: "In the current climate of increased scripting of curriculum and reliance on high-stakes tests as mirrors of children's aptitudes, small stories from classrooms are emblems of resistance" (p. 217).

These "emblems of resistance" give us a different way of understanding both students and teachers. Rather than view students as what I have called "walking sets of deficiencies"—students who do not have two parents, speak English, or have books at home; students who do not get to go to museums or on vacation to mind-expanding places; and students whose parents do not have a formal education—thriving teachers recognize that all students, including students of diverse backgrounds, have assets that they bring with them to school, and they build on these assets.

In the pages that follow, I tell the stories of these teachers within the context of an educational system that, in too many cases, has gone terribly wrong: a system that has substituted test scores for learning, rigid standardization for high standards, and punitive accountability for social justice. In spite of these problems, the teachers highlighted here have found joy in teaching our most vulnerable and marginalized students.

NOTES

Maimon, G. 2009. 217.

Part I

Recognizing the Current Context of Public Education

What does it mean to be a teacher in the current sociopolitical context? Chapter 1 lays the groundwork by reviewing federal policy over the past three decades and what it has meant for teachers, students, and schools. The high-stakes testing culture resulting from an increased demand for accountability has led to teacher surveillance as well as punitive measures like closing schools and characterizing schools as "underperforming" and teachers as "unsatisfactory." These policies have created a climate of uncertainty and frustration among teachers and students and hold serious implications for public education, including narrowed curriculum, teacher deprofessionalization, and even fraud triggered by the intense pressure on teachers and schools to produce better test results.

The public at large is often confused about which of the many "solutions" offered for tackling the problems of underachievement and failure among students—charter schools, for-profit schools, others—are the best options. Chapter 1 also reviews research related to teachers' attitudes, beliefs, and staying power and discusses the nation's demographics, which have changed dramatically over the past century, especially in schools: students of diverse backgrounds are now the majority in most cities and even in many suburbs.

It is not simply federal policy that has changed schools so radically. Societal barriers such as structural inequality, lack of access to decent housing and meaningful employment, and poor health care are also in the mix. Stubborn ideologies concerning race, ethnicity, native language, social class, and other social differences also play a part in creating a context that makes it difficult for the most vulnerable students to be successful. Conditions in the schools themselves, from a lack of resources to uninteresting and mindless curriculum, among many other factors, also create a stifling climate for both teachers and students.

How teachers are prepared for the profession, and evaluated once they enter it, is the subject of Chapter 2. Teachers often feel unprepared to teach students of diverse backgrounds, students who are learning English as a second language, and students with special needs, even though more states are requiring (and colleges and universities are offering) courses to address these populations. What is often missing is teaching from a social justice perspective, a topic also addressed in this chapter.

Assessing teachers has become a hotly contested issue, as schools and states consider such approaches as merit pay and value-added assessments. This is discussed in Chapter 2 as well, along with what professional development should ideally be.

Chapter 1

Surviving in Today's Schools

Taking Stock of Where We Are

Novice teachers who join the profession with enthusiasm and high hopes may not be prepared for what they find when they first enter a classroom: rigid and unquestioned insistence on standardized tests as the arbiters of excellence, unparalleled surveillance of teachers' work, a dizzying array of mandates to reach AYP (Annual Yearly Progress), and as a result an oftentimes joyless environment. While these things have all become "normal" parts of schooling, they do not define what schools should or can be. Before the present-day push for inflexible accountability and standardization, a push that began in earnest with the publication of *A Nation at Risk* (National Commission of Excellence in Education 1983), most schools were quite different.

> *When a novice teacher is in the snare of a toxic, dysfunctional system, the system will win every time.*
>
> —Joan Richardson
> (2009, p. 4)

Now please do not misunderstand me: I don't mean to imply that there was ever an idealized era in which all schools worked flawlessly, all students were successful learners, and all classrooms were staffed by caring, sensitive, and competent teachers. Given the history of public education as well as the dismal experience of many students in our public schools, especially immigrants, students of color, and students living in poverty, such a claim would be disingenuous. These are for the most part the students who have been least well served by our public schools. This is a major reason we find ourselves in the current predicament, precisely because too many youngsters are left behind, cheated out of the equal education to which they are entitled. That the parents and advocates of these children should demand more is no surprise. They know their children deserve more, and they expect no less.

However, their demands have largely either fallen on deaf ears or led to what we have today: teaching to the test, more scripted curricula, the firing of teachers, and the wholesale closing down of schools.

But demands from communities poorly served by public schools are not the only, or even the major, reason for the current obsession with accountability and standardization. Forces more sinister and self-serving than powerless parents are also at play, including big business interests, conservative think tanks and foundations, and educational testing companies. Chief among the critics of public education spearheading the current reform efforts have been those who believe that schools should be treated like any other free-market business. As a result, vouchers, charter schools, and other privatization schemes are the order of the day. The number of children in charter schools more than *quadrupled* between 1999–2010 (Aud et al. 2012). The historic role of public schools—to prepare young people for productive lives in a civil society—although never fully realized by any measure has been all but overshadowed by the modern fixation on accountability and marketization. In too many cases, such policies result in lifeless, dreary schools with unmotivated students and anxious teachers.

This situation is eloquently described in *A Declaration of Professional Conscience for Teachers*, written by Kenneth Goodman in 1990, and it is even truer today. Goodman states, in part:

> There are strong pressures today to dehumanize, to depersonalize, to industrialize our schools. In the name of cost effectiveness, of efficiency, of system, of accountability, of minimal competency, of a return to the basics, schools are being turned into sterile, hostile institutions at war with the young people they are intended to serve.

The tendency to treat schools as if they were simply another business is not new, as we see in the following quotation from a 1912 edition of *The American Teacher*:

> We have yielded to the arrogance of "big businessmen" and have accepted their criteria of efficiency at their own validation, without question. We have consented to measure results of educational efforts in terms of price and product—the terms that prevail in the factory and the department store. But education, since it deals in the first place with human organisms, and in the second place with individualities, is not analogous to a standardizable manufacturing process. Education must first and foremost measure its efficiency not in terms of so many promotions per dollar of expenditure, nor even in terms of so many student-hours per dollar of salary, it must measure its efficiency in terms of increased humanism, increased power to do, increased capacity to appreciate (Gruenberg 1912, p. 90).

A more recent critic, Henry Giroux (2010), besides being disdainful of the education-as-business metaphor, also condemns what he has called "the triumph of management over leadership" that perpetuates a situation that "increasingly relies on punishment models of governance when dealing with teachers and unions while simultaneously using harsh disciplinary measures against those students viewed as disposable because they are poor, black, or viewed as flawed learners."

It is not my purpose to provide a comprehensive review of the troubling story of current federal education policies, but a brief review helps us understand how such policies are wreaking havoc on the lives of students, teachers, and the educational system as a whole, and envision another kind of education, one that is joyful and liberatory.

Federal Policy and the Marketization of Schooling

Using the civil rights–like discourse of challenging "the soft bigotry of low expectations," President George W. Bush in 2002 promoted the passage of No Child Left Behind (NCLB), a federal law that was to change dramatically how education was viewed, funded, and assessed. NCLB was followed by Race to the Top (RttT), a policy proposed by President Obama a decade later yet surprisingly similar to NCLB in its punitive character and reliance on standardized test scores. Although it is true that countless children have suffered the consequences of "the soft bigotry of low expectations," the proposed remedy, in the minds of many teachers, parents, scholars, and the public, has worsened the problem. Rather than more meaningful teacher education and professional development, smaller classes, better pay for teachers, and more resources for poor schools, NCLB and RttT put in place an unparalleled program of mandated standardized tests that has significantly changed the nature of teaching and learning for millions of teachers and students around the nation. Most notably affected have been students in under-resourced schools and the teachers who work with them.

The newest federal government mandate is the Common Core State Standards (CCSS), adopted by all but a few states even before the standards were complete. The Common Core is supposed to address the lack of rigor and quality of the texts students currently read. By concentrating on depth rather than breadth, it is meant to create a more demanding curriculum comprising both fiction and nonfiction texts, encourage collegial pedagogical and curricular conversations, give writing a more central role in the curriculum, and most important, discourage teaching to the test. Many teachers, administrators, professional organizations, and policymakers have endorsed these goals.

Although the Common Core has the potential to raise expectations for student learning and enhance the quality of the curriculum, it comes with several potentially troubling problems. One is the claim that it will raise student achievement. Yet, according to a recent study by Joshua Goodman (2012) at Harvard's John F. Kennedy School of Government, changes to state standards over the past twenty years have had little, if any, impact on student achievement. Goodman found that from 1994 to the present, standards have not been linked to student growth except in relation to eighth graders in schools characterized by ineffective teaching. He concludes, "Little is known . . . about how the quality of written standards translates into improvements in curriculum, pedagogy, and student achievement" (p. 1). This is a cautionary tale about rushing headlong into unproven policies.

Another problem is that the Common Core will be accompanied by a slew of new tests, expected to be in full use by the 2014–15 school year. More grades will be tested and there will be more tests per grade. Whether the tests will be better or more relevant than current tests is debatable. According to FairTest, the new tests are "a mixed bag, only marginally better than other tests" (The National Center for Fair and Open Testing 2012a, n.p.). In any case, their effects may be just as detrimental as previous testing programs, because states may continue to use student scores to evaluate both school and teacher effectiveness. The tests will also be expensive: a study about the potential costs of implementing the Common Core found that while test-development costs will be covered by the federal government, states will probably incur over $10 billion in one-time costs in preparing teachers for the new standards, buying new textbooks and other materials aligned with the standards, and upgrading technology (Accountability Works 2012). All this at a time when states are increasingly facing other unfunded mandates.

In a critique of the Common Core, Thomas Newkirk (2013) has made a number of serious allegations about its purported goals, design, implementation, and possible outcomes. First, he finds an inherent conflict of interest, because the testing companies engaged to write the standards (the College Board and ACT) also intend to design tests to accompany the standards. Newkirk asserts this is comparable to asking pharmaceutical companies to write health standards. Also, the Common Core will be a bonanza for publishing companies, who can now "align" their products with the standards, a process that has already begun. While one of the problems that the standards are supposed to tackle is that reading texts are not complex enough, Newkirk suggests that the Common Core will exacerbate the problem, explaining that it has taken the top five percent of students "and made it the new norm," thus creating unrealistic expectations and more blame for teachers and schools (p. 2).

Another of Newkirk's criticisms is that while one of the goals of the Common Core is to help the U.S. catch up with nations such as Finland and Singapore in student achievement, those countries do not use standardized tests in the same ways we do. He poses a thoughtful question: "Are standardized tests compatible with the more complex goals of twenty-first century literacy?" (p. 4). His response is that standardized tests are not suitable for assessing such skills as expressive abilities, speaking, writing, interpersonal skills, and creativity in general, all of which will be sorely needed in the coming years in our postindustrial economy. Wayne Au, who has written persuasively on the dangers of the marketization of education (2009), is also wary of the direction the Common Core seems to be taking, particularly with regard to the social studies. Claiming that it will inevitably lead to standardized high-stakes tests similar to those associated with NCLB, Au worries that the seeming flexibility it provides will disappear once the tests appear (2013).

Diane Ravitch (2013), an influential voice against high-stakes testing, has also come out against the Common Core: "I have come to the conclusion that the Common Core standards effort is fundamentally flawed by the process by which they have been foisted upon the nation." First, because most states accepted the Common Core as a condition for receiving Race to the Top funding, she believes little thinking has gone into the standards' implementation. In addition, she strongly believes that the standards should be thoroughly reviewed and tested before being implemented and free of any mandates that teach teachers how to teach, because "there are many ways to be a good teacher, not just one." In addition, the standards were neither a grassroots effort nor developed by the states, but rather by two organizations generously funded by the Gates Foundation, Achieve, and the National Governors Association. And like Newkirk, Ravitch also believes that, given the arbitrary cutoff scores, the implementation of the CCSS will see a precipitous decline in test scores.

Despite these powerful and commonsensical critiques of the Common Core, teachers, school systems, and other educational organizations around the country are looking for ways to make the CCSS more meaningful and less restrictive than former standards. Although particular texts are recommended by the Common Core, there are no mandated texts. However, the standards *do* recommend an approach for *how* texts should be selected. At the same time, publishing companies are jumping on the bandwagon and developing texts to go along with the CCSS. In many cases principals and school districts have ordered only those texts recommended by the CCSS, which seems contrary to their stated purpose.

Still, since specific texts are not required but only recommended, the Common Core may be more flexible than mandates like NCLB. For example, Teaching Tolerance (TT), a project of the Southern Poverty Law Center (SPLC) "dedicated to reducing prejudice, improving intergroup relations and supporting equitable school experiences for our nation's children" (tolerance.org) believes that the Common Core offers a good opportunity to embed culturally responsive texts and strategies into instruction. They believe that *what* texts students read is just as significant as *how* they read these texts (a major stated goal of the CCSS). Consequently, Teaching Tolerance is working on *Perspectives for a Diverse America,* a free web-based anti-bias K–12 literacy curriculum that pairs the relevance of multicultural content with the rigor of the Common Core standards (see http://www.tolerance.org /magazine/number-43-spring-2013/perspectives). *Perspectives* maintains the CCSS approach to text complexity and fiction/nonfiction ratio and improves on that approach by adding criteria for selecting texts that reflect the diversity of the students and families in our nation.

We can only hope that the Common Core will result in better outcomes than either the NCLB or RttT and that policymakers will not once again blame students and teachers for the longstanding and intractable problems of poverty, racism, and structural inequality. Unfortunately, our national testing policies have not led to the promised results. In too many cases high-stakes testing has led to cheating, fraud, unhealthy competition, higher dropout rates, a constricting of the curriculum, and a decline in creative pedagogy (see, for example, *How Standardized Testing Damages Education,* National Center for Fair and Open Testing, 2012b). To top it all off, student achievement has not been noticeably improved. A review by the Center on Education Policy (2010) found that although there has been some progress in narrowing reading and math gaps, it has been uneven. Gaps by race, ethnicity, and income have remained significant and persistent. An especially damaging report from the National Center for Education Statistics (2011) found that the "achievement gap" between Latino/a and White students has been unchanged for *two decades*. In addition, there has been a decided drop in teacher resilience and resolve to remain in the profession. (For incisive and comprehensive critiques on these and other consequences of NCLB and RttT, see Au 2009; Darling-Hammond 2010; Nichols & Berliner 2007; Ravitch 2012. Also see information about the impact of high-stakes tests from the National Center for Fair and Open Testing, FairTest, 2012b & 2012c.)

Given this damaging context, we ask a great deal of teachers if we expect them to be joyful, professionally fulfilled, and committed to their students. Greg Michie (2012), a talented teacher and writer who returned to the classroom after twelve years in teacher education, eloquently describes what the transition back to a public school was like. Although he returned to the classroom because that is where his heart is and he had frequently returned to schools to observe student teachers, he was unprepared for the often invisible destructive effects of tests on a school's culture, including eliminating or reducing recess in order to keep the school quiet, and, when tests are web-based, severely limiting the use of computers for other students (Michie, 2012).

Since the passage of NCLB, teachers and students have found themselves in the crosshairs of educational policy, and they have been its greatest victims. What was once viewed as a noble albeit poorly compensated profession is now vilified by many in the general public. Teachers are blamed for everything from students' low test scores to their bad behavior. This is both grossly inaccurate and eminently unfair. Although there are certainly incompetent and uncaring teachers everywhere, the vast majority of teachers are hard-working, competent, and caring. Students too, especially the most vulnerable, are blamed for their failure to learn, with little mention of the meager resources and lack of opportunities in crumbling schools. Instead of doing something about the school, state, and national policies and practices that have largely caused these problems—including poverty and the lack of adequate health care, housing, and employment—the tendency has been to focus exclusively on the perceived shortcomings of teachers and students.

A graphic example of the blame game is the ubiquitous term *achievement gap* that has found its way into every debate over the deficiencies of public education. The term is used as if students alone were responsible for their failure to learn, while little attention has been paid to the context in which this failure occurs. Jacqueline Irvine (2010) has suggested that instead of focusing on the "achievement gap," we shift the focus to "the teacher quality gap; the teacher training gap; the challenging curriculum gap; the school funding gap; the digital divide gap; the wealth and income gap; the employment opportunity gap; the affordable housing gap; the health care gap; the nutrition gap; the school integration gap; and the quality childcare gap" (p. xii). Until such gaps are addressed, achievement differentials will remain significant.

Linda Darling-Hammond (2010) too has suggested that in contrast to the attention given to the "achievement gap," we focus instead on opportunity gaps, that is, "the accumulated differences in access to key educational resources—expert teachers, personalized attention, high-quality curriculum opportunities, good educational materials, and plentiful information resources—that support learning at home and at school" (p. 28). Such opportunity gaps are the result of inequality created and sustained in schools and society, and exacerbated by the current sociopolitical context.

Sociopolitical Issues in Schools and Society

To understand how we have reached the point where all the responsibility for failing schools seems to fall on students and teachers, we first need to understand the various barriers that get in the way of an equal education, including the most impenetrable barrier to equitable schools: the ideological one.

Societal Barriers

Societal barriers to equal education have existed since the beginning of what is now the United States. These barriers have been created and kept in place through various means: the denial of state-supported education to enslaved Africans and American Indians; racial segregation, either by the enforcement of Jim Crow laws in the South, as in the case of African Americans, or by tradition and legal obstacles, as in the case of Mexican Americans and some Asian Americans in the South and Southwest; residential housing patterns in the North and Midwest that kept children of diverse backgrounds in inferior schools; and unequal opportunities for a high-quality education by either separating children from their families, as in the case of Native Americans forcibly removed to boarding schools, or by offering substandard schooling that prepared students of numerous ethnic backgrounds for little more than menial labor. (For discussions of inequality in education in the United States, see Spring 2013 and Nieto 2005a.)

The legacy of such societal barriers lingers, however. Although racial segregation is no longer permitted by law, many barriers remain in place through policy, practice, and tradition. A recent report from the Civil Rights Project at UCLA, for instance, found that in spite of the nation's gains in integrating public schools from the 1960s to the 1980s, segregation has returned with a vengeance. Moreover, racial segregation is increasingly accompanied by segregation of the social classes, and this "double segregation" is having an enormously negative impact on African American and Latino/a students, who are more likely to attend impoverished and racially segregated schools. Black students still face tremendously high segregation, particularly in the South, while Hispanics now attend the most segregated schools in generations in terms of both ethnicity and resources. The report concludes that segregation is closely and systematically linked with unequal educational opportunities. According to the study's authors, "The consensus of nearly sixty years of social science research on the harms of school segregation is clear: separate remains extremely unequal" (Orfield et al. 2012, p. 7). Another recent report, this one from the Center for American Progress, found that a "comparability loophole" in federal district policy, not just differences in property taxes, leads to local district budgeting policies that create and sustain inequality. According to the report, "we are living in a world in which schools are patently unequal" (Spatig-Amerikaner 2012, p. 1).

The problem is deep-seated, and solving it requires redistributing resources and carefully rethinking policies that unfairly benefit some students at the expense of others. Current "reforms," however, focus on policies that have done little to remedy the situation: more testing, taking over failing schools, firing teachers indiscriminately, chartering more schools, setting up shortcuts to teacher accreditation, and hiring enthusiastic but poorly prepared teachers through such programs as Teach for America.

Equal education is more a political problem than an educational one. It is not simply a matter of firing teachers, giving students more tests, or providing poor families with vouchers for private schools. According to economist Richard Rothstein (2004), the quality of a school explains only about a *third* of the variation in student achievement. The remainder is explained by factors such as poverty, lack of quality preschool and afterschool programs, and inadequate employment, health care, and housing. These "out-of-school factors" also include poor nutrition, unhealthy neighborhoods, and limited prenatal care, among others (Berliner 2009). Without these resources, many children living in poverty are doomed not just to educational failure but also to a life of diminished possibilities. In a more recent blog, Rothstein (2011) asserts that current nonschool factors such as the economic downturn, a weak labor outlook, and high unemployment will have an even greater impact on education than do school factors. He writes: "I make a discouraging prediction: academic achievement gaps between advantaged children and the various categories of disadvantaged children will grow in coming years, and education policy will be powerless to prevent this." In the same vein, Jean Anyon (2005) has explained that "macroeconomic policies like those regulating the minimum wage, job availability, tax rates, federal transportation, and affordable housing create conditions in cities that no existing educational policy or urban school reform can transcend" (p. 2).

Eliminating poverty is a tall order but it is clear that more can be done. Stephen Krashen, speaking about the impact of poverty on student learning in a 2011 commencement address at Lewis and Clark University, suggested that rather than focus on improving teacher quality, as the federal government has done, the best way to improve learning is to reduce poverty. He cautioned:

> The fact that American students who are not living in poverty do very well shows that there is no crisis in teacher quality. The problem is poverty. . . . [T]he best teaching in the world will have little effect when students are hungry, are in poor health because of inadequate diet and inadequate health care, and have low literacy development because of a lack of access to books.

Going a step further, a report from the Children's Defense Fund (2012) warns of the sobering future that awaits African American and Latino boys: unless dramatic changes in education and the opportunity structure are made, an African American boy born in 2001 has a one in three chance of going to prison in his lifetime, a Latino boy one in six. The report also points out the high cost of poverty: "Every year we maintain current poverty levels costs us $500 billion a year in lost productivity" (p. 2). Linda Darling-

Hammond's analysis of the inequality of school funding (2010) is a good example of the old dictum "penny wise and pound foolish": "States that would not spend $10,000 a year to ensure adequate education for young children of color spend $30,000 a year to keep them in jail" (p. 24).

It should come as no surprise that poverty has an enormous impact on student learning, on school conditions, and on the general quality of life of our nation. According to the U.S. Census Bureau, forty-six million Americans, or one in six, are living below the federal poverty rate, the highest number in our history (DeNavas-Walt et al. 2011). The Children's Defense Fund (2012) states it even more starkly: *children under five are the poorest age group in the nation.* At the international level, the United States also fares poorly: the Organization for Economic Development and Cooperation (2011) found that our nation has the highest overall poverty rate and the highest childhood poverty rate of any major industrialized nation in the world. Even more disturbing, in the past three decades the wealthiest Americans made the most income gains of any group: the richest one percent made an average $1.3 million after-tax dollars, compared with $17,700 for the poorest 20 percent.

It is unfortunate, given these realities, that the blame game continues to be used against children living in poverty. A prime example is the work of Ruby Payne (2005), an educator whose self-published book on poverty has sold well over a million copies and whose ideas have spread around the country through thousands of professional development seminars. Using a framework that emphasizes a deficit view of children and families living in poverty, Payne's work is a salve to school systems and teachers eager to find a cultural explanation for why students fail. If it's part of students' "culture," these educators may reason, then there is little they can do about it. Paul Gorski (2008), in a thorough review of Payne's work, has countered that Payne fails to base her approach on creditable research, while also failing to acknowledge the root causes of poverty. In addition, Mistilina Sato and Timothy Lensmire (2009) suggest that teachers can challenge the misinformation on poverty by emphasizing students' competence, focusing on teachers' cultural identities, and developing a professional development model based on ongoing collaborative work among teachers.

Children living in poverty face an uphill battle to obtain a decent education. Teachers who work in overcrowded and poorly resourced schools characterized by low morale also pay a price. In these circumstances, it is easy to understand how they struggle to find joy in teaching.

School Conditions

Anyone who has stepped foot in a school with guards and metal detectors at the door, filthy and nonfunctioning bathrooms, overcrowded classrooms, as well as few books, computers, and other resources, knows that the physical environment influences learning. The physical condition of a school also affects its emotional environment. Are there aesthetically pleasing plants, posters, and welcoming signs? Is there respect for parents and families of different cultures? Do they feel welcome? Are there signs in various languages and is the staff friendly? These things make a tremendous difference in how schools are experienced by those who work and learn there as well as by visitors.

While the condition of a school alone does not determine whether students and teachers are engaged or disaffected, it is hard to imagine being enthusiastic and productive in a depressing environment. Well-resourced public schools and elite private schools seem opulent by comparison, with expanded curricular choices, smaller classes, rich resources (books, libraries, computer labs), music and art instruction, large athletic fields, and many opportunities to participate in a variety of sports and other extracurricular activities.

A school's emotional environment is even more vital. Whether schools are open or forbidding, friendly or unwelcoming, joyful or fearful, largely depends on the policies and practices enacted in a school as a whole and in particular classrooms. Negative policies and practices include unfair disciplinary policies, unequal distribution of services such as special education and classes for the gifted and talented, poor access to high-level curriculum, high rates of retention, and inadequate outreach to families, among others. As one more example, many schools have cut back on music and art in spite of research revealing that exposure to the arts is tied not only to emotional well-being but also to higher student achievement in mathematics and reading (Americans for the Arts 2010). And students in poorly resourced schools and communities are often afraid to walk to school and, once in school, remain afraid for their safety. How can learning take place in this situation?

The Ideological Barrier

Conventional wisdom rules much of what happens in public education. Our received ideas about students and their intelligence, capabilities, and learning potential often have more to do with ideology than with science, research, or reality. Two of the most damaging (and unfounded) societal ideologies are that students' social and cultural identities and backgrounds determine their intelligence and ability, and that intelligence is fixed and unchanging. These ideologies find their way into school policies and practices through the actions of educators, administrators, and policymakers. Students themselves may come to believe negative perceptions about their identities and abilities. It is also unfortunately true that racism is still a fact of life in the United States. A recent poll by the Associated Press found that racist attitudes have *increased* slightly since Barack Obama was elected as the first Black president of our nation. Specifically, 51 percent of Americans expressed prejudice toward Blacks whether they recognize these feelings or not. Most Americans (57 percent) also express anti-Hispanic attitudes (Ross & Agiesta 2012).

Biases and stereotypes about race, ethnicity, and social class affect everyone, even the most well intentioned, and unless teachers and administrators make a concerted effort to face and change these biases, they may unintentionally act on them. This can lead to what Patty Bode and I have referred to as "the expectations gap" (Nieto & Bode 2012, p. 13), that is, the expectation that students will perform based on others' perceptions of their backgrounds rather than on their true ability. It is by now a well-known and amply documented fact that African American and Latino/a students living in poverty are recommended by their teachers for gifted and talented programs in far lower numbers than White and Asian students are, even though the former may be just as gifted. The same is true of placement in AP and honors courses in high schools. Conversely, students of color are far more likely to be placed in special education than are their peers (Oakes 2005; Harry & Klingner 2006), fulfilling what Alfredo Artiles (2011) has termed "the racialization of ability." This kind of tracking often results in permanent placements that are almost impossible to change as the years pass, even if they have been made on the flimsiest of evidence.

It is worth keeping in mind that nonacademic factors play a role in tracking: whether a child speaks English or not, and among those who do speak English, whether they speak Standard English or Ebonics; whether a child is obedient and well-behaved or not; the social skills of the student; and the like. Unless students have parents who are well versed in school policy, speak English fluently (and understand educational jargon), and feel comfortable in confronting school officials about these inequities, the situation remains unchanged.

Limiting ideologies are also the foundation for assumptions about families and whether or not they are interested and involved in their children's education. Parents who do not attend parent-teacher meetings or accompany students on class trips may be seen as indifferent even though any number of other reasons—lack of child-care, lost pay if work is missed, discomfort about visiting schools because of their own negative experiences as students—may be at work.

Another policy influenced by ideology is the curricular offerings available to students. Well-resourced schools with middle-class students typically have a broader range of course options than do poor schools, even though the students who attend the latter schools may be just as able and intelligent as their middle-class peers. Yet the kinds of courses students take, especially in high school, have a direct relationship to how prepared they will be for college. Too many students who attend poorly resourced schools are not only deprived of the option of taking particular courses but may be unaware (because of the lack of counseling services available to them) that certain courses are essential for postsecondary education. When senior year rolls around, young people who thought they might be going to college are left with few options for doing so.

Because they are based on deficit perceptions about what students are capable of accomplishing, it is evident that negative ideologies get in the way of student learning. Unless these ideologies are confronted at both the individual and institutional levels, little is likely to change. However, as pointed out in the previous section, negative ideologies alone are not responsible for the dismal state of public education for the most vulnerable populations. Taken together, social and school conditions and negative perceptions and expectations of students are a poisonous brew that gets in the way of the nation's stated ideals of equal education.

Students and Teachers in U.S. Public Schools

The ability of teachers to influence student learning has been proven time and again, not only through anecdotal evidence (who among us have not had a teacher who changed our life in positive or negative ways?), but also through research (see Nieto 2003 and 2005b). Given the current context in which many teachers work, it might be hard for them to believe that they hold tremendous power, in fact wield more power over the lives and learning of children than almost anyone or anything else. As far back as 1978, researchers found positive and long-term effects of first-grade teachers on the adult success of disadvantaged students, an impressive finding given the obstacles with which many of these students cope every day (Pederson 1978). A frequently cited report from 1996 states that "what teachers know and do is one of the most important influences on what students learn" (National Commission on Teaching and America's Future 1996). A more recent study by Spyros Konstantopoulos and Vicki Chung (2011) finds that the cumulative effects of high-quality teachers on students' lives are considerable and that their influence persists through the elementary grades. Even more conclusive, Caroline Chauncey's review of the research on the issue (2005) finds that teacher quality has far more of an impact on student learning than class size, per-pupil spending, students' socioeconomic backgrounds, or previous academic performance. This is powerful evidence that teachers, in spite of the current sociopolitical context, can make an enormous difference in the lives of their students.

Teachers: Between a Rock and a Hard Place

There are currently over 3.5 million teachers in U.S. public schools. A large majority (approximately 84 percent) are women, and about the same percentage are White (Aud 2010). A MetLife survey conducted in 2010 found that a majority of teachers (59 percent) were satisfied with teaching as a career and three-quarters of them said they wanted to continue to work in education beyond retirement. Within this rosy picture, however, 50 percent of teachers in urban schools were less satisfied with teaching as a career, and newer teachers were less satisfied than veteran teachers. One explanation may be that a substantial majority of teachers (69 percent) felt that teachers' voices were not being heard in the current climate of reform. Even more sobering, *Teaching for a Living*, a nationwide survey of nearly nine hundred teachers conducted by Public Agenda and Learning Point Associates (Johnson et al. 2009), found that 40 percent of K–12 teachers in the nation were disheartened and disappointed with their job. Of these, more than half taught in low-income schools.

A 2012 MetLife survey produced more negative results. In the two years since the previous MetLife survey, teachers were decidedly more dissatisfied with their career. Teacher satisfaction dropped by 15 points in those two years, the most dramatic decrease in job satisfaction in two decades. This, along with an increasing percentage of teachers who said they would leave their job, sends an unequivocal message about low teacher morale. Reductions in jobs and services (including substantial cuts in art, music, foreign language, and physical education), increasing class size, inadequate compensation for the work they do, and job insecurity are some of the reasons for the low morale. (For example, 34 percent of teachers surveyed feel insecure about their job, compared with just 8 percent in 2006.) In contrast, teachers who are very satisfied "are more likely to feel their jobs are secure and say they are treated as a professional by the community. They are also more likely to have adequate opportunities for professional development, time to collaborate with other teachers, more preparation and supports to engage parents effectively, and greater involvement of parents and their schools in coming together to improve the learning and success of students" (p. 5).

These surveys make it clear, first of all, that teachers are greatly influenced by the context in which they work as well as by their experiences in their schools. A factor barely mentioned but enormously significant in both surveys is that the majority of teachers in urban schools, who are White, teach students who are largely Latino/a and African American. In the 2010 MetLife study, for instance, highly satisfied teachers, most of whom work in middle-class and affluent schools, had a strong belief in the success of their students and greater confidence in their own ability to help their students succeed. They were also more likely to have high expectations for their students. The same was not true of many of the teachers who worked in low-income schools with students of diverse backgrounds.

These findings were corroborated through research by Douglas Ready and David Wright (2011), who used nationally representative data to explore the links between teacher perceptions and children's sociodemographic backgrounds. Holding students' social and academic backgrounds constant, the researchers found that teachers in high-poverty schools with lower-achieving students often *underestimated* their students' abilities. On the other hand, teachers *overestimated* the skills of White students compared with Hispanic students, even when English was their primary language. These expectations influenced their interactions with their students and drove important decisions related to placement in academic programs. Although some of these misperceptions disappeared over time, such decisions have important consequences in both the short and long term. The researchers concluded that the characteristics of classrooms are more strongly associated with teacher biases than with teachers' own backgrounds.

It is evident, then, that in spite of the significance of teacher quality on student learning, not all children have access to qualified teachers. According to Linda Darling-Hammond (2010), "In the United States, teachers are the most inequitably distributed school resource" (p. 40). The most highly qualified teachers tend to be in the best-resourced and most middle-class schools, while the most inexperienced, least qualified, most underprepared, tend to be in the most challenged schools. Darling-Hammond contends that the "achievement gap" would be dramatically reduced if low-income students of color were assigned to highly qualified teachers. It should also be noted, however, that teachers in different schools have different access to mentoring, professional development, curricular materials, and other resources. Therefore teachers in high-poverty schools, like their students, often suffer from a lack of adequate resources and support.

Given this toxic context, how can teachers thrive? Before we begin to answer this question, we need to know something about the students in our public schools.

Students in U.S. Public Schools: Change and Diversity

Our society is changing from a largely White, European American population to one that is tremendously diverse. Our neighbors now hail from all over the world, some displaced by war, others driven by hunger, still others in search of a free and democratic society or simply a decent job and a good education for their children. Our public schools are usually the first to reflect these demographic changes, from the many languages heard in school hallways to the complexion of the students in those hallways. Every urban, suburban, town, and rural school is now diverse in numerous ways.

The Condition of Education (Aud 2012), the annual report mandated by Congress and prepared by the National Center for Education Statistics, found that as of 2011, there were 49.5 million students in U.S. schools; 54 percent were White, a marked change from 1990, when 67 percent were White. The greatest increase was among Hispanics[*]: 23 percent of the entire school population in 2011 was Hispanic compared with 12 percent in 1990. Students for whom English is a second language now number over 5 million, from about 3.7 million just a decade earlier. The number of immigrants, currently estimated at over 50 million, is also having a significant impact on schools. One in four public school students now speaks a language other than English at home. In addition, immigrant children account for one-third of all children living in poverty, and nearly a third of all immigrant families lack health care insurance (Camarota 2012). The number of students with special needs and disabilities, 6.5 million, has also increased substantially in the past several decades.

Preschool enrollment is an increasingly important indicator of later school success. One study (Reynolds et al. 2011) found that providing preschool services for low-income families had significant economic benefits that exceeded costs, sometimes by as much as $10.83 per dollar invested, up to age 26. Yet access to preschool is not equal. The percentage of Asian children enrolled in preprimary programs was 71 percent, noticeably higher than the percentage of Hispanic children (56 percent, the lowest percentage among all racial/ethnic groups) (Aud et al. 2012).

[*]**Please note** in this book, depending on the context, I use both *Hispanic* and *Latino/a* to refer to those of Caribbean, Central American, and South American descent and others whose native or heritage language is Spanish (or, in some few cases, an indigenous language of South America). Government publications generally use Hispanic, while most Latino/a scholars prefer Latino/a.

Conclusion: Context Always Influences Teaching

The demographics of student and teaching populations have changed greatly over the past several decades, the change most notable among students. While about 45 percent of students in U.S. schools are students of color (Latinos/as, African Americans, Asian Americans, and American Indians, as well as biracial and multiracial students), only about 17 percent of teachers are teachers of color (Aud et al. 2012). Not only are the demographics divergent, but also many teachers (of all backgrounds, not just White) have had little personal or professional experience with the populations they teach. Teachers of *all* backgrounds are responsible for teaching *all* students effectively; however, without personal or professional experience with diversity, miscommunication, mistrust, and discomfort between teachers and students of different backgrounds are common.

There is no question that teachers and students are influenced, positively and negatively, by societal, educational, and ideological contexts. These contexts include insufficient resources, punitive school policies, and unquestioned negative ideologies about the abilities of students and teachers alike. The "expectations gap" of students of some backgrounds certainly has a negative impact on whether or not they thrive in school. At the same time, the "expectations gap" of teachers held by many in our society has an impact on whether or not teachers can be effective, competent, and caring. A study of over 1,200 K–12 teachers nationwide (Richards 2012) found that the five top stressors associated with teaching are teaching needy and unmotivated students without the needed support; having too many responsibilities; lacking control over decisions that affect students; and being constantly subject to accountability measures. The results of these stressors included physical exhaustion, a waning enthusiasm for and idealism about teaching, self-doubt about abilities and job security, and negative effects on personal relationships. Researcher Robert Bullough (2011) has written forcefully on the toll taken on teachers in an atmosphere of incessant stress and inflexible accountability: "Where educational ends are test-score dominated, narrow, and uninspiring, educators find investing fully in their work difficult, and aspirations lower and performance flattens" (p. 16).

But context is not destiny; although there are many improvements that can and must be made in many of the nation's most troubled schools, these conditions can be positively affected by teachers willing to work in conjunction with their students, their students' families, and community members to change them. How some teachers manage to do so, and to thrive in the process, is the topic of subsequent chapters. This is not to take the responsibility away from administrators, policymakers, and others, but rather to say that while larger structural changes that can equalize opportunities for all students are crucial, teachers can, and will, continue to make a difference in their students' lives.

In the chapters that follow, we learn how a group of teachers push back on a toxic policy context and negative expectations and instead challenge both the societal and the school conditions they face on a daily basis to build strong and nurturing relationships with their students.

NOTES

Accountability Works. 2012.
Americans for the Arts. 2010.
Anyon, J. 2005.
Artiles, A. J. 2011.
Au, W. 2009
Au, W. 2013
Aud, S., Hussar, W., Johnson, F., Kena, G., Roth, E., Manning, E., Wang, X., & Zhang, J. 2012.
Berliner, D. C. 2009.
Bullough, R. V., Jr. 2011. 15–30.
Camarota, S. A. 2012.
Center on Education Policy. 2010.
Chauncey, C., ed. 2005.
Children's Defense Fund. 2012.
Darling-Hammond, L. 2010.
DeNavas-Walt, C., Proctor, B. D. & Smith, J. C. 2011. 60–239.
Giroux, H. A. 2010.
Goodman, J. 2012.
Goodman, K. S. 1990.
Gorski, P. 2008. 130–148.
Gruenberg, B. 1912. 90.
Harry, B. & Klingner, J. 2006.
Irvine, J. J. 2010. xii.
Johnson, J., Yarrow, A., Rochkind, J., & Ott, A. 2009.
Konstantopoulos, S. & Chung, V. 2011. 361–386.
Krashen, S. 2011.
MetLife. 2010.
MetLife. 2012.
Michie, G. 2012a.
National Center for Education Statistics [NCES]. 2011.

National Center for Fair and Open Testing (FairTest). 2012a.
National Center for Fair and Open Testing (FairTest). 2012b.
National Center for Fair and Open Testing (FairTest). 2012c.
National Commission on Excellence in Education. 1983.
National Commission on Teaching and America's Future. 1996.
Newkirk, T. 2013.
Nichols, S. L. & Berliner, D. C. 2007.
Nieto, S. 2003.
Nieto, S. 2005a. 57–78.
Nieto. S., ed. 2005b.
Nieto, S. & Bode, P. 2012.
Oakes, J. 2005.
Orfield, G., Kucsera, J., & Siegel-Hawley, G. 2012.
Organization for Economic Development and Cooperation. 2011.
Payne, R. 2005.
Pederson, E., Faucher, T. A., & Eaton, W. W. 1978. 1–31.
Public Agenda and Learning Point Associates. 2009.
Ravitch, D. 2012.
Ravitch, D. 2013.
Ready, D. D. & Wright, D. L. 2011. 335–360.
Reynolds, A. J., Temple, J. A., White, B. A. B., Ou, S.-R., & Robertson, D. L. 2011. 379–404.
Richards, J. 2012. 299–316.
Richardson, J. 2009. 4.
Ross, S. & Agiesta, J. 2012.
Rothstein, R. 2004.
Rothstein, R. 2011.
Sato, M. & Lensmire, T. J. 2009. 365–370.
Spatig-Amerikaner, A. 2012.
Spring, J. 2013.

Chapter 2

Professional Development

Preparing for the Real World

Challenges created by the growing poverty and inequality in society, as well as changes in public education that are making life more difficult for students and teachers alike, necessitate that professional development play a major role in preparing and sustaining teachers for the real world in their classrooms and schools. This is not to imply that there is one best way to be prepared to teach. As in everything else, there is no magic formula. Deborah Ball and Francesca Forzani (2010) assert, "The fact is that we do not know the best way to train people to do this work skillfully. This is a serious collective problem" (p. 8). The amount of content area knowledge, educational theory, classroom practice, and ongoing support needed to become an expert teacher are all debatable; what is not is that all teachers need all this and more to become effective in the classroom. An especially daunting challenge is developing the skills, aptitudes, and enthusiasm for teaching students different from themselves. To make matters worse, teachers who work in the most impoverished schools serving the most vulnerable students are the least well compensated: the Office of Civil Rights surveyed over seven thousand school districts across the nation and found that teachers in schools that serve the top quintile of African American and Latino/a students get paid about $2,500 less than their peers in other schools (U.S.D.O.E. 2012). It seems that in many ways, the odds are stacked against many of the teachers who want to make a difference in the lives of our most vulnerable and underserved students.

In this chapter, I discuss what it means to teach with a social justice perspective. Following this is a discussion of the nature of teacher learning today, from preservice to inservice, the impact of typical models of professional development on both teachers and students, and what might be more effective approaches to teacher learning. We end with an exploration of the hotly debated topic of evaluating teachers.

Learning to Teach Students of Diverse Backgrounds

A MetLife survey (2011) of several thousand teachers found that a solid 91 percent believed that strengthening programs and resources to help diverse learners should be a priority; 59 percent indicated this is one of the *highest* priorities. Given the tremendous increase in the population of students of diverse backgrounds, this is not surprising. Unfortunately, although teacher preparation is now better in this regard than it was a number of years ago, too many teachers still feel unprepared to teach students who are different from themselves. The same survey found that while 61 percent of teachers say they are able to differentiate instruction according to students' needs, this still leaves nearly 40 percent who are not.

Many teachers report feeling unprepared to teach students of diverse backgrounds even if they have had a course or two on the topic. A survey of over six hundred first-year teachers (Rochkind et al. 2008) found that although they said their coursework on diversity was comprehensive and useful, 40 percent felt underprepared for the challenges of dealing with diversity in their classroom. No other aspect of their preparation showed as great a gap. As one teacher said, "I was completely unprepared for dealing with the poverty issues and social issues that occur at my school" (p. 11). Another study (Zientek 2007) found that all teachers, whether traditionally prepared or not, needed positive support systems; some classroom experience before beginning to teach; and instruction on curriculum design, diversity, lesson planning, and assessment, among other topics.

Learning to teach students of diverse backgrounds is about much more than methods. Specific approaches and strategies can be very helpful, but methods alone have never solved the problem of underachievement. In fact, the case can be made that a singular focus on methods might even exacerbate the problem if it leads teachers to believe that if the methods do not work, the problem must be the students. Much more significant than methods are teachers' attitudes and beliefs about their students, their relationships with them, and their knowledge about their families and backgrounds. This requires above all developing a social justice perspective.

Teaching from a Social Justice Perspective

All classrooms today are diverse, although some may not appear so at first glance. Beyond the issues of race, ethnicity, gender, and native language—differences that are typically visible—diversity also encompasses differences in social class, religion, sexual orientation, ability, and other areas. The best way to be prepared to teach students who embody all these differences is to develop a *social justice* approach to teaching. This is more a stance than a set of strategies or lesson plans. It requires being open and flexible, willing to learn, and humble. One also needs to become a *multicultural person* rather than just being a *multicultural teacher* (this is discussed in more depth in Nieto & Bode 2012).

Defining Social Justice in Education

The term *social justice* has been thrown around a great deal in the past couple of decades, in the process becoming little more than a meaningless mantra. But social justice is more than a term: in education, it is a set of attitudes, beliefs, and behaviors in relation to teaching, learning, and students that form the foundation of one's pedagogy.

I define social justice as having four components:

1. It challenges, confronts, and disrupts misconceptions, untruths, and stereotypes that lead to or exacerbate structural inequality and discrimination.
2. It provides all students with the resources they need to learn to their full potential. This includes both *material* resources (books, curriculum, adequate funding, etc.) and *emotional* resources (believing in their ability and worth, caring for them as individuals and learners, honoring both their individuality and their group membership, having high expectations for them, and giving them the cultural and social capital to succeed, among others).
3. It draws on students' talents and strengths. This requires having a critical perspective while also rejecting deficit theories about children of particular backgrounds, and understanding that all children have strengths that can enhance their education.
4. Finally, social justice in education is about creating a learning environment that promotes critical thinking and supports agency for social change, in effect providing students with an apprenticeship in their role in a democratic society (Nieto & Bode 2012).

A social justice approach also means being aware of the sociopolitical context of education and society, particularly issues of inequality, poverty, racism, and other biases, as discussed in Chapter 1. This is especially significant because the policies enacted at local, state, and national levels may be in conflict with teacher preparation programs that focus on social justice. Bilingual education is a good example: while a teacher education program may support bilingual education as an approach to teach students for whom English is a second language, the state may prohibit this approach, as has happened in California, Arizona, and Massachusetts. It is little wonder that prospective teachers are conflicted about what they learn in their teacher education programs and what is expected of them in their schools.

The Political Nature of Social Justice Teaching

Many years ago, Paulo Freire (1970) stated that teaching is always political because it determines who benefits and who loses when decisions about pedagogy, curriculum, policies, and practices are made. According to Marilyn Cochran-Smith (2010), teaching and teacher education are political and ideological activities "in that they inherently involve ideas, ideals, power, and access to learning and life's opportunities" (p. 3). That teaching is political is obvious if one asks questions such as: Who has access to quality education? Who does not? Why? What opportunities and supports are available for teacher learning? How are these doled out? Who has access to them?

One way to become more effective with students of diverse backgrounds is to focus on teaching as an ethical endeavor. This philosophical and intellectual mindset is built on the understanding that teaching should above all be concerned with equity and fair play. This is a message echoed by Lilia Bartolomé (1994), who decries the "methods fetish" in teacher education and professional development as fundamentally harmful. She advocates instead that teachers need to learn the histories of their marginalized students because by doing so,

> these teachers and prospective teachers come to realize that an uncritical focus on meth-
> ods makes invisible the historical role that schools and their personnel have played (and
> continue to play), not only in discriminating against many culturally different groups, but
> also in denying their humanity.

For Bartolomé, dehumanization happens when students are robbed of their language, culture, history, and values. No method can change this; only a reorientation of teaching can help. Rather than particular methods, Bartolomé suggests that it is a teacher's "politically clear educational philosophy" that will make the difference in teaching students of diverse backgrounds (p. 179).

In a related vein, Kenneth Zeichner (2003) has suggested that in order to narrow the "achievement gap," teachers should, among other things:

- have a clear sense of their own identities
- have, and communicate, high expectations for all their students
- be committed to making a difference for their students, and believe they can do so
- work at forming a close bond with their students
- explicitly teach students the culture of the school while also helping them maintain a sense of ethnic and cultural pride and identity
- teach a curriculum that is academically challenging and multicultural
- understand that learning is collaborative and interactive
- encourage families to become involved in the education of their children.

Social Justice Pedagogy

These ideas are not new, although they may go by different names. Martin Haberman (1991), in an incisive and influential article written over twenty years ago, focused on the practices of teachers working in high-poverty schools. Haberman critiqued what he called "the pedagogy of poverty," a basic urban style that included giving instruction, asking questions, giving directions, making assignments, and monitoring seatwork. In spite of its widespread use, this pedagogy has little success and students leave these classrooms with minimal life skills. Unsupported by theory, by research, and by the best practices of successful urban teachers, the "pedagogy of poverty" is instead a set of negative attitudes and beliefs—in reality, a philosophical stance—based on a deficit perspective about urban students enacted through pedagogy. Haberman suggested that teachers change their attitudes and beliefs about their students; give their students a role in planning what they will be doing; and help them learn about human differences, discuss difficult and controversial issues, and apply ideals of fairness and equity to solving problems and real-life issues. Unfortunately, the situation has not changed a great deal since Haberman wrote his now classic article. In a more recent piece (Haberman 2010), he lamented,

> It is a source of consternation that I am able to state without equivocation that the overly directive, mind-numbing, mundane, useless, anti-intellectual acts that constitute teaching not only remain the coin of the realm but have become the gold standard.

Clearly there is a long way to go in promoting a social justice perspective in both preservice and inservice education.

How teachers learn to teach with a social justice perspective depends on the kinds of teacher education programs they attend, the inservice professional development they receive in their schools and beyond, and the culture of collaboration in their schools.

Professional Development

Certainly, all teachers would be in a better position to work effectively with low-income students of color if they received appropriate preparation, but this is not always the case. The problem may begin with their own lack of experience with diversity, but it is often exacerbated during their preparation at colleges and universities.

In reviewing research on teacher preparation, the American Association of Colleges for Teacher Education (AACTE) (2009) found significant links between good teacher preparation and student achievement. In another review of a broad range of studies on inservice professional development, Ruth Chung Wei and her colleagues (2010) found that the kind of sustained teacher learning that increases student learning requires from 49–100 hours of contact on a single focus. Unfortunately, in most cases, teachers received *less than eight hours* on any given topic.

Student learning must be the bottom line of professional development, but teacher satisfaction can and must go hand-in-hand with student learning. Good and meaningful professional development, both before one enters the profession and later when one is teaching, are signposts of student success and teacher sustainability in the profession. In her exhaustive review of state, local, and district studies,

Linda Darling-Hammond (2010) found that teachers' academic background, preparation for teaching, certification status, and teaching experience have the greatest influence on student achievement. In a more recent review by the Alliance for Excellent Education on the educational systems of Finland, Ontario, and Singapore (all among the most high-achieving nations), the researchers found that what they had in common were coherent and complementary policies in recruitment, preparation, induction, continuing professional and career development, and teacher retention (Rothman & Darling-Hammond 2011).

In the United States teacher education programs and continuing professional development have come under increased scrutiny in the past couple of decades, by both critics and supporters. In addition to those outside the profession critical of teacher preparation, teachers along the spectrum from preservice to novice to veteran are frequently dissatisfied with professional development, especially in their preparation to teach students of diverse backgrounds.

Teacher Preparation Programs

Any good preparation program needs to acknowledge the importance of learning how to teach students of diverse backgrounds. Developing a social justice perspective is a necessity, yet many programs offer a plethora of methods courses and little else. Instead, prospective teachers need to be shown how to be advocates for their students and collaborators with their colleagues. A good example is the UCLA Teacher Education Program, one of the most highly regarded in the nation for preparing candidates to work with diverse populations. In follow-up surveys of over a thousand teachers, Karen Hunter Quartz and her colleagues (2009) found that most graduates of the program defined themselves as social reformers or activists. They became teachers not simply because teaching was compatible with their lifestyle or offered material benefits (such as they are) but because they wanted to make a difference. The majority had remained in the profession for ten years after completing the program, although many now held other jobs in the field.

Most teachers go through traditional teacher education programs in four-year colleges. Although these programs make an effort to teach preservice teachers to work effectively in urban schools with students of diverse backgrounds, many teachers enter the profession with little experience in working in these communities. What teachers need, according to researcher Peter Murrell (2001), is an orientation as "community teachers" who "draw on a richly contextualized knowledge of culture, community, and identity in their work with children and families in diverse urban communities" (p. 4). Community teachers not only have a deep knowledge of their students' cultures and communities and promote robust learning among them, but they also recognize their own cultural, political, and racial identities and privileges in relation to the students and families they serve.

Because most traditional teacher preparation programs are part of students' undergraduate education, they are only two years long, hardly enough time to develop the kind of teacher envisioned by Murrell. In response to the criticism that too many teachers have been shortchanged with regard to both a solid general education background and meaningful preparation in pedagogy and subject matter, many teacher education programs in the past decade or two have added a fifth year or master's program. Even a fifth year, however, is inadequate if not accompanied by consistent and relevant experience in schools.

A growing number of teachers are now being prepared in nontraditional programs such as Teach for America and teacher academies. These programs are criticized for how quickly teachers enter the classroom—usually after a summer intensive, followed by coursework for a year or so as they teach full-time in their own classroom, often with little supervision or support. In addition, these programs traditionally place inexperienced teachers in the most challenging schools (those with large classes, a scarcity of resources, and other problems). The majority of students in such schools are students of color living in poverty, while the majority of novice teachers have had little experience with these populations. This is a poor recipe for preparing teachers to work in urban schools with students of diverse backgrounds.

Although job-changers with rich life experiences who have joined the field in nontraditional ways tend to be highly regarded by both peers and administrators, the evidence is mixed on the effectiveness of nontraditional pathways into teaching. One study found traditionally certified teachers felt better prepared than nontraditionally certified teachers to communicate, plan, and use instructional strategies (Zienteck 2007).

Inservice Professional Development

What works in professional development has become fairly evident in recent research. Using a national probability sample of over a thousand math and science teachers, Michael Garet and his colleagues (2001) found that three core features of professional development significantly increase teachers' knowledge and skills: a focus on content knowledge; opportunities for active learning; and coherence with other learning opportunities. Unfortunately, these things do not always happen in the typical professional development provided in schools. As emphatically stated by Heather Hill (2009), "The professional development 'system' for teachers is, by all accounts, broken" (p. 470); she suggests it is time to abandon the kind of professional development that exists only to fulfill state licensing requirements. This includes induction and mentoring programs, as well as one-shot, large-group lectures and workshops, especially on topics that teachers have not defined as important to their continued professional learning.

The content of professional development is frequently not what teachers want or need. One study found that in a three-year period, fewer than 23 percent of teachers received even *one day* of professional development focusing specifically on English language learners and students with disabilities (Darling-Hammond & Richardson 2009), even though the growing presence of English language learners and students with special needs makes this an essential topic. A study by Wei and her colleagues (2010) found similar results: only 42 percent of the teachers had access to professional development on teaching students with disabilities, only 27 percent on ELLs.

Mentoring and Induction Programs

Good mentoring programs can be enormously effective in retaining new teachers. In Public Education Network interviews (2004) the two hundred plus teachers participating said mentoring was the most useful form of assistance they received in their first years on the job. The most effective programs were ones in which regularly scheduled common meeting times were held and teachers were partnered by subject area and grade level. But even when available, mentoring programs are not *equally* available. Ruth Chung Wei and her colleagues (2010), examining data from the 2008 Schools and Staffing Survey (SASS) and other sources, found that teachers in urban and rural schools with the highest number of students of color and the highest percentage of students receiving free and reduced-price lunches participated in induction programs less often than teachers in suburban schools and schools with fewer low-income students and students of color. Once again, those in the most privileged schools, both students and teachers, were the primary beneficiaries.

Induction programs are becoming increasingly popular but they differ in intensity and duration. Programs where novice teachers are assigned to work with an in-school mentor tend to last only a year or two. Informal types of induction are generally less successful than more formal, comprehensive, sequential, and structured induction. To evaluate the impact of comprehensive programs, the National Center for Education Evaluation and Regional Assistance conducted a national large-scale randomized study in school systems that had not previously had them. One intriguing finding was that for the first two years there was no significant impact on student learning but by the third year there was (Glazerman et al. 2010). This points to the importance of long-term rather than one-year induction for new teachers, the typical model in most schools.

Teacher Collaboration

Collaboration, although generally highly valued by teachers and principals, is not always promoted. For example, in a 2010 MetLife survey, 69 percent of teachers and 78 percent of principals indicated that greater collaboration among teachers and school leaders would lead to major improvement in student achievement. Also, in schools with a culture of higher collaboration, teachers were more satisfied with their career. Yet, on average, teachers spend less than three hours a week in structured collaboration with other teachers. In another study that analyzed eleven years of data on North Carolina teachers, C. Kirabo Jackson and Elias Bruegmann (2009) found that student achievement rose in all grade-level classrooms when a high-quality teacher joined the faculty. The researchers argued that peer learning is the likely explanation. Carrie Leana (2011) goes so far as to call collaboration "the missing link in school reform." She suggests that focusing on highly skilled individual teachers may be missing the mark because the result may be "undervaluing the benefits that come from teacher collaborations that strengthen skills, competence, and a school's overall social capital" (p. 30). Study groups are another form of collaboration and can help teachers learn about their students of diverse backgrounds.

Luis Moll (2010) promotes study groups as an opportunity for teachers to think together about their students and students' families in order to help change and shape their classroom practice to best meet the needs of students of diverse backgrounds.

That teachers appreciate collaborating with their peers is evident. Jane Coggshall, Amber Ott, and Molly Lasagna (2010) found that teachers who think of themselves as effective prefer to work in a school with a great deal of collaboration and guidance from instructional experts. Teacher learning communities—teams, study groups, other formats—have many potential benefits: they bridge the gap between research and practice, improve student learning by giving teachers a venue to address problems of practice, and foster positive change in teaching practices. Professional loneliness and lack of peer support are key reasons that teachers leave teaching. According to the National Council of Teachers of English (2010), "teachers who work collaboratively with colleagues are much more likely to remain in the profession" (p. 17).

It is time to take collaboration seriously by making it an explicit part of professional development and providing the resources that collaboration requires. Tom Carroll (2009) makes the point that quality teaching is not an individual accomplishment but a whole-school goal:

> The idea that a single teacher, working alone, can know and do everything to meet the diverse learning needs of thirty students every day throughout the school year has rarely worked, and it certainly won't meet the needs of learners in years to come (p. 13).

The Problem of Assessing Teacher Quality

That teachers make a difference, sometimes an extraordinary difference, is indisputable. It is difficult nowadays to find a report, commission, or research study that does not single out teacher effectiveness as the most important ingredient in student learning. Unfortunately, rightwing critics of public education, as well as the media and popular press, frequently use this reality in negative ways to suggest that privatization, "choice," and more testing are the cure for incompetent teachers. In his book *Bad Teacher! How Blaming Teachers Distorts the Bigger Picture,* Kevin Kumashiro (2012) describes how scapegoating public school teachers, teacher unions, and teacher educators masks larger systemic problems of inequality, racism, and the marketization of public education. All teachers are maligned, and students, particularly students of color and those living in poverty, suffer the negative consequences of attending a school designated as "failing," having their school closed, or having their teachers reassigned or fired.

Much in the way students are blamed for the "achievement gap," teachers are blamed if their students do not perform well on standardized tests, as if issues of poverty, racism, lack of resources, and other inequities played no part in creating this gap, as if standardized tests measured all that should be measured. In a critical report on value-added measures, Sean Corcoran (2010) cautioned, "Not all subjects are or can be tested, and even within tested subject areas, only certain skills readily conform to standardized testing" (also see Annenberg Institute Press Release 2010).

The negative press about teachers has been one of the catalysts for recent assessment efforts, most notably those based largely on student scores on standardized tests. The goal of such approaches is to punish ineffective teachers and reward effective teachers with merit pay, class assignment, and other benefits. Some cities have gone so far as to publish teachers' names and their students' average test scores, thus lowering morale and increasing acrimony among administrators, teachers, and families. Given the high-stakes nature of these measures, value-added assessments are having a chilling effect on the teaching profession, creating more stress and another reason teachers say they are leaving the classroom.

Here's a real-life example. Kim Cook is a first-grade teacher with nearly twenty-five years of experience who currently teaches at Irby Elementary School, in Alachua, Florida. Florida's recent adoption of Senate Bill 736 mandating that 40 percent of a teacher's evaluation must be based on student scores on the FCAT, the state's standardized test, has led to some strange and implausible outcomes. Cook received an unsatisfactory score even though she was selected as Teacher of the Year by her peers. Even more disturbing, she had never taught a single student who took the FCAT! (Strauss 2012). Obviously using student test scores to evaluate teachers is at best an imprecise and at worst an irrational approach to evaluating teachers.

Critics of value-added measures, including leading educational testing experts, caution against relying on test scores to evaluate teachers (see, for example, the fact sheet from the National Center for Fair and Open Testing, or FairTest, 2012d). Eva Baker and colleagues (2010) point out that student test scores remain inaccurate measures of teacher performance and that such scores should not dominate the information used by school districts in making decisions about the evaluation, discipline, and compensation of teachers. Richard Rothstein (2010) has an especially critical take, asserting that before we can make teacher quality the focus of a national campaign, there need to be better ways of assessing good and bad teachers. He writes that using students' test scores as the chief measure of teacher quality is "a terribly dangerous idea" for several reasons, including the narrowing of the curriculum, the incentive for teachers to focus only on reading and mathematics, the pressure to "teach to the test," and the misidentification of ineffective teachers because students' test scores can be influenced by so many other factors besides poor teaching (p. 2).

Another critical report asserts that "placing excessive emphasis on test scores alone can have unintended and undesirable consequences that undermine the goal of developing an excellent teaching force" (Hinchey 2010, p. 1). The report recommends that instead policymakers carefully consider a number of other issues such as the purpose of the test and the need to use many other measures and involve all key stakeholders. Another report suggests that since teacher differences account for no more than 15 percent of differences in students' test scores, teacher evaluation should be accomplished through formative approaches that focus on identifying both strengths and weaknesses and improving teaching (Mathis 2012). Even proponents of using value-added measures concede that there are serious concerns with using this approach, including incentives for schools and teachers to cheat, adopt teaching methods that focus narrowly on tests, and ignore nontested subjects (Hanushek & Rivkin 2010).

In a recent review of the literature on value-added assessments, Linda Darling-Hammond and her colleagues (2012) found that the characteristics of the students teachers work with have a great deal to do with teachers' assessments. For example, teachers of grades in which students who are learning English are "mainstreamed" as well as those who teach large numbers of students with special needs are the least likely to show added value. Their conclusion: value-added assessments are not appropriate as a primary measure for evaluating individual teachers. They suggest instead that more productive ways of evaluating teachers are examples of student work, observations, videotapes, artifacts, and student surveys, among others. A recent publication attempts to face the quagmire of teacher evaluation squarely by involving those who have been most often left out of the conversation: teachers. Aptly titled *Everyone at the Table: Engaging Teachers in Evaluation Reform* (Public Agenda and the American Institutes for Research 2013), the book provides a research-based methodology and practical strategies for involving teachers and promises to be a more collegial approach to teacher evaluation.

Conclusion: What Does Professional Development Mean to Teachers?

An interesting study based on surveys of teachers found "convergence and contradiction" in their perceptions of the current policy reform agenda: "what teachers think are good indicators of effectiveness—and what they think will make them more effective—are not always aligned with what policymakers or researchers think" (Coggshall et al. 2010). In many instances, the teachers were overwhelmingly opposed to some of the more punitive reforms in place, including focusing on standardized testing and tying teacher rewards to students' test performance. Not surprisingly, the researchers concluded that teachers' voices do not have a strong influence on the policy agenda. This is not news, but that it was so clearly demonstrated in this study should give pause to researchers, policymakers, and administrators intent on pushing policies that have little resonance for teachers.

What do the teachers I interviewed think of the professional development they receive in schools? In most cases, the most memorable and exciting professional development experiences they mentioned came not from inside the school but from outside, typically through programs like those offered by the National Writing Project and the National Board for Professional Teaching Standards or subject matter conferences, reading groups, community service projects, travel, and other experiences. Geoffrey

Winikur received a grant from the National Endowment for the Humanities that proved to be an excellent learning experience, unlike typical professional development he described as "putrid." Several teachers said they were largely dissatisfied with the professional development offered in their schools, finding it haphazard or irrelevant. They found their own ways to keep informed and abreast of new trends, materials, and strategies.

Some of the best professional development happens serendipitously. Walking around the neighborhood in which a school is located to discover the resources it offers can be far more productive than sitting passively through a presentation that teachers neither asked for nor want. John Nguyen mentioned the day he and a group of his colleagues went to a museum and, by appreciating and analyzing the art they saw there, were able to make some important connections with who and what they teach.

What did these teachers want from professional development? They needed to be kept up to date with technology, learn to be more effective with English language learners and students with special needs, learn how to be better organized, and have the opportunity to work with others to help make changes in the school. They needed support, resources, modeling, guidance, and more time to collaborate with peers. Several also said that they appreciated peers who offered workshops and other learning opportunities. Clearly, these teachers wanted something meaningful, different, and respectful of their professionalism and their time. Traditional professional development did not fill the bill.

NOTES

American Association of Colleges of Teacher Education (AACTE). 2009.

Annenberg Institute for School Reform. 2010.

Baker, E. L., Barton, P. E., Darling-Hammond, L., Haertel, E., Ladd, H. F., Linn, R. L. Ravitch, D., Rothstein, R., Shavelson, R. J., & Shepard, L. A. 2010.

Ball, D. L., & Forzani, F. M. 2010. 8–12.

Bartolomé, L. I. 1994. 173–195.

Carroll, T. 2009. 8–13.

Cochran-Smith, M. 2010. 447.

Coggshall, J. B., Ott, A. & Lasagna, M. 2010.

Corcoran, S. P. 2010.

Darling-Hammond, L. 2010.

Darling-Hammond, L., Amrein-Beardsley, A., Haertel, E., & Rothstein. J. 2012. 8–15.

Darling-Hammond, L. & Richardson, N. 2009.

Freire, P. 1970.

Garet, M. S., Porter, A. C., Desimone, L., Birman, B. F., & Suk, K. Y. 2001. 915–945.

Glazerman, S., E. Isenberg, S. Dolfin, M. Bleeker, A. Johnson, M. Grider, & M. Jacobus. 2010.

Haberman, M. 1991. 290–294.

Haberman, M. 2010. 45.

Hanushek, E. A. & Rivkin, S. G. 2010.

Hill, H. C. 2009. 470–476.

Hinchey, B. 2010.

Irvine, J. J. & Hawley, W. D. 2011.

Jackson, C. K., & Bruegmann, E. 2009. 85–108.

Kumashiro, K. K. 2012.

Leana, C. R. 2011. 30–35.

Mathis, W. 2012.

MetLife. 2010.

MetLife. 2011.

Moll, L. C. 2010. 451–460.

Murrell, P. E. 2001.

National Center for Fair and Open Testing. 2012d.

National Council of Teachers of English. 2010.

Nieto, S. & Bode, P. 2012.

Public Agenda and American Institutes for Research. 2013.

Public Education Network. 2004.

Quartz, K. H., Olsen, B., Anderson, L., & Lyons, K. B. 2009.

Rochkind, J., Ott, A., Immerwahr, J. Doble, J., & Johnson, J. 2008.

Rothman, R. & Darling-Hammond, L. 2011.

Rothstein, R. 2010.

Strauss, V. 2012.

U.S. Department of Education. 2012.

Walton, P. H., Baca, L., Escamilla, K. 2002.

Wei, R., Darling-Hammond, L., & Adamson, F. 2010.

Zeichner, K. M. 2003. 99–114.

Zientek, L. R. 2007. 959–1001.

Part II

Profiles of Thriving Teachers

Enacting your core commitments to social change through education requires enormous creativity, fortitude, and perseverance, but it also demands sufficient professional autonomy and supportive social networks.

—Karen Hunter Quartz and colleagues

The popular media is full of stories of bigger-than-life teachers who, in the space of a couple of hours, work magic, turning hostile students into successful and enthusiastic ones while providing audiences with the happy ending they expect. These "media teachers," so unlike the real live teachers in our schools, may face some challenges— temporarily disengaged students, envious colleagues, angry parents— but they quickly overcome these obstacles through resolve and sheer gumption. And they always survive on their own, with nary an assist from colleagues, administrators, or families. Theirs is a solitary quest and a personal achievement. These super teachers are an impossibly unrealistic picture of what it means to teach in real schools with real students today. Most movies about teachers, whether fact or fiction, do not even mention standardized tests or the supersurveillance to which teachers and their students are now subjected.

The twenty-two teachers interviewed for this project are not cardboard replicas of media teachers. As inspiring as they are human, they face every day with realism and hope but also, if they are fortunate, with support, whether from colleagues, administrators, the parents and families of their students, or their own friends and family members. They read students' papers through the wee hours of the morning, dutifully hand in the same information administrators have requested in three different ways, grapple with thorny problems of pedagogy and instruction, organize field trips and fundraisers, and spend their own money to buy the materials no longer provided by financially strapped schools. The work they do is sometimes exciting, frequently enlightening, often frustrating, and sometimes tedious. But it is work most teachers find rewarding in spite of everything. Good teachers are not media stars; they are the unsung heroes of our nation.

In Chapters 3 through 8 I introduce you to several of these teachers, tell you who they are and why they do what they do. Although different in many ways, the teachers share many values and perspectives. Each chapter highlights particular issues that define the teachers in that chapter, but each teacher could just as easily have been presented in any of the other chapters. Whether it is being a culturally responsive teacher; understanding teaching as a moral endeavor; or any of the other dispositions, values, and practices these teachers embody, they all speak passionately and decisively about what it means to be a teacher today.

Chapter 3

It's *Whom* You Teach, Not Just *What* You Teach

The best piece of advice I received during my teacher preparation program many years ago was "start where the kids are at." This advice almost seems redundant. Where else *would* we start? At the same time, I was urged to leave my "cultural baggage at the door." That these pieces of advice were contradictory didn't seem to occur to my professors. Yet soon after beginning my teaching career in an intermediate school in Brooklyn, New York, it became clear that leaving my cultural baggage at the door—in essence, leaving my identity behind—was not only difficult but also impossible, because my identity, knowledge, and experiences were the best ways to connect with my students. This is true of all teachers, not just teachers of color teaching children of color, but for the connection to take place, all teachers need to truly get to know their students.

Given the kind of preparation they receive for the profession as well as their own limited experiences with diversity, many teachers do not *know* "where the kids are at." Instead, as we'll see in Roger Wallace's reflections in this chapter, some teachers start where they *would like* their students to be. The result may be that teachers do not recognize where their students already are. At the same time they negate their students' identities, teachers may also negate their own identities by failing to bring themselves fully into their teaching. Getting too close to our students, we've often been told, violates professional standards and the distance needed to maintain control in the classroom. But when teachers negate their own identities—believing that they must be "professional" or "neutral"—they deprive their students of the opportunity to get to know them more deeply and in the process to form meaningful relationships with them.

This chapter focuses on Angeles Pérez and Roger Wallace, teachers who epitomize what it means to "start where the kids are at," while also recognizing that it is almost impossible, as well as counterproductive, to leave their identities out of the classroom. They know that *whom* they teach is as or more important than what they teach and that whatever they teach—geometry or art, reading or math—is also about themselves and their view of the world.

Starting Where Kids Are At

Although vastly different in many ways, Angeles Pérez and Roger Wallace nevertheless share this truth: *relationships are at the heart of teaching*. Nel Noddings's influential work on the relational aspect of teaching has transformed how many teachers and researchers understand the need to create caring classrooms in order to build strong bonds with students. Since first published in 1992, her book *The Challenge to Care in Schools* has provided an alternative to the primary focus on methods and content that has been the yardstick by which teachers and their classrooms have traditionally been assessed. Throughout her body of work, Noddings has insisted that relationships are as important as the content in the curriculum.

Many scholars have since documented how caring manifests itself in schools around the nation and with different populations. Angela Valenzuela's study of Mexican and Mexican American students and their teachers in a Texas high school (1999) found that students benefited academically from their teachers' acts of kindness and thoughtfulness, from bringing in tacos to feed hungry students to being available to help them whenever needed. In a school with few examples of success, she found that the students who benefited from their teachers' care also benefited academically. Valenzuela calls this "the politics of caring": not simply saying "Good job!" or patting students on the back (particularly when accompanied by low expectations and cultural and racial stereotypes) but believing in students, showing an interest in their well-being, demanding only the best from them, having high expectations of them, and supporting them in meeting those high expectations.

Similarly, in research with Puerto Rican middle school girls, Rosalie Rolón-Dow (2005) proposes *critical care*, an approach founded on a historical understanding of students' lives and their sociopolitical realities. For her, caring is not just an individual phenomenon but an institutional one. In the same vein, Mari Ann Roberts (2010) explores the ethic of care in a group of African American teachers of African American students. These teachers showed a genuine concern for the future of their students, while at the same time providing support for their present success. Roberts describes this as *culturally relevant critical teacher care* to highlight the significance of taking students' identities into account when interacting with them. In both studies, the researchers make it clear that care is *not* colorblind, that it necessarily takes into account students' identities, their histories, and their realities. Likewise, in his work with high school students of diverse backgrounds in summer and afterschool programs, Ernest Morrell (2008) emphasizes developing students' sense of efficacy through researching conditions in their schools and exploring how those conditions limit their educational opportunities.

There are many other factors besides care or lack of care—poverty, limited curricular and extra-curricular opportunities, poor health care and nutrition, stressors in the home, the nature of the community, among others—that also influence how students relate to school, but the research on teachers' relationships with students make it clear that care matters a great deal. Caring goes beyond superficial acts of charity. It is a genuine love for students that entails recognizing their talents, their identities, and their needs. It also means demonstrating an interest in their families and their communities by interacting frequently with them, attending community events, and becoming in some sense a member of those communities.

Bringing Your Identity into the Classroom

Parker Palmer, whose work focuses on education, social change, and spirituality, has famously written, "We teach who we are" (1998, p. 1). His statement captures what is at once the essence and also a taboo of teaching. The conventional wisdom is that teachers are supposed to be "professional," detached, and objective. Except for kindergarten teachers, who are permitted the luxury of demonstrating their love for their students, even forgiven for hugging them and being their surrogate parents while at school, all other teachers are urged not to get too close to their students. One need only look at the advice given to novice teachers: "Don't smile until Christmas!" they are warned, or they will forever lose the respect of their charges. Angeles Pérez is indignant at this advice, saying, "Don't smile until Christmas?! That means you never really made a connection with them until Christmas!" This is a good reminder that teaching is *always* about relationships and about being oneself, whether on the first day of school or the last.

Many of the teachers I interviewed also spoke about how they develop strong bonds with their students by bringing themselves completely into their teaching. John Gunderson, a high school teacher of psychology and history in southern California, explained that what's important to him is the students:

> *Teaching is about relationships. It's not about knowing how to do a lesson plan. It's about knowing how to create an environment to foster humanity, to foster human relationships; when you do that, the content will be so much easier to transmit because you're in a conversation with people and with that conversation you are telling a story.*

María Ramírez Acevedo, an early childhood education teacher in Milwaukee, spoke about her culture being important not only to her but also to her students: "It's important to know where you come from. I've always been proud of being Puerto Rican, and I think it's important for children to learn that as well."

For María Federico Brummer, a high school teacher in Tucson, Arizona, it's about proudly representing her Mexican American identity and community. Being a mentor to her students is vital to María because, as a young student herself, she felt she'd sometimes been judged negatively because of her identity. She shares her own story about being counseled not to apply for college while at Tucson High School, the high school where she now teaches. She wants her students to understand that the advice she was given was counterproductive, even racist, and that they, like her, can overcome the stereotypes on which such advice is based.

All the teachers I interviewed identified the connection with students as a primary reason they thrived in the classroom. Amber Bechard, a language arts teacher in a public middle school in an urbanized suburb with a very diverse student body who had previously taught kindergarten children in a privileged private school, found that regardless of the students' ages, socioeconomic circumstances, or identities, "it's this interaction, this experience that we have together, that I think makes teachers thrive." John Nguyen, a high school teacher in New Haven, Connecticut, credited being honest for his close relationship with students. He explained: "They know that if they ask me a question, I'm very honest with them, unless it's a political issue. Then I'll give them both sides, but I won't tell them where I stand. For the most part, anything else is fair game." That kind of honesty is another example of bringing one's identity into the classroom.

In this chapter, we see how Angeles Pérez and Roger Wallace create classrooms founded on caring for students through their willingness to bring themselves fully into the classroom.

Two Models of Caring

Saying that relationships, the *whom* of teaching, are essential in no way diminishes the centrality of content knowledge, the *what* of teaching. Teachers must be competent in teaching content, and they need to remain curious, excited about learning, always on the lookout for both information and pedagogical approaches that will keep them current and fresh. Being knowledgeable about one's subject matter is indispensable—but it is not enough. Good teachers understand that knowing their students well and tailoring their pedagogy to the students in their classroom make a difference in the quality of the education students receive.

Angeles Pérez and Roger Wallace, although separated by age, gender, ethnicity, geography, years in the profession, and experience, nonetheless epitomize what it means to focus on relationships. Their stories hold lessons for all of us who care about children of diverse backgrounds and their future.

Angeles Pérez

When I interviewed fourth-grade bilingual teacher Angeles Pérez in 2010, she was in only her second year of teaching language arts, social studies, and ESL (English as a second language) in a K–5 Title 1 school in the Sheldon, Texas, Independent School District, where 87 percent of the students are

Angeles Pérez is now an instructional specialist in the Aldine Independent School District, in Houston, Texas. She began her career in the Sheldon Independent School District, where for three years she was a fourth-grade bilingual teacher in a self-contained classroom. Angeles has a bachelor's degree in Spanish and a master's degree in educational administration and technology leadership. She has worked with English language learners, special education students, and gifted and talented students. In her current position, Angeles provides interventions for struggling students. The ELL population at her current school is more than 70 percent, the number of students at or below the poverty line more than 80 percent. Serving students from diverse backgrounds and in challenging situations is Angeles's passion. She loves what she does and, more important, loves her students. She hopes one day to obtain a position that will allow her to have a larger impact on students from various backgrounds living in urban areas.

Latinos/as and 96 percent are classified as economically disadvantaged. Angeles purposely chose this school because although many of the students live in poverty, she believes strongly that they deserve excellent teachers. She was indignant that these children have to attend poorly resourced schools and often have inexperienced teachers who do not want to be there. She asked, "What about the kids that it's not their fault? Because they're economically disadvantaged, they're going to get stuck with the leftovers?" In making this statement, Angeles is reflecting the hard reality that many effective teachers tend to teach in middle-class schools while those who are least experienced and least effective end up in high poverty schools. This is not to say that these teachers cannot *become* excellent teachers, but only to point out that teaching in difficult circumstances places a great strain on new teachers and also jeopardizes the future of the students they teach.

Angeles recognized that although long on enthusiasm and energy, she was short on experience. Yet, at just twenty-two years old, she was wise beyond her years. The big difference between Angeles and other novice teachers is that she purposely chose to teach at her school, recognizing that although lacking in experience, she had the knowledge, the desire, and the kinds of attitudes that could make a difference in the lives of her students. Bilingual, bicultural, and with some of the same experiences as her students, she was different from them in that she had attended good schools as a child and wanted to make certain that her students had the same chance. Her husband, a Mexican American who is a vice principal at another school, made the same choice to work in a high-poverty urban school with mostly Mexican and Mexican American students.

Although Angeles went to Catholic or private schools all her life and graduated from "a really affluent school" where she took many honors courses, she never felt that she fit in, one reason being she didn't have any role models:

> *In my high school, you could count the Hispanics on your hand, so I was either told I needed to be in ESL (when I spoke perfect English) or I hung out with the ESL kids. When I wanted to take an honors class or I wanted to test out of something they were like, "Are you sure?" I just felt it was a bad experience.*

Angeles bubbled over with enthusiasm when describing her students: "I'm their biggest fan." About teaching, she said, "I come out of school and I feel like a really cool person because these kids just bring you up and I like to think that I do the same for them." For example, given the low status of bilingual programs in most schools, Angeles was ecstatic when one of her students won the spelling bee *in English* at her school. While most of the previous winners had been fifth graders, he was in fourth grade. Beaming with pride, she said: "I don't mean to brag but my student just won the spelling bee! I can't believe it! That for me is so big that I feel like *I* won the spelling bee! Their success is my success, I guess."

Angeles's Approach

Angeles builds relationships—with one student at a time and with her entire class—by creating a learning community that is nurturing and accepting. For example, she has instituted the last ten minutes of the day as "hanging out with Ms. Pérez time" because she wants to make sure to learn something about each student's interests and experiences. No student is invisible in her class. Angeles remembered the mother who came to her in tears, confiding that before her son was in Angeles's class, he had never been happy in school:

> *He had told his mother that since my name is Angeles, I was an angel for him because he's never had a teacher understand him. That day, I cried my eyes out because it just goes to show that they know when you care, and if you show them you care, they will work for you.*

Describing some of the strategies she uses to build relationships with her students, Angeles recognized that students need to be cared for not just as students but also as individuals:

> *I make it a point to greet them at the door every day. I'm at the door, I'm smiling. And at the end of each day, they run to give me a hug and it's the best feeling because they care so much about me. They will work for me because they know I work for them. I love them.*

Believing that students need to determine their own learning, Angeles helps each student set high goals at the beginning of the year, and she works with each one individually to help her or him meet those goals. "I pride myself on getting them to set their goals and they're not low goals, they're high goals." She's as thrilled as the students when they reach their goal. Then she helps them set the next one.

Using her students' identities in the curriculum is another significant strategy in Angeles's teaching. She jokes that she's a Puerto Rican transplant in a heavily Mexican American community. She challenges the stereotype that all Hispanics are alike and she has made it her responsibility to learn about her students' Mexican and Central American backgrounds; if her students' identities are visible in the curriculum, learning is more exciting and students become better writers and more enthusiastic learners. Her students are her greatest teachers. For example, when she discovers a Mexican holiday or piece of history or phrase in Spanish that she didn't know, she asks her students about it and finds a way to incorporate this information into the curriculum, especially in writing: if it's a topic they know something about, or something that interests them, they'll become more enthusiastic writers.

Angeles gave an interesting example of how she learns about her students' culture. One day a student asked her if they should "hacer sangría," or *make sangría*. To Angeles, *sangría* was a Spanish alcoholic beverage made with wine and fruit, but to her students, *sangría* means indenting a paragraph using two fingers. "So now I have *hacemos sangría* as part of our writing process." She also created a legends curriculum that highlighted La Llorona, a famous character in Mexican folklore, doing research and locating appropriate books. As she said, "Finding out about La Llorona was so exciting!"

Believing that her identity is important in her role as a teacher, Angeles is a role model for her kids. She is not only bilingual and comfortable in a variety of cultural settings but also college-educated and successful. She is proud that some of her students want to be teachers so they can be "like Ms. Pérez." Angeles feels that showing young people greater options in life is crucial: "Seeing me, especially how young I am, these kids are so amazed at having a successful young Hispanic teacher, especially female, that they just love me and it shows them they can be that way."

At the same time that Angeles focuses on culture, language, and identity, she insists that each student is an individual and it's her responsibility to figure each student out and then tap into his or her interests. She spoke about the importance of going beyond the surface: "You could know their name, you could know the kinds of things that they like, but you've really got to get to know where their walls are. How they put up their walls." She says it's her job to learn "how to really just destroy that wall and never let that wall go up again, and then you've really got to take yourself out of the picture." She tries never to humiliate her students if they misbehave or to threaten to call home or to call them out if they haven't done their homework, knowing that their "walls will go up" immediately. In these cases, she meets with students about these things individually, often during her lunch hour. "Everything has to be about the student."

Angeles also spoke about students who are reluctant to raise their hand in class because they feel that their English is not good enough or that they're not the smartest kid in the class. She makes sure to respect their feelings, while at the same time finding other ways to assess them and, eventually, helping them feel comfortable enough to participate in a more public way.

Angeles says that high test scores, AYP, and other mandates are not foremost on her mind; they are just givens. Although she does not teach to the test, she is certain that her students will do fine on the mandated tests because she has taught them well. For her, succeeding as a teacher goes beyond having students score well on tests: "I guess I'm thriving in that my kids are successful, not only based on the state standards, which is big in Texas, but beyond that, they learned and they were excited to learn." She mentioned a student who at the beginning of the year was certain he couldn't make it to fifth grade and identified as a nonreader, insisting that he couldn't, wouldn't, read. "He's reading fifth-grade books now," she said proudly.

Although the students she taught her first year did very well on the state test (unusual and unexpected for a first-year teacher), thriving is about more: "I feel as if I'm thriving in that the TAKS in Texas is on the side burner; I know they're going to succeed in that." Happy as she was with the test results, seeing her students learn to accept who they are and be happy with themselves was her greatest achievement.

Not everything was peaches and cream in the beginning. Being in the bilingual program, Angeles sometimes felt isolated: "In bilingual you're in a little corner, you're shipped off to the side, you're not the main focus: especially your first year nobody wants to take you seriously." As a first-year teacher, she frequently second-guessed herself and was afraid to venture outside the prescribed curriculum. She also felt that the other teachers thought she didn't know very much or thought of her as "silly." By the second year, that attitude had mostly disappeared, primarily because of how well her students had done on the state test. By the time she was interviewed, Angeles had become both more flexible and more confident. She said she now was focused on fighting for what was best for her kids.

Roger Wallace

When he was interviewed in 2011, Roger Wallace, a veteran teacher, had been the only African American male teacher at Fort River School, in Amherst, Massachusetts, since he had begun teaching there (he retired in 2012 after serving thirty-nine years). Originally planning to become a juvenile justice lawyer, Roger did well on his law boards, gaining admission to the prestigious University of Virginia Law School. But something happened on the way to law school: Roger got hooked on teaching.

A member of the Clark University basketball team, Roger started hanging out with kids from the neighborhood, coaching and playing ball with them. He had always had a knack for talking with kids, and in his senior year, during a semester-long internship in an afterschool program in Worcester, Massachusetts, he realized his passion. He found the work so rewarding that he thought, "Where can I work with kids *before* they get into a great deal of trouble?" Roger also loved economics, history, and math, and wanted these subjects in his life as well. He realized that to help kids before they got into trouble and to keep learning the things he loved "it had to be in a school."

Roger Wallace was born the youngest of four children in Springfield, Massachusetts. He was a student in the A Better Chance (ABC) program for underserved urban youths with academic promise. Through ABC, he attended Wilbraham Academy, an independent school, from 1966 through 1969, and then attended Clark University, in Worcester, Massachusetts, graduating in 1973. His love for educating children was acquired on the basketball courts around the city. At Clark he met Jacqueline Davis, who agreed to marry him. They are the parents of two daughters who are excellent educators in their own right. Roger taught one year at Elm Park Community School, in Worcester, Massachusetts, before leaving for Fort River Elementary School, in Amherst. In his thirty-nine years at Fort River he endeavored to make each year, for each student in his classroom and for the school community, a journey not through the curriculum but of self-discovery. Roger was instrumental in shaping the Amherst-Pelham School System's determination to meet the challenges of teaching students of diverse cultures and social classes. Shortly after his retirement, to recognize the impact he has had on so many students, teachers, and community members, the annual Roger Wallace Excellence in Teaching Award was established to honor an elementary school teacher in the Amherst-Pelham School District.

Immediately after graduating from Clark University, Roger became a teacher. His mother was pleased with his decision: "My mother always told me when I was little, 'You should be a preacher because you never shut up.' I said, 'Mom, preaching and teaching are not far apart.' So that made her happy." Raised in Springfield, an urban area in western Massachusetts, Roger was one of four children of a single mother who for several years relied on public assistance. This experience left an indelible mark, influencing not only his life but also his teaching. As a sixth-grade teacher in Amherst, a socially diverse college town of about 35,000, he wanted his students to understand that some families need more help than others and that some are more fortunate than others. He would speak with his students about this:

> *To admit that you're poor growing up is something most people don't want to do. The government may have given my mother assistance. I can't tell you how much but my brothers and my sisters and I have more than paid it back in our taxes. The government made a good investment. So when you look at someone and you know they have free lunch or reduced-price lunch, take a pause before you open your mouth.*

Roger has a legion of fans in town. Given the scarcity of African American teachers in the school system, people of color in the community frequently want him to teach their children (although the same is true of many White children and their families, who know his reputation as an exceptional teacher). The school's student body is quite diverse, about 65 percent White, with African Americans, Latinos/as (primarily Puerto Ricans, Guatemalans, and Salvadorans), Cambodians, and the children of international graduate students making up the remainder. Roger's students range from those who are very wealthy to those who live in poverty.

There is no greater calling than teaching for Roger, and he says he has certain responsibilities as a Black man: "I remember my cultural history and what was important to my grandma and granddad and my mom." One of the responsibilities he takes seriously is being who he is with all his students. He feels a special responsibility for African American and other students of color: "I do know that in sixth grade, the expectation is that an African American child, particularly a male, but male or female, is coming to my class." Most of the Black children in his school have had Roger as a teacher. But many White parents, knowing his reputation as an excellent teacher, also want their children to be in his class.

Another part of Roger's cultural legacy is to accept all children for who they are rather than what he, or anyone else, expects them to be. He explained that some White teachers expect children of color to be just like the White kids despite their unique individual and cultural differences. Although it's not always easy to explain to White teachers why some strategies might not work with their students of color or working-class students, he attempts to do so:

> *Look, it ain't going to work, they ain't never going to be White. Can you teach them* as they are *instead of "I'll teach them when they become what I want them to be and then they'll be ready to learn"? They're* ready *to learn, they need to learn* now. *So if you want to be a successful teacher of kids of diverse backgrounds,* put your stuff away.

"Putting your stuff away" is about listening to students; learning from them; and discarding any negative preconceptions, biases, and untested assumptions about them. Recognizing that everyone harbors biases, Roger nevertheless encourages teachers to walk into a classroom with fresh eyes and an open heart.

Roger's Approach

Given his feelings about the importance of identity, it is no surprise that Roger is known as a culturally responsive teacher. He is highly respected by parents and by his peers, and recently he was recognized with the town's prized Martin Luther King Award. An active member of the school district's Diversity Committee, he also helped formulate the district's social justice framework, an important document on which he worked with colleagues to affirm the district's commitment to diversity and equity.

Diversity and social justice are at the heart of Roger's teaching philosophy and pedagogy. He is direct with his colleagues when it comes to these concerns:

> *Some of my peers, when cooperative learning was the thing, couldn't figure out why sometimes kids of color fought against that. Because they don't get a cooperative attitude at home. It's, "Boy, you better take out the trash now!" It's not, "How do you feel about that? Could you share that experience with your neighbor?" Many parents of color, particularly those with blue-collar roots, they're not playing that game. It's momma's way or the highway.*

In this Roger underscores Lisa Delpit's (1988) caution on "teaching other people's children": that rather than a one-size-fits-all mentality about pedagogy, teachers need to fit the pedagogy to the students instead of the other way around. Roger said that many of his students of color have spoken to him about why some things don't work for them, "particularly all that cooperative learning stuff." They wanted to hear things from the teacher's mouth, not from their peers: "Have the teacher tell me, because that's the authority figure." This doesn't mean that Roger doesn't use various strategies in his teaching, but rather that he first thinks about how certain approaches will work and how to introduce those strategies.

Roger communicates with his students every day through the lessons he plans, the feedback he gives, and the pedagogy he uses. The most important way to communicate, he says, is to listen: "I'm a good listener and that's a real key thing for a good teacher." He's proud that if his students have a question or a concern, they can call him on either his home or cell phone. "I do that with every child, every child, 24/7. Not just the Black kids, not just the poor kids, not just the White kids, every kid has my number. I would say that out of my eighteen students this year, at least thirteen or fourteen have called me."

Roger is also clear that he can never know what impact his lessons, his pedagogy, or his philosophy will have. Deeply religious and very involved in his church, Roger often used biblical metaphors during our interview to describe his teaching. He compared himself to a sower of seeds, acknowledging that sometimes there are obstacles:

> *We know that oftentimes the seeds can't find a place to root because the ground is too rocky. There's going to be rocks in the way of making children independent, empowered learners so you move the rocks away. Then there are the children for whom you throw the seeds out, the earth covers them correctly, and you begin to see the sprouts and they grow and they're growing at a good pace for them. I use that analogy. I do read the bible—I'm a man of God—and I know that that's my job.*

Roger also communicates often and openly with parents, because he recognizes that all parents try to do the best for their kids despite sometimes tremendous obstacles. Being from a one-parent home himself, Roger has little patience with teachers who attribute a child's lack of success in school to having a single parent. "Excuse me?! Have you met the momma? Do you want to meet a single parent who did both jobs? Meet *my* momma." While he acknowledges that there are disadvantages to having just one parent, he is grateful for the tenacity, resilience, and determination of his mother, who made sure that all her children went to college and were able to have successful lives.

Roger sees himself not only as a teacher but also as a friend, a neighbor, and a counselor. For him education is not a 9 to 3 job; he says he has the "country doctor philosophy." When students call him at home, the only thing he asks in return is that they learn phone etiquette. He practices with them by pretending to be Mrs. Wallace, and he makes sure they learn to be respectful when they speak with her. Rather than a hurried, "Is Mr. Wallace there?" he encourages better manners: "Hi Mrs. Wallace. This is Jerome. How are you?" And after a response, "Is Mr. Wallace home? May I speak with him?"

Recognizing the importance of reaching out to families, Roger builds relationships with them by meeting them where they feel comfortable. He gave a humorous example:

> *I like to have parent conferences in laundromats. If I know a parent goes to a laundromat on Thursdays, I show up with clean hands and a willingness to fold everything but the underwear! Now you may laugh but I have parents who will tell you that they've had their parent conference with me in the laundromat. I'll say, "Just sit down and look through the papers while I fold your clothes." It's what I do. That's why I think I thrive.*

Because family outreach was a significant part of Roger Wallace's success, parents knew they could count on him to do everything possible for their child. As a result of his efforts, he created enormous good will and respect in the community over his nearly four decades of teaching.

Conclusion: Teaching Is an Act of Love

Angeles and Roger differ in many ways to be sure. Angeles was the youngest and most novice teacher I interviewed, Roger the most veteran. They teach in tremendously different sociopolitical contexts, and their backgrounds differ in early upbringing, language, and ethnicity. What they have in common is more important than those differences. Both teach in ways that respect and honor their students' identities and transcend gender, race, and experience. It is an outlook that views each child, regardless of background or circumstance, as a learner capable of great things, now and in the future.

What can we learn from Roger and Angeles? Even in these brief glimpses into their world, we have seen that for these thriving teachers *teaching is an act of love*. Effective teachers know that students who feel loved and valued are free to learn. In both Angeles's and Roger's classrooms, teaching is about more than content; it is also about caring for their students' well-being. They focus their energies on *whom* they teach, not only on what they teach.

Angeles Pérez explained that she loved her students and they loved her in return, and it was because of this love that they worked hard. She called her students her "buddies" and her "babies." When asked what thriving meant to her, she kept going back to the students: it meant getting them excited to learn or seeing them believe in themselves. Our interview took place near the end of the school year. Angeles said, "Especially this group, I don't know what I'm going to do when they go."

Communicating with her students' families is also key to Angeles Pérez's success as a teacher. She said that she had been told in a training session to contact parents twice a month and she tries to do so: "I call the parents for good, I call the parents if I see something concerning. I don't just call them because their kids didn't do their homework." She has also gotten several parents to volunteer in her classroom and the school, realizing that a teacher can't expect parents to come in for no reason: "You've got to call them. You call them, you get them excited." The important thing for her is to personalize communication with families. She also gets her students involved because the more excited they become, the more likely it is that their families will become involved. In many schools like Angeles's, teachers and administrators bemoan the fact that parents don't show up for school-sponsored events because "they don't care." Angeles's experience belies this claim:

> *We had a Dad's Night; three hundred dads showed up! That was amazing and it was because all week I was building it up with any student I saw in the hallway. We had so many dads we didn't know what to do! You've got to get them excited. When parents came to pick up their kids, we're telling them, "It's going to be so much fun, come!" I load the kids in the car, I'm like, "Hey, you've got to come today. You're coming, right?*

For his part, Roger made it clear that loving his students is indispensable to being a teacher. He knows some people might consider his philosophy "soft": "Oh, this is a nice teacher from the seventies, touchy-feely." But for Roger, teaching as an act of love is anything but soft; it is about pushing each student to the limit. He goes so far as to visit his students' homes to help them organize their rooms so that they can study more efficiently or help them with a problem they might have. "They don't pass two vocabulary tests and see if I don't show up at their house and say, 'Where do you study your vocabulary? How do you study? Let's go to your room and organize.'"

Roger says that to be successful with students of color, you have to love them for seven hours a day, 180 days a year, and you have to stick with them no matter what. "To teach kids of diverse backgrounds, you have to be someone who can shuffle a lot of cards." Those cards include being effective with White students as well, many of whom have been changed forever by having had Roger as a teacher. He remembers each and every student he's taught all these years and he keeps records of all of them. He also spoke about teaching the children of former students, and about the many former students who come back to visit him.

Roger said that students often ask him which class has been his favorite over the many years he's been teaching. He tells them that *every* class is his favorite, because he gives his all to each student he has ever taught and no two groups of kids are alike. Although he has had challenging students every year, he views these challenges in terms of something his stepfather, a skilled carpenter, told him: "There's never a bad piece of wood. There's only wood that needs extra planing. You have to find the right purpose for the piece of wood." That has become Roger's philosophy about his students: he pushes for excellence with each student by listening and learning from them. That is what it means to love his students.

NOTES

Delpit, L. 1988. 280–298.
Flores-Gonzalez, N. 2002.
Morrell, E. 2008.
Noddings, N. 1992.

Palmer, P. J. 1998.
Roberts, M. A. 2010. 449–467.
Rolón-Dow, R. 2005. 77–111.
Valenzuela, A. 1999.

Chapter 4

"If I Haven't Taught Them How to Be Good People, That's Failure"

Teachers' Perspectives on the Moral Dimensions of Teaching

Whereas the discussion of school reform has been organized and controlled largely by corporate interests—including publishing companies and foundations, both with vast sums of money to influence educational policy and pedagogy—the moral dimension of teaching has generally been missing in the public discourse, and teachers have had little say in such matters. In contrast to standardization, achievement mandates, and other instrumentalist views on the purposes of public education, teachers spend a great deal of time thinking about ethical issues. Who are they teaching and why? What can they do to promote not only learning but also empathy, caring, and civic courage among their students? What role do they play in developing positive and inclusive attitudes in their students about their peers and, as they get older, their fellow citizens? As the editors and authors of a book on this topic make clear, knowledge and skills are not enough if they are not used for both individual and public good (Murrell et al. 2010). This chapter presents the perspectives of Carmen Tisdale, Amber Bechard, and Adam Heenan—caring and courageous teachers who know that some of the current practices labeled as "education reform" do little to take into account nonquantifiable issues such as teaching moral responsibility and being culturally responsive to students' identities. This chapter focuses on two aspects of the moral dimensions of teaching: *teaching as instilling values of empathy and responsibility* and *teaching as culturally responsive pedagogy*.

Instilling Values of Empathy and Responsibility

One of the responsibilities the teachers I interviewed take most seriously is to instill in their students enduring values that will help make them moral human beings leading consequential lives. These values include empathy with and responsibility for others, values consistent with an ethic of care (Noddings 1992) but often overshadowed by the undisputed focus on individualism that characterizes much of modern life in the United States. John Gunderson, a high school teacher in Southern California, bemoaned the exclusive focus on standardized tests that has taken over education. He was passionate that a single-minded emphasis on AP classes, honors classes, and testing does not necessarily result in students' leading a more moral life. Instead, "We need to focus on being a whole child and work on the true meaning of learning besides just regurgitating information."

Although they certainly want their students to shine intellectually, Amber Bechard, Adam Heenan, and Carmen Tisdale also recognize that trying to understand others who are different from us and demonstrating responsibility for others are important human values that need to be nurtured.

Carmen Tisdale

A teacher at Carver Lyon Elementary School, in Columbia, South Carolina, Carmen Tisdale had been teaching for eleven years when she was interviewed (primarily in South Carolina, with a year in California and three in Virginia). Carmen defines teaching as a moral commitment: "I'd like to think that I'm giving my students goodness for their hearts along with the education I'm providing." She rated helping develop her students as moral human beings at the top of her list of reasons she teaches. "I just want them to be good people and if I haven't taught them how to be good people, that's failure to me."

When I asked what thriving meant to her, Carmen responded:

> *I think thriving is when you are giving your children the best that you have and you feel that it has helped them intellectually and socially. That you're not only building their education and their intellect, but you're building their character. The first day of school I tell my children how important it is to be a person of good character and to be a good person in the world. I say, if you have a good heart, it speaks volumes about you, so much more than if you are the smartest kid in my class.*

All teachers recognize that their profession is undervalued and that they will likely not become famous or rich; they also recognize that teaching, even in the best of circumstances, is a difficult job. But even in challenging circumstances, teachers want to make their mark. Carmen described teaching as "hard and heavy because there's so much more to it than a book and a pencil." She is aware of the heavy moral responsibility she has as a teacher:

Carmen Tisdale is currently a second-grade educator at Carver-Lyon Elementary School, in the historic Waverly community of Columbia, South Carolina. She has been teaching for twelve years and has also taught first and third grade. Carmen is committed to going beyond the classroom to impact the education of young children. She has served as the elementary representative-at-large on the Executive Committee for the National Council of Teachers of English and is also a member of the Early Childhood Education Assembly of that organization. She is a National Board Certified teacher and former Teacher of the Year. Her passion is culturally relevant teaching; she believes that when done with fidelity, this focus is the key to successful academic achievement.

> *I think to be a good teacher you need to love your children in spite of themselves, in spite of whatever they bring to you. You love them unconditionally and you tell them that you love them. But what about the children who aren't getting a lot of love? Our job is to reach those children. Teaching is so much more than putting information into their heads. You're helping to form people who are going to lead this world, and if you look at it that way, you take it more seriously.*

Carmen underscored that some children are harder to love than others, particularly a girl like Geneva, a student who had challenged Carmen's patience and good humor to the limit: "My gosh! That's a whole other ball of wax!" Nonetheless, knowing that she wanted to make a difference in her students' lives made her "go in the next day and try to love Geneva more." Loving Geneva in the tougher moments made a difference. A couple of years after Geneva went on to another school, a substitute teacher handed Carmen a note from Geneva telling Carmen how much she loved her. When Carmen expressed surprise, the woman told her that Geneva hadn't asked about anyone else at Carmen's school but "she asks about you every time I see her."

Adam Heenan

A social studies high school teacher in a large urban high school in Chicago, Adam's students are largely Latino/a and African American. Although Adam is White, he is comfortable with students of diverse backgrounds because as a child he attended schools with large numbers of African American students. In addition, he has learned Spanish and he teaches from a decidedly multicultural and social justice perspective.

Adam Heenan is a teacher and education activist in Chicago. He currently teaches financial literacy and American law at Curie Metropolitan High School, where he is also the elected delegate to the Chicago Teachers Union. In 2012 he was recognized as one of three Chicago Public Schools Service-Learning Teachers of the Year, and he is currently a Mikva Challenge Action Civics Instructional Leader in Chicago Public Schools. Adam has previously taught at a South Side charter school, as well as in his hometown of Kankakee, Illinois. He is an active member of CORE (Caucus of Rank and File Educators). In 2011, Adam started the UseYourTeacherVoice Project on YouTube. He also blogs and tweets @ClassroomSooth on issues of teaching and learning in Chicago and nationwide. In his free time, Adam reads comic books and rides motorcycles but not simultaneously.

When a high school senior, Adam was nominated by the superintendent of his school district for the Golden Apple Award, a scholarship that pays a large part of the cost of college for a hundred Illinois high school students who want to pursue teaching and agree to teach for at least five years in what is euphemistically called a "school of need." Adam was thrilled because he had already been considering teaching as a career. "This was a way for me to serve my community and do what I love and make it my career and what I am as a person."

Adam also talked about the values that are important to him as a teacher, the same values he wants to instill in his students: "Honesty and resilience, dignity, resourcefulness, and consistency: those are the things that have been able to construct my teacher identity so far." He emphasized that he was not speaking about standards as currently defined in many school districts: "I have high expectations, I just have them with my kids, they know I have them; I don't need standards to tell them."

Although idealistic about the values he hopes to instill in his students, Adam is realistic about the relative importance of his classes. He knows that his students have many demands on their lives, both in and outside school, and realizes that every teacher believes his or her subject is the most important. "My assignment probably isn't the most pressing thing in the world to them and I need to respect that." Nevertheless, for Adam, the intrinsic values that he tries to model for his students are even more essential:

> *So beyond that, do I think they come away from my classroom being better human beings? Yeah, I think so. I think they're better off because I am here. That sounds so egotistical! But I like to think that my students come away learning from my class even if they didn't learn exactly what I had in mind. They come away with a broader worldview.*

Adam used the example of a project on homelessness that his students were doing in his economics class. He expected them to develop empathy for others, learn research skills, take responsibility for their work, and take initiative, all while being innovative. The students had to demonstrate what they had learned and also develop an action plan. Adam explained that he wanted this project to benefit their community; it was not just for a grade: "For me they have to create something of value for other people, not just themselves."

Amber Bechard

Amber Bechard had been teaching kindergarten in a very privileged private school in Massachusetts when her husband was told he was being transferred to Chicago. Knowing that she would be teaching a much more diverse student body, she took a class in multicultural curriculum with me. For the first time she, as a White woman, felt she had permission to teach with a multicultural perspective, something she then tried out in her nearly all-White kindergarten class before moving to Chicago. "I just needed someone to say, 'You don't have to be Black to do this.' I needed you to say it's okay if you

As the thirteenth of fifteen children in a blended family living in what her mother described as "abject poverty," **Amber Bechard** recognizes how her background influenced her determination to become a teacher and influences her still. Although surrounded by a loving family with a strong work ethic, she was not expected to pursue postsecondary education. Her parents and older siblings, she said, "took this bold ambition with a grain of salt" since nobody in the family had ever attended college, and most hadn't even finished high school. She identifies with her students, many of whom are first- and second-generation immigrants (mostly Mexican but also Filipino/a and Eastern European) because, although they have different racial and ethnic backgrounds, she sees their dreams as very similar to hers. Currently an eighth-grade language arts teacher at JFK Middle School, in Plainfield, Illinois, Amber is also an adjunct professor at Dominican University and the University of St. Francis. She earned her doctorate in education (in curriculum and instruction) from Aurora University, in Illinois, and has received National Board Certification in early adolescent literacy. Special education, multicultural and literacy education, and teacher education are her passions. She has received two Fulbright scholarships and several other awards that included travel to a number of places around the country as well as to Mexico, Peru, and South Africa. She has developed curriculum units, collaborated on community initiatives, served on district committees, and presented at state and national conferences. Someday she hopes to move full-time into higher education, where she finds the inspiring energy of developing teachers nourishing and hopeful.

don't know it. It's okay for me that I grew up in a relatively privileged life." The freedom to bring up these conversations about race and privilege was relevant even in her all-White kindergarten class.

Amber was hired to teach language arts to middle school students in Plainfield, an urbanized suburb in the Chicago area that was rapidly becoming extremely diverse. Rather than being intimidated by the dramatic change in her teaching context, Amber was fascinated by the things she was learning. She loves teaching her middle school students as much as she had loved teaching her kindergarten children.

Working with her colleagues in other subject areas, Amber instills values of responsibility and empathy through the curriculum. After her eighth graders read the memoir of Aaron Elster, a Holocaust survivor (Elster and Miller 2007), she had them write their own memoirs, after gathering recipes, anecdotes, photographs, and stories and prompting their parents to tell their immigration stories. These memoirs included photo collages of their families and friends. "In my classroom I teach what I'm supposed to teach, what the state tells me to teach that's good for kids, but I also teach kids to embrace themselves and each other." The art teacher had the students make beautiful covers, and they also learned how to bind their books. "They left the last day of the school year with their yearbook in one hand and their memoir in the other, and they valued who they were, and they valued their stories." This was true even of the boys ("fourteen-year-old boys going off to high school with their ego in one hand and their memoir in the other"), who one might think would not care about such things.

However, Amber and the other eighth-grade social studies teachers also wanted the students to understand what it means to have a moral obligation to others. Extending the study of memoir, they invited Aaron Elster to speak to the class in person. The students took charge of the entire activity, planning the visit, placing posters all over the school, and highlighting the event with quotes from the memoir as well as relevant quotes from the Dalai Lama and Thomas Jefferson.

> *Three hundred and thirty eighth graders sat in complete silence while this man walked in, and then gave him a standing ovation without being coached. Just on his arrival! Then he spoke, and on three occasions, he broke down in tears. At the end of the talk, a hundred kids purchased his book even though they already knew the entire story. They valued his story, they valued his message. For eighth graders to value the story of an eighty-seven-year-old man who was a ten-year-old escapee from the Polish ghetto was amazing.*

A postscript to this story: when the Illinois Holocaust Museum opened a few years ago, with Bill Clinton the star attraction, Aaron Elster invited the team of teachers who had used his memoir in the curriculum to the museum opening. He gave them all tickets and they got to sit with the survivors.

When Aaron and his son approached them, Aaron said, "I want to introduce you to these teachers from JFK." His son said, "Oh, this is the school you haven't stopped talking about." Aaron responded, "This is the school that has touched me in a way that no other school ever has. I speak all the time and I've never been so impacted. The kids really understood and respected my message."

Culturally Responsive Pedagogy

Spurred by such books as Gloria Ladson-Billings's *The Dreamkeepers* (2009; first edition, 1994) about effective teachers of African American students, the field of culturally responsive pedagogy has expanded to include Latino/a, American Indian, and students of other racial and ethnic backgrounds (Irvine 2003; Gay 2010, first edition, 2000; Irizarry, 2011a). Culturally responsive pedagogy is not a specific set of strategies to use with students of a particular background but rather a mindset that respects and honors students' cultures, experiences, and histories and finds ways to include them in the curriculum. Culturally responsive teaching affirms students' identities and at the same time expands their world; it respects and admires students and their communities and also holds high expectations for them. It means learning about students' cultural and family practices and values and infusing those practices and values in the curriculum. It means teaching students that their voice is just as important as anybody else's. In the end, it means believing that students are capable of achieving high standards and worthy of a quality education. (Chapter 10 discusses culturally responsive education in more depth.)

The teachers I interviewed for this book demonstrate their cultural responsiveness in many ways. María Brummer, a high school teacher in Tucson, explained that in order to teach her students well, "I need to know where they're coming from. I need to know what their goals are in life." For María, this means, at the very least, understanding who they are as cultural beings. John Gunderson, a high school social studies teacher in Southern California, teaches a psychology course in which he has his students create "a playlist of their lives" that will not only reveal who they are but also allow them to explore who they might want to be. "My big thing is trying to bring that human side into it and make it personal and try to tie it into their real life and their world and make them think." Geoffrey Winikur, a high school teacher in Philadelphia, creates cultural responsiveness through the curriculum: "I love the idea of having a curriculum that really embraces the notion of diversity."

Carmen Tisdale

Feeling a responsibility to give back to her community is a major reason Carmen is a teacher. She teaches in a predominantly African American school because she believes that children need to see their culture and race reflected in the professionals around them, something many children of color do not get to see. As a child Carmen experienced a sense of joy and pride when she saw other African

Americans in positions of responsibility and status, and she wants the same for her students. "As a Black woman, I have to convey to them—especially at the school I'm at now, it's not just African American, it's low socioeconomic—that they are valuable and that they are smart and that they can be so much more."

Offered four jobs when she returned to South Carolina, Carmen chose Carver Lyon Elementary: not only was the student body African American, so were the majority of staff members and the principal. Carmen believes that having these role models in school will prompt her students to look beyond the limited choices they see around them, and she reminds them of these possibilities frequently. She mentioned that one of her first graders, Jamal, had told her he wanted to be a bus driver:

> So I'm always the one to say, "I want you to think about owning a fleet of buses." There's nothing wrong with being a bus driver, there's nothing wrong with being anything that you are if that's what you truly want to be and you're good at it, but I feel he's saying that because that's what he knows and he rides the bus every morning. He sees that person driving the bus and he knows that it's a job. I think it's my place—not that it's not anybody else's place—but it's my place to show him that he can be more and that he needs to be more.

Carmen also spoke about being a "Black Momma," something that connects culturally with her African American students and that also demonstrates that she cares about them:

> We just have—and I'm sure all cultures do—a certain way of talking, there's a rhythm to it. I could tell when my White kids in my previous school would first come to my classroom, most of them were culturally shocked, because they were not used to what I termed "Black Momma." It is just who I am. We all bring our culture to the classroom whether we realize it or not.

About using this approach in her current class, she explained, "I might say, 'Get your behind over there and sit down.' That's what your Black Momma would say and it's not to say every Black Momma would say it." Carmen said that just using Black dialect created a mutual understanding with her students.

Referring more specifically to the controversy about Ebonics (see, for example, Delpit & Doudy 2002; Miner 1998), Carmen spoke about maintaining a balance between language that is socially accepted in general society and helping children understand that their language is also a legitimate form of communication:

> *I know I have to teach them language that is accepted in school, but I also give them confirmation that their home language is a real language. There is nothing wrong with it. In some ways, I feel I offer them validation of who they are, and I understand them just because of who I am. They get to see themselves and experience the familiar while learning outside of their box.*

Besides being their teacher, Carmen sees her job as being a family member as well. She is their mom and more at school: "You know how it is, you're the social worker and advocate; you are the momma. 'I'm putting shea butter on your little ashy face. That's what your momma does.'" In turn, her students feel perfectly comfortable in saying, as if they were at home, "Ms. Tisdale, I need some shea butter." She says, "I really am a part of that village it takes to raise a child."

Carmen incorporates African American culture in her classroom in other ways as well. During Black History Month, her brother, who is a rapper, composed a rap for her students about famous African Americans. "It showed how much children learn through music!" One of Carmen's students, April, had a learning disability. Well into the school year, April still did not know all the letters of the alphabet. Carmen was teaching the class about Rosa Parks and asked April who was the lady who refused to give up her seat to a White man. April thought hard, beat herself up for not knowing, and looked for help from the other kids, who all said, "Michelle? Michelle Obama?" (Carmen explained that ever since Barack Obama was elected President, Michelle Obama was the answer to everything.) She said to April, "No, come on April, you can get it. You can get it."

> *Then I began to rap the song and she said, "Rosa Parks!" because that was the name that was coming next. It was just a beautiful thing, and throughout the whole unit, whenever I would mention anyone in the song, they would break out in song. I had to wait until they got to the end of the verse because they all would join in.*

What made the experience especially meaningful was that the students didn't just learn a watered down version of Black history, which is the norm in most history books:

> *I stretched their learning and made them see their own possibilities as we did research projects and wrote letters to some of the people in the rap song. I was able to show them that these are real people who live real lives today. They could be one of these people.*

The children even heard back from Tom Joyner, Carmen said.

Amber Bechard

Carmen Tisdale is African American, as are most of her students, and this helps to explain both her support and her success with them. But what about teachers who don't share the same culture as their students? Many teachers have had neither personal nor professional experiences with students whose identities are different from theirs and may feel uncomfortable trying to be culturally responsive. Amber Bechard used to be one of these teachers.

She began to learn about multicultural education shortly before moving to Chicago and brought her excitement for multicultural education with her from Massachusetts to Illinois, along with her confidence in broaching difficult conversations about diversity and privilege:

> *Having had those conversations with five- and six-year-old kids gave me the courage to have them with my colleagues and with fourteen- and fifteen-year-old kids in my middle school which is now a very relevant conversation because the demographics are so different, the students so diverse.*

Her new school in a suburb of Chicago was not what she expected. While the racial and ethnic diversity was growing significantly, it was a fairly new issue for the community. Thirty-two languages were spoken in the school, by students of a great many ethnicities, and Amber felt "being willing to talk about our differences and value our differences is very, very important. Being comfortable enough to do that." Still, teachers were for the most part silent and unsure about what to do with regard to the changing demographics. Because of the course she'd taken on multicultural education, Amber "wanted to welcome these students and respond to these students." She jumped in and started all sorts of projects, as well as beginning (and a few years later successfully completing) a doctoral program in multicultural education.

Amber also promoted a multicultural perspective in the school. She started a multicultural club, the first one in the district, and now three of the seven middle schools have multicultural clubs. In the spring, they have a culture fair at which the students and families display the projects they've developed as well as videos they've made. One student made a video depicting prejudice through music. Another interviewed fellow students about why they sit with students of the same race at lunch. Others have done projects on their family genealogy.

Amber spoke animatedly about the culture fair and how it has generated so much excitement in the school and community. The previous year, "parents were jumping on board":

> *I had a group of African American parents who did a huge display on Barack Obama and another display on the Little Rock Nine. This year the African American parents did a huge display on hair; they had some mannequin heads and they did braids. And I*

had another family from India, the mom does henna. She had a table set up and she was painting henna on the kids. And this one mother from Indonesia, she brought in Thai dancers and Indonesian dancers. We had the praise dancers from a local church, ethnic foods, student projects, art projects, poetry, projects from the social studies teachers. This was our third annual culture fair and it's now held at two different schools.

Administrators are trying to take the fair districtwide. For Amber, a really rewarding experience "starts real little, as a passion, and it explodes beyond. So now it's not just the Amber Bechard Diversity Show [laughing], it's the district's." As a result of the fairs and the efforts of many individuals, the district now has a diversity committee.

Because of her passion for teaching and for multicultural education, Amber has been a catalyst for what started "real little" and has grown in her school and the larger community. She spoke about the ramifications of something as simple as starting a Culture Club in one school:

The reward, I think, comes from the tiniest little thing, like the kid who said this year, "I never knew I was related to Billie Holiday. That's really cool. I'm going to do my project on that." Then the mom who says, "Next year let's do this between three schools so that we can have the high school, the middle school, and the elementary school all together and we can make this even bigger."

More parents are visiting the school. Especially rewarding for Amber was "to see that when you start a little fire, when *you* start a little fire, it can really get big. And it's getting bigger. It's awesome!"

Adam Heenan

For Adam Heenan, being able to talk naturally about race and other differences with his students is about creating a culturally responsive space. "We have to build a community about trust before we even get there." Adam is comfortable having these discussions for a number of reasons, among them his being Jewish and having grown up in a predominantly Black community. He can relate to what it means to be a minority in certain contexts and feels confident

that recognition of my heritage as a minority group has enabled me to talk with students about our collective definitions of "minority" and "diversity" in new ways. In other words, we can take collective ownership of the many ways in which we are diverse as a class: ethnicity, religion, gender and sexual identity, disability, and in other ways.

His comfort with diversity also stems from the relationships he has built over time with students of color: "They tell me I am real, they tell me I am not trying to fake it."

For Adam, becoming a culturally responsive teacher means establishing close and caring relationships with his students from the start. He told how this came about with Jhesyka, who he had been warned was a "difficult" student:

> *There is a girl and her name is spelled J-H-E-S-Y-K-A, and I'm like, how do I say that name? And I put it on the board of the teachers' room and ask, "Has anyone had this student? J-H-E-S-Y-K-A and how do I say her name?" And Mr. Roosevelt says, "Oh yeah! I had that student, her name is pronounced 'Jessica,' be careful around her, she's one of those students, kind of rambunctious, be ready for her!" I go in the first day of school and go down the list of the kids' names, taking attendance, and I say her name, and she does this double take. Like I imagine no one has ever probably got her name right on the first day, right? And I had such a great relationship with her from day one. And maybe it is kind of a hidden curriculum for the other students, that there is a teacher who cared enough to research how to say this girl's name.*

Being culturally responsive also means including in the curriculum topics that are of consequence to students. Issues that impact the daily lives of students of color include discrimination, exclusion, and marginalization, topics not generally discussed in most classrooms. Adam said that he broaches topics such as race, class, gender, and privilege, but when I asked whether he thought all teachers should discuss these issues, he was cautious: "I think it depends on *who* is talking about it and *how* they are talking about it." He feels some teachers don't really understand poverty and discrimination, and they don't see their students as their equals. These teachers can do more harm than good having these conversations. "I think they are very much of the pull-yourself-up-by-your-bootstraps mentality and would never admit that some people don't have bootstraps or don't have boots. Which is my camp, right?" But if teachers are willing to genuinely listen and have honest discussions about race and class, he said they should, with this caveat:

> *When the topics are broached haphazardly, without a comfortable space, most often the outcome will not be beneficial to anyone; it could result in further misunderstandings and deeper prejudices. Teachers can do it, as long as they are careful and have a good understanding of diversity and an appreciation for what multiculturalism is and can be.*

Conclusion: Teaching Is an Ethical Endeavor

There are many lessons to be learned from Adam Heenan, Amber Bechard, and Carmen Tisdale, but the major one is obvious: teaching is always an ethical endeavor. Teachers need to be aware that their actions, attitudes, and practices may have untold and longstanding repercussions, however unintended, on their students' lives. Whether it is teaching students responsibility for themselves and for their neighbors or learning about students' identities in order to become culturally responsive educators, the ethical nature of teaching is unmistakable. Although Carmen, Amber, and Adam are extraordinary teachers, they are no different from many other caring and compassionate teachers. They are, however, unequivocally committed to teaching as a moral enterprise, and they demonstrate this commitment in innumerable ways in their teaching, their relationships with their students and their students' communities, and their collaboration with colleagues.

Unfortunately, in the teacher-bashing environment so prevalent today, these kinds of qualities and commitments are too often invisible, even though for students school isn't just a kind of 9-to-3 affair but (as Adam said) "their *lives*!" Adam, Amber, and Carmen see their job as a moral endeavor to help their students be all they can be while also caring about others. They know that a quality education is the only way children from marginalized communities can hope to have a chance of living a consequential life.

In an era when there is so little talk about ethics in education, these teachers stand out as exemplary educators who respect and affirm students' identities and communities and who dare to believe in these students, honor who they are, and teach them to be responsible and moral human beings.

NOTES

Apple, M. 2006.
Darling-Hammond, L. 2010.
Delpit, L. and Doudy, J. K., eds. 2002.
Elster, A. & Miller, J. E. 2007.
Garland, S. 2011.
Gay, G. 2010.
Irizarry, J. G. 2011b. 188–214.

Irvine, J. J. 2003.
Ladson-Billings. 2009.
Miner, B. 1998. 79–88.
Murrell, P. E. 2001.
Nichols, S. L. & Berliner, D. C. 2007.
Noddings, N. 2005.

Chapter 5

The Quest for Knowledge

Teacher Learning In and Out of the Classroom

Is teaching an art or a science? Are teachers born or made? Can one learn to be an excellent teacher? These questions lie at the heart of an enduring debate in education.

Whether teaching is an art or a science has probably been disputed for as long as teaching has been a profession, and doubtless the issue will never be resolved. Clearly, teaching is an art because it has artistic and creative elements; anyone who has ever seen a master teacher in action can attest to the improvisation, the flexibility, the sheer inventiveness, that characterize teaching. These are things that cannot be measured, put down on paper, or copied. Teaching is also a science: at its core is a logic, a scholarly tradition, and a research base that informs both new and practicing teachers, as well as teacher educators, about effective pedagogy and curricula.

Perhaps a better way to define teaching is as a *craft*, with elements of both science and art. Craftspeople need to know the techniques and materials with which they work, as do teachers. But craftspeople also develop the creative impulse that lifts their work from mere imitation into art. Like teachers, craftspeople are concerned with not just the product but also the process of their craft. They need to keep abreast of the state of the art in their field: what innovations and technologies are available? What materials and pedagogies are likely to improve the work?

The underlying issue is teacher learning. No matter how good they may be intuitively—whether or not they are "born teachers"—good teachers know that their work cannot remain static; it needs to improve constantly based on new techniques, materials, technologies, and innovations, as well as critical reflection on and assessment of these things. At the same time, they know that intuition, creativity, and imagination are equally indispensable. The way to improve their craft is to remain vigilant about new theories and perspectives, ever ready to learn and always on the lookout for new advances. This means being intellectuals and researchers, artists and scientists. As Carmen Tisdale thought about her own learning, she linked it with making changes in her pedagogy: "You're thriving when you continue to grow. When you become stagnant and you're using the same lesson plans you used ten years ago, there's a problem."

Learning as a Lifelong Journey

Learning is an indispensable part of being a teacher. This entails redefining teaching as an intellectual activity and teachers as intellectuals, something that is far from how teachers are currently viewed. Henry Giroux (1988) has written cogently about what this means:

> In the final analysis, teachers need to develop a discourse and set of assumptions that allow them to function more specifically as transformative intellectuals. As intellectuals, they will combine reflection and action in the interest of empowering students with the skills and knowledge needed to address injustices and to be critical actors committed to developing a world free of oppression and exploitation (p. xxxiv).

The ways in which teachers go about continuing to learn are varied and depend on their interests and the availability of resources. Of course, teacher preparation is an important part of developing and sustaining new teachers in both the science and the art of teaching. Inservice professional development can also help teachers keep informed and updated. Nevertheless, what typically goes by the name of "professional development" is not always what teachers want or need to improve their craft. Many teachers find that participating in self-directed learning such as teacher inquiry and reading groups, becoming involved in professional organizations, attending and presenting at conferences, mentoring novice teachers, taking and teaching university courses, and so on, are more meaningful and satisfying than one-shot professional development sessions. In the former types of activities, professional collegiality is crucial. Learning from peers is one of the most effective ways for teachers to learn, as has been illustrated both theoretically and in practical terms through numerous examples in teacher research (Cochran-Smith & Lytle 2009); teacher leadership (Lieberman & Friedrich 2010); teacher writing (Nieto 2005b; Freedman et al. 1999), and teacher support groups (Long et al. 2006).

Amber Bechard, as enthusiastic a learner as one could ever find, is always learning. Having completed her doctoral studies after teaching for a couple of decades, she is still on the lookout for opportunities to extend her education. Even her summers are full of learning experiences: "Teachers typically think they have the summer off, but for me, summer is the time to refuel my brain and change my perspective and enhance my learning, so I find teacher seminars." At the time I interviewed her, Amber was preparing to attend a National Endowment for the Humanities summer seminar on the philosophy of Hannah Arendt. She has received a Freeman grant as well as a number of Fulbright grants, and has traveled to China, South Africa, Peru, Mexico, and Japan, bringing back new perspectives and resources to enrich her curriculum and classroom. In addition, she pursued National Board Certification in language arts and found it "a very reflective process" and a powerful learning experience. Amber became a teacher because she loves learning, and she continues to be a teacher because she wants to share that passion with her students, both her middle school students and her graduate students at a local university where she is an adjunct professor. "I would hope my middle school students, and my grad students, would say, 'Yeah, she's thriving. Look at that passion! You can't *not* catch it!'"

Hyung Nam, a high school social studies teacher in Portland, Oregon, says he probably wouldn't have lasted long as a teacher if, in his first year, he hadn't come across Rethinking Schools, an organization of progressive teachers with headquarters in Milwaukee, Wisconsin. As a beginning teacher, Hyung was struggling not only because of his lack of experience but also because he was teaching at a school with few resources. When he found out that two of the founders of Rethinking Schools, Bill Bigelow and Linda Christensen, were then teaching in Portland, he sought them out and discovered a Portland area Rethinking Schools TGIF (Thank Goodness It's Friday) gathering in which a teacher study group was just beginning to explore the topic of globalization. He joined at once. The group met twice a month for several years, sharing ideas about how to teach these things to their students and collaborating on creating curriculum. (The project eventually resulted in the book *Rethinking Globalization* [2002], edited by Bill Bigelow and Bob Peterson.) Hyung's relationship with Rethinking Schools has had a profound influence both on his teaching and his life: "Having colleagues share ideas and resources and learn from one another really made me feel that I could teach."

Geoffrey Winikur, a high school English teacher in Philadelphia, has also been an active participant in several out-of-school learning experiences. Although teachers too infrequently get to work long-term and consistently with their colleagues, Geoffrey believes this kind of work is essential ("I love the adult relationships in teaching"); he has taken courses offered by the National Endowment for the Humanities and used those experiences to develop curriculum for his classes on African literature and film and the Atlantic slave trade.

Like Alicia Lopez, who you will read about later in this chapter, Geoffrey also writes poetry derived from his teaching experiences, an activity encouraged by the Philadelphia Writing Project (the local site of the National Writing Project), in which he is an active participant, having been introduced to it by his mother who was involved in the organization when she was a teacher. He and his colleague Christina Puntel teach a Philadelphia Writing Project summer institute, which keeps him on his toes as a learner. "We really learned a lot about curriculum design through working together. When you can really talk deeply with somebody, that's a gift."

John Nguyen and Alicia Lopez epitomize what it means to learn to teach and teach to learn. Through their words and reflections, you will see the many ways they keep their teaching fresh and new.

John Nguyen has always wanted to be in education. A major influence in his decision to become a teacher was his grandfather. John studied to be a teacher at the University of Connecticut–Storrs. In addition, he completed a semester abroad in London, England, earned credits in Vietnam, and student taught in Hartford. While at UCONN, John took a year off and volunteered with Americorps National Civilian Community Corps (Domestic Peace Corps). He was stationed in Maryland and worked on community service projects in Texas; New England; Washington, D.C.; New Orleans; and Baltimore. He finished his UCONN master's degree in Washington, D.C., where he interned at the National Council for the Social Studies. He stayed in the D.C. metro area and taught social studies at T.C. Williams High School, in Alexandria, Virginia. After teaching there for three years, John moved back to Connecticut to teach social studies at James Hillhouse High School, in New Haven, for eight years. While at Hillhouse, he volunteered to rebuild homes in New Orleans after Hurricane Katrina. He was also selected to participate in the sister school exchange program between Connecticut and Shandong Province, China. After eight years of teaching, John was promoted to assistant principal and is currently in his third year. In 2007, John was honored with the Milken National Family Foundation Educator Award.

John Nguyen

Inspired by his grandfather, a chemistry teacher in Vietnam, John Nguyen decided in eighth grade that he too wanted to be a teacher. By this time, he and his family had emigrated to the United States and were living in Connecticut. John began his teaching career in Alexandria, Virginia. When I interviewed him, he had been teaching civics and social studies for eleven years in New Haven, Connecticut, the last eight at James Hillhouse High School. Hillhouse's student body of approximately nine hundred is about 80 percent African American, 19 percent Latino/a, and 1 percent "other." One of only two schools in the city not designated as a magnet school, it is a default choice for most of the students. "If you don't get into all the other schools, you come to our school."

At the beginning of his time at Hillhouse, John was severely tested by his students. Some of his class sizes were extremely large; although by city law classes were supposed to have no more than twenty-seven students, one of his classes had fifty-five. There were also discipline problems. In one class, students would throw things at one another while he was writing on the board. Laughing, John commented, "That was my first lesson—never to write on the board again! I would always use the overhead or some sort of projector." He was called awful things as well. But though it was a demanding first year, he found "the right people" to help him out. Learning from mentors and peers was enormously helpful in those first years.

In spite of the difficulties he had, John had purposely chosen to teach in New Haven because of the diversity. He didn't "want to teach in a homogeneous school like most of Connecticut." He mentioned the irony of teaching in a "diverse school" that is not diverse at all but "almost homogeneous African American." Still, he "wanted an area where I could make a lot of impact and change. Most definitely, I'm glad I chose this school." John has never taught AP or honors classes, preferring "to teach the students for the most part that have been neglected."

Self-Initiated Learning

An enthusiastic learner, John set about learning to be a teacher at the improbable age of thirteen, when he was in eighth grade. It was the summer of the Tiananmen Square uprising, and shortly thereafter the Berlin Wall came down. These were eye-opening events. "I realized there's a world outside of Connecticut and they're fighting for what I took for granted, which was democracy." Years later, John went to both China and Germany, visits that have strengthened his teaching.

In high school, completely on his own, he volunteered for the AIDS Quilt Project in Connecticut, the only high school student to do so. He also volunteered for both Habitat for Humanity and Amnesty International. During college (the University of Connecticut at Storrs), he took a year off to join AmeriCorps, which upset his parents because they were afraid he wouldn't return to school. But as he said, "I wanted to be a teacher, so of course I was going to go back to school!" During his year with AmeriCorps, John helped clean up after floods in New Orleans, set up a teen center in Baltimore, and release fish in the streams of New England. He and his AmeriCorps peers were twice invited to the White House. "I knew all of those experiences would make me better. I knew I was going to be a teacher but I didn't know what kind of teacher, and AmeriCorps really showed me that I wanted to be a social studies teacher."

Creating Curriculum Through Learning

Five months after Hurricane Katrina devastated the Gulf Coast, John, then a teacher, went to New Orleans during his February break to work with Habitat for Humanity. His Habitat group of ten (they dubbed themselves "The All-Star Team") gutted six houses in five days, while the rest of the over one hundred volunteers did only thirty. When he returned from his week in New Orleans, he created a PowerPoint presentation for his students: "I encouraged my students to become not only better students but, more important, better people."

John is a quintessential student, always curious and eager to learn, and this is also what he wants for his students. He has used everything he's learned in his life to develop curriculum and hone his instructional practices. In his pedagogy, he often uses photography and music. He likes to play games with his students, especially as a review technique, explaining: "Every day I have a question of the day. I have no problem missing a whole day of class if they're responding and relating to it." His students also contribute challenging questions. One day, a student asked why the death of a Yale student got more publicity in the news than a death of a Hillhouse student. "It ended up being an amazing lesson about media and socioeconomic issues. To this day, I've never forgotten that lesson and the students involved. It was one of those days you cherish as a teacher."

John's visits to Washington, D.C., have motivated him to create various activities related to politics and government. One of his favorites is "The Top Ten Favorite Amendments." The students learn about and discuss the Amendments to the Constitution, summarize them, evaluate them in writing, and then rank their top ten favorites, matching a picture with each. John also has them create political commercials. Another favorite activity is to have students select two Supreme Court cases and explain, in a PowerPoint presentation, whether or not they agree with the decisions and why or why not.

Another way John keeps learning is by making good use of as many community resources as he can. He became friends with a judge he met while on jury duty several years before, and convinced her to speak to his classes. Her visits are now a favorite annual event. "She's an amazing speaker. She's definitely one of the highlights. She won them over by bringing them candy. [Laughing.] She relates to the kids. I think by the fifth class she's tired but she does five classes for me."

Having a full life of other interests and goals is important not only for one's mental health, but also for one's ability to thrive in the profession. Finding a teacher more conscientious than John Nguyen would be difficult, and finding one who began preparing for his teaching career in junior high school would be almost impossible. Yet John has learned that being a good teacher means making time for himself as well, not only for his ongoing learning, but also just to have a break:

> *You need to have your own personal space and personal time. It's nice during your first few years to be so obsessive about teaching so it gets you better, but there also has to be a time when you have to step away from it. It's hard to do. It took me a bunch of years to figure that out.*

He believes teachers should take the day off if necessary rather than teach badly.

Passing on a Passion for Learning

John grew up in Danbury, Connecticut in what he calls the "slum/refugee area," which helps him understand his students' backgrounds and experiences:

> *I go back there as a reminder of where I came from, and I always tell my students my personal story so they understand our backgrounds aren't that much different. We build that connection right away. Despite our differences, we have more similarities than differences.*

Building on these similarities, John develops close relationships with his students. But unlike John, given their often negative experiences with public education, many of his students are unmotivated learners. John sees it as his job to motivate them. His love of learning influences how he teaches and how he views his role:

> *I always tell my students that once, as a teacher, you stop trying to learn, you become a bad teacher. Same thing with the students; I try to suggest that to them. They should always be in quest of knowledge—that's the biggest thing. It's disappointing to see some of my colleagues stop learning. For me, that's what keeps me thriving, just to see more and more things out there.*

Being the only Asian American teacher in a school in which both the students and the staff had preconceptions about what that means, John's first year at Hillhouse was difficult. "Most of my students didn't know what to make of me." Their only previous knowledge of Asians had been either "the Chinese takeout delivery guy" or a particular character on a TV show. John has worked hard at confronting their preconceptions. "That's the first thing: dispelling stereotypes, and we continue to do that throughout the year." Even one of his colleagues, an African American alumna of Hillhouse who became a teacher at the school, at first had her doubts that he would make it there. "She's like, 'There's no way that Asian guy is going to survive.'" She is now one of his closest colleagues.

Doubts about his future as a teacher were shared by his principal who, at one point in his second year, told him that he didn't think John would make it as a teacher ("He actually thought I should leave"), but fortunately for both the students and the profession, John stuck with it. He is loved by his students, admired by his colleagues, and has won the respect of the community.

Alicia López

Seventeen-year veteran Spanish and French teacher Alicia López (my daughter) grew up with teachers as parents and decided early on she did not want to be a teacher. She remembers her father and me working all the time, agonizing over our students, our curriculum, and our classes. Entering college with a firm resolve to major in psychology, she took her first course in the subject and quickly decided it wasn't for her. She graduated with a double major in anthropology (following in her father's footsteps) and French (a language her mother had always loved) and no idea what she would do with these interests. She took a job in an office in order to earn enough money to return to France, where she had spent her junior year. On the night of her twenty-second birthday, November 4, a couple of months before she was to leave for France, I invited Alicia to hear Jonathan Kozol speak at the University of Massachusetts about his then new book, *Savage Inequalities*. "That was really the turning point for me," she says.

Alicia López started her teaching career at private schools in New York, where she taught French and Spanish for nine years. However, she always knew that ultimately she would teach in public schools, and when she and her family moved back to Amherst, Massachusetts, she was happy to be hired at Amherst Regional Middle School. Until this year, she taught mostly Spanish and some French; this year she is teaching English Language Learners. She embraces the new challenge and feels prepared for it, having several years ago received her master's in multicultural education with a focus on second language acquisition. Alicia finds teaching ELL students gratifying in a completely different way from teaching foreign language. She loves the students' motivation and drive to learn English, and she is constantly amazed by their positive attitude given the struggles they face every day. Alicia definitely considers herself a middle school teacher: she believes that students at this age need adults who support them, love them, and "get" them. Besides, middle school students keep her young and make her laugh. Alicia recently joined a group of Latina moms who dance traditional Latin American dances, and she is thoroughly enjoying the experience. She has three beautiful, smart, wonderful children who are in sixth, fourth, and second grades—Celsito, Clarita, and Lucia. She would like to dedicate her part in this book to them and to her husband of fourteen years, Celso.

By the time we walked out of the auditorium, Alicia had decided she had to be a teacher—that teaching was the most important thing she could do with her life. She was ready to cancel her trip to France until I convinced her a couple of years away would do her good and the opportunity to teach would be here when she got back. Two years later, back from Paris and living in New York City, no education courses on her transcript and without a teaching certificate, she couldn't find a job as a teacher in a public school. So she began her teaching career as the co-director of an afterschool program in the Bronx sponsored by Aspira, a Latino/a education and leadership organization. Her students were all students of color, mostly Latinos/as who had dropped out of school. She learned a lot about inequities in education based on race, ethnicity, and social class.

On-the-Job Learning

Within a year of returning from Paris, Alicia got a position as a French teacher in a setting that couldn't have been more different from her job with impoverished youths of color in the Bronx: an elite private school for girls on Manhattan's Upper East Side. There were no more than a dozen students in each class, and the school encouraged a great deal of dialogue and provided students and teachers with tremendous resources and learning opportunities. The evening after her first interview, she called me and said, "My students in the Bronx would be *brilliant* in this school!" She recognized that the sociopolitical context of people's lives—circumstances over which they often have little control—can have a dramatic impact on their educational success or failure.

Alicia soon discovered that teaching was for her: "I was hooked from the beginning." Spending at least three hours each evening preparing for her classes, she was exhausted but fulfilled. "I think it was in the first week or two, my department head passed me in the hall one day and said, 'I hear only good things about you.' That made me feel really good. I thought, 'Okay, I can do this and I like it.'"

Alicia's experiences at the school were draining, eye-opening, and gratifying. They were also disconcerting because of the tremendous disparities she saw between her previous experience in the Bronx, with young people who lived in abject poverty, and her current students, who were "for the most part very wealthy, very White." Many of the girls came from privileged families who would jet off to Paris for the weekend or owned entire islands in the Caribbean. It was "almost like living in two worlds because I would go to work at this very wealthy Upper East Side school and then I would take an hour and a half subway ride home to my little railroad flat in Brooklyn." At the same time, it was an incredibly enriching experience. She learned to become a teacher with on-the-job training; supportive mentoring; small classes; and generous resources for materials, conferences, and other professional development opportunities. She also loved her students; many years later, some remain in touch.

Two mentors, one in the school, one external but arranged by the school, helped Alicia acclimate to teaching. They offered support, consolation, pep talks, a shoulder to cry on. She also had access to excellent professional development that included well-known speakers, a generous budget for materials, and the opportunity to attend numerous conferences (she attended the yearly People of Color conference sponsored by the National Association of Independent Schools, traveling to places as nearby as Rhode Island and as far away as California and Puerto Rico, one year heading a delegation of seven teachers and two students). Now that Alicia is a public school teacher and has experienced tight budgets and time constraints firsthand, she appreciates these opportunities even more: "It was always all expenses paid and we just didn't have to worry about anything."

Alicia was also the advisor for the student multicultural club CAFÉ (Cultural Awareness for Everyone) and later helped initiate a faculty diversity committee, experiences that prepared her for subsequent leadership experiences at the school and beyond.

After seven years, when she and her husband and baby had moved to Flushing (closer to the school but still more than an hour's subway ride away), she took a job at another private school, this one in Queens, where she taught for another three years.

Then, so they could be closer to family, Alicia and her young family moved to Amherst, Massachusetts, where she immediately found a job as a Spanish and French teacher at the Amherst Regional Middle School. (Since 2012, she has been an ESL teacher.) Although she did not yet have teacher certification, she was eligible for a waiver because she was a native speaker of Spanish and also fluent in French and had ten years of on-the-job experience and excellent references. She has since earned her certification and a master's degree in language, literacy, and culture and helped teach graduate-level courses for practicing and preservice teachers at the University of Massachusetts.

Learning Through Professional Organizations

The Amherst regional schools educate some thirty-five hundred students, including speakers of over thirty native languages. There are three elementary schools in Amherst, as well as a middle school and high school that also enroll students from a number of smaller surrounding towns. The middle school has nearly seven hundred students and is fairly diverse; about 60 percent of the students are White, 40 percent students of color, including Latinos/as, African Americans, Asians, American Indians, biracial students, and the children of the many international graduate students enrolled at the local university.

Although Amherst is known primarily as a middle-class town with many faculty members from the five colleges in the area as well as other professionals, there are also sizable populations of working-class families, families living in poverty, wealthy families, lesbian- and gay-headed families, and multi-generational families. Even in a self-described liberal town like Amherst, with a highly-regarded public school system, the schools, like those in big urban cities, have struggled to meet the learning needs of English language learners, students with special needs, and children living in poverty. These are the students who each year fall short on the MCAS (Massachusetts Comprehensive Assessment System, the state's standardized tests) and who also have higher rates of suspension and other disciplinary actions.

Given this dynamic context, teacher learning is an important aspect of staying on top of things happening in Amherst, in Massachusetts, and in the nation. Alicia has continued her education in numerous ways, but by far her most rewarding professional development experience has been with the Western Massachusetts Writing Project (WMWP), co-sponsored by the National Writing Project and the University of Massachusetts. She first enrolled a number of years ago and discovered it was just what she needed:

> *I hit a rut and thought, I don't know if I can do this another year. I'm bored, I'm tired of the discipline issues—because in middle school there's so much social behavior. That's when I did the WMWP summer institute. I felt like that really rejuvenated me. When I went back in September, I was ready to start again. I had so many great ideas. I got to talk with these teachers every day and it was very stimulating intellectually.*

After that first year, she was asked to be an institute facilitator and has been one for the past three summers. Each time, she experiences the same sense of renewal, and she loves seeing how the other teachers are also revitalized and inspired. Organizing the institute, working with and learning from her peers, and communicating throughout the year with teachers from many cities and towns in Western Massachusetts have all been tremendously engaging:

> *I think all teachers should do it. It's free professional development. A group of teachers come together and focus on their personal writing and research for their classes. You research a topic that you want to find out more about and you present a workshop on it. It's supposed to be an inquiry workshop on something that you're trying to find the answers to in terms of your class. You have the chance to listen to all these teachers' workshops, and I get so many great ideas.*

What makes the National Writing Project a meaningful professional development model? First, most professional development offered by school systems does not provide systematic, ongoing peer support. Peer-initiated, the NWP gives teachers the opportunity to work closely with colleagues in order to improve their teaching, their writing, and their research skills. In her first institute, Alicia developed a curriculum on Puerto Rico for her Spanish classes. Although she could not put it into practice that first year (she was teaching French, not Spanish), she shared it with a colleague who used it immediately, and she herself used it in subsequent years.

An even more crucial aspect of the NWP is that it honors teachers' intelligence, professionalism, and creativity. Curricula emerge from the interests, experiences, and questions of the participants. In the past participants were either paid a stipend or received academic credit from the partnering university. Given the current economic downturn, stipends have diminished, but the NWP has restored some of the money and is working hard to raise more. Participants maintain contact for at least a year, meeting several times to review their research projects, attend the state and national conferences, and support one another in other ways.

Although many of the teachers are English teachers, many others are not; the NWP welcomes teachers of foreign language, English language learners, math, science, art, any subject, as well as elementary school teachers. The subject matters less than the process, reflection, and camaraderie. For Alicia and many other teachers, the National Writing Project is a lifeline that keeps them motivated and excited about teaching.

Alicia has also learned a lot from her colleagues at the Amherst regional middle school: "They're the most hard working teachers I've ever worked with." Even when she gets to school very early, sometimes before seven a.m., there are "a bunch of cars there already, and there are people there late every day."

Another experience that helped Alicia become part of her new school was being part of an inquiry group. (The practice, unfortunately, was since replaced with more traditional professional development.) Once a month, on a Thursday morning, the students would get to sleep a couple of extra hours while various inquiry groups focused on a teaching problem or organizational or curricular issues affecting the school. All professionals in the building participated, not just classroom teachers. Alicia chose the group investigating why English language learners and students in special education were falling behind their peers. Over a period of five years, the group developed a number of recommendations concerning the kinds of attitudes, practices, materials, and structures to better serve these students.

Learning from and About Students

Connecting with her students is essential for Alicia; it's what helps her thrive. This means not only keeping informed about her craft but also learning about her students and sharing her life with them. She talks with students about her family because she wants them to feel comfortable doing so as well. She feels teaching is in some ways like parenting:

> *When I became a parent, everything changed for me as a teacher. I realized that every kid in my class is someone's child or grandchild, it's someone's special person. Just the thought of anyone saying or doing anything that made my son feel uncomfortable or sad in class broke my heart. That really transformed my teaching.*

One way Alicia begins to learn about her students is by writing a letter to them the first week of school:

> *I tell them that I'm Spanish and Puerto Rican and that I was born in New York and grew up in Belchertown. I tell them about my family, things that I like to do, foods I like to eat. I usually pick foods I know they will recognize if I write them in Spanish. Then I ask them as their first homework assignment to write me a letter telling me about themselves. Right away, that opens up how the students respond to me. Those letters, for me, provide an instant connection with my students.*

Alicia loves getting the students' letters ("I can't wait to get home and read them") and rereads them after she gets to know the students better:

> *I go back to them when I know a little bit more about them. I find out more things about them and sometimes I'll mention those things to them if I'm talking to them one-on-one. Or sometimes I'll just keep it in the back of my head to remember. Like this person lives in*

> *an apartment, not a house, so when I do my unit on housing, I have to remember to teach*
> *the word for apartment too because they don't teach that in the book. Things like that.*

She stresses the importance of mentioning her culture and identity in the letter she writes to her students: "It's a part of me and I think it's important for them to know." Different students relate to different parts of her letter. Some will say, "Oh, yeah, I was born in New York too." Or, "Oh, I grew up in Leverett" (a small town not unlike Belchertown). Her Latino/a students share, "I'm Salvadoran" or "I'm Puerto Rican" or "My mother is Puerto Rican even though I don't speak Spanish." Upfront about her own identity, Alicia finds that her students almost always mention their ethnicity in their responses. White students will write, "My family is German and Scottish and Irish" or whatever it may be.

At the beginning of the year, Alicia asks students what other languages are spoken at home, because she believes bilingualism and multilingualism need to be acknowledged as strengths. She can also use this information in class from time to time ("How do you say *apple* in Swahili?"). Although she tries not to make students feel they are the "representatives" for their entire cultural group, she does feel it's important to do little things every day that acknowledge their identity, so that students feel more connected both to the school and to her. She loves to see them get excited about learning Spanish, "making a little light bulb go off in their heads, that's what keeps me going, helps me thrive."

Alicia also makes it a point to be available to students after school and is active in extracurricular activities and other nonschool events. Shortly after arriving at the middle school, she volunteered to be the faculty advisor for Latinos Unidos, a student club. She has organized trips to Latino/a communities in Boston and New York, activities that hadn't happened for several years until she began them again. On one Boston trip the students helped out at a food shelter, saw "In the Heights" (a musical about Latinos/as in New York City), and had dinner at a local Dominican restaurant. She holds a fundraiser for each trip so that students whose families cannot afford the cost are able to go. The fundraisers range from the traditional bake sale to more explicitly cultural activities like "Salsa Socials" at which people learn to dance salsa to music provided by a volunteer DJ and enjoy refreshments provided by a local Mexican restaurant. Many parents volunteer to help.

For Alicia, connecting with students means getting to know *all* of them:

> *We were doing a clothing unit during which the students shop online. Curtis said, "Can't*
> *we shop at a place where we really shop, like I shop at Salvation Army." I said, "Wednesday*
> *is family day, half price!" And he said, "You go there, Ms. López? Cool!" And he put up*
> *his hand to give me five. Actually, he put up his fist, because I had taught them how to say*
> *chócalo, "pound it.") He was so excited that I shopped at Salvation Army. He's a White*
> *student from one of the small towns nearby. But he made that connection with me.*

A year after having him in class, she ran into him at the new Goodwill Store in town. "He was so excited! He came over and gave me a big hug and introduced me to his mom and grandmother. It was very, very cute. Just that willingness to find out more about your students and make that connection with them is really what it takes."

Learning who students are pays off in other ways as well. If students are accepted for who they are, they are more likely to want to learn. The day before I interviewed Alicia she had been out to a local restaurant and the server turned out to be a former student:

> When he saw me, he spoke to me in Spanish and I thought that was great, because it's been six years since I first had him. He just finished his first year of college and he still addressed me in Spanish! He was an average student and he wasn't the greatest Spanish student but I think he was happy to see me. It's little things like that, and the students who come back to visit after they've gone to the high school and say, "We miss you so much, we wish you could be our teacher." Or students in eighth grade will ask me at the end of the year, "Will you come with us to the high school? Will you be our teacher there?" It's those moments that keep you going.

Conclusion: Teachers Thrive When They Keep Learning

Learning to teach is not something that happens only in college courses or that ends when a teacher begins working in a school. Instead, learning to teach is a lifelong journey with ups and downs, twists and turns, and numerous surprises. Teacher learning is not having one's nose stuck in a book for hours every day; as John Nguyen and Alicia López illustrate, teachers also need to be open to new experiences, think critically about them, learn from colleagues and seek their support and advice when things get hard, and most of all, do all these things in the service of one's students.

Alicia and John demonstrate that teaching is both an art and a science. In their words and actions, we see that teaching is an art. Otherwise, how could John make his students understand that his identity as an immigrant from Vietnam and their experiences as African American young people living in poverty are more alike than different? How else could Alicia reach a student who had no visible connection with her life? These are not things one can learn in a book. Yet John, with his determination at a young age to learn everything he could so that he could be a better teacher, shows as well that teaching is a science, as does Alicia's transformative experience with the National Writing Project, an experience that while giving her the opportunity to work closely with colleagues, has also taught her new skills, approaches, and theories.

These teachers, and the others in this book, demonstrate in numerous ways that one cannot be a good teacher without also being a good student. As Paulo Freire (1998) has asserted: "Whoever teaches learns in the act of teaching, and whoever learns teaches in the act of learning" (p. 31).

NOTES

Bigelow, B. & Peterson, B. 2002.
Cochran-Smith, M. & Lytle, S. 2009.
Freedman, S. W., Simons, E. R., Kalnin, J. S., Casareno, A., & the M-Class Teams. 1999.
Freire, P. 1998.
Giroux, H. A. 1988.

Lieberman, A. & Friedrich, L. D. 2010.
Long, S., Abramson, A., Boone, A., Borchelt, C., Kalish, R., Miller, E. Parks, J., & Tisale, C. 2006.
Nieto, S. 2005a. 57–78.
Nieto, S. 2005b

Chapter 6

"I Hope I Can Become *That* Teacher"

Teaching to Honor Language and Culture

When I spoke at the Center for English Learners at Loyola Marymount University, in Los Angeles, I asked Professor Magaly Lavadenz, the director, to recommend a thriving teacher I could interview. I was disappointed (and a little surprised) when she said she couldn't. It turned out it wasn't because she didn't know such a teacher; she knew too many and couldn't choose just one! So I conducted a group interview with nine bilingual and ESL teachers—Carmen Alcazar, Griselda Benítez, Angela Fajardo, Jennifer Fleming, María Guerrero, Katie Shibata, Maricela Meza Buenrostro, Gabriela Olmedo, and Leticia Ornelas. We spent an invigorating couple of hours speaking about their motivations for becoming teachers, their struggles and triumphs, the lives of their students, and the state of bilingual education in California, the first state to eliminate bilingual education, through Proposition 227, in 1998.

This chapter focuses on the joys and challenges of teaching emergent bilingual students. Given the growing number of such students in our nation, whether one works in a preschool, an elementary school, or a middle or high school, one will inevitably teach English to such students. That is why it is crucial for all teachers, not just ESL and bilingual teachers, to be aware of and affirm the strengths and needs of these students. In spite of the best efforts of teacher educators and scholars to prepare all teachers to understand the complexities of second language learning and the numerous academic and emotional challenges faced by emergent bilingual students (see, for example, Freeman, Freeman, & Ramirez 2008; Freeman & Freeman 2011), too many teachers are still unprepared to do so.

This chapter reviews the focus group interview with the LMU teachers, recounting their experiences, hopes, and fears, as well as some of their significant insights about working with emergent bilingual students. Before doing so, I review some of the terminology that has been used to describe these students, as well as a brief demographic portrait of such students.

What's in a Name? Emergent Bilingual Students

Who are the students learning English in our schools? The simple answer is that *all* students in U.S. schools are learning English, whether they are native speakers of English or learning English as a second, third, or fourth language. Even native speakers of English never completely master the language: there is always more to learn, more vocabulary, more books, more poetry, more genres. More typically, of course, we think of students learning English as immigrants who do not yet speak English fluently. This is true but incomplete: not all students learning English are immigrants. Many have been born and raised in the United States and speak another language at home and in their communities. Their first exposure to English may be when they enter kindergarten (or first grade, as in my case). Conversely, some immigrants are already native English speakers—students from the English-speaking Caribbean, among other places—or have learned English proficiently in their home country. Other students know English to some extent but not well enough to be in a classroom where all the instruction is in English.

Labels for these students have changed over the years: *non-English speaking* (emphasizes what they do not know rather than what they know); *language minority* (their language is a minority in the United States); *limited English proficient* (with the unfortunate acronym LEP); *ESL* (English as a second language); or *bilingual* (a misnomer in most cases, because it refers to the program in which they're enrolled rather than to their language proficiency). In some places (Florida is a good example) the acronym *ESOL* (English for Speakers of Other Languages) is used, a more accurate term that includes students who speak more than one language besides English. More recently, the label *English Language Learner* (ELL) has come into vogue. Although it is a convenient term (and I've used it myself on occasion), I dislike it because it implies that the only thing these students are doing is learning English, that all the other content they need to learn is insignificant until they become fluent English speakers. Since it generally takes five to seven years to become fully fluent in another language, students cannot put their academic learning on hold while they learn English. They must learn English *in addition*.

A more accurate term that has become popular in the past several years is *emergent bilinguals*:

> English language learners are in fact *emergent bilinguals*. That is, through school and through acquiring English, these children become *bilingual*, able to continue to function in their home language as well as in English, their new language and that of school. When officials and educators ignore the bilingualism that these students can and often must develop through schooling in the United States, they perpetuate inequities in the education of these children (García, Kleifgen, & Falchi 2011, p. 6; emphasis in original).

Although no label is completely appropriate, in this book, I refer to students learning English as *emergent bilinguals* because the term makes clear that students are not a blank slate but instead come to school with a language or languages. It also refers to the students' language identities rather than to the program in which they may be placed and acknowledges that while they may be in the process of learning English, they also have other assets, including their cultural knowledge and prior experiences that can enrich their education.

Emergent Bilingual Students in the United States

Our nation has undergone a tremendous change in demographics in recent decades as more immigrant families enter the country, as well as to the higher birth rates of some already here. They arrive by plane, car, boat, raft, even on foot; they are documented and undocumented; some are refugees of war and some are refugees of economic plight; they are skilled and unskilled workers; some arrive with little or no formal education and others are highly educated professionals; they come from a wide variety of countries and their ethnic and racial identities are enormously diverse, as are their social class backgrounds and their political affiliations. The children of all immigrants, despite their many differences, share an eagerness to learn English, to fit in with their peers, and to succeed in school.

The numbers tell the story. In 2010, the U.S. Census Bureau reported that while the general population had grown by just 34 percent in the previous thirty years, the number of people age five and older who spoke a language other than English at home had increased by a massive 140 percent (U.S. Census Bureau 2010a). Nearly 13 percent of U.S. residents are immigrant born, and 20 percent of the population speak a language other than English at home (U.S. Census Bureau 2010b). Although Spanish is the language spoken by the great majority of those who speak a language other than English (some 60 percent), the number and variety of languages spoken in the nation—from Aleut to Yiddish—is an astonishing 380 or so.

Immigrants and others whose native language is one other than English have influenced every area of life in our nation, from our dietary preferences to the kinds of small businesses found in our cities and towns to voting patterns in local and national elections. The institution most impacted is our public education system.

The Loyola Marymount University Teachers

The teachers I spoke with at LMU shared common values about teaching as well as important insights about their work with emergent bilingual students. Several overarching themes emerged from our conversation:

- In their teaching they wanted to replicate or rewrite their autobiography as it pertained to learning English.

- They wanted to make a difference for their students.
- They were committed to affirming the values of their students' communities.
- They were disillusioned with the current state of public education, particularly the emphasis on testing and standardization.

Replicating or Rewriting Their Autobiography

Teachers and other professionals select a life journey based on their autobiography. In his succinct statement "I teach who I am," Parker Palmer (1998, p.1) captures the essence of teachers' work and purpose in life. I found this as well, in research I did with high school teachers in the Boston public schools (Nieto 2003). They were brought to smiles or tears as they recalled caring teachers who made them feel worthwhile or insensitive teachers who, through a careless word or gesture, turned them off to school. Whether their own experiences as students were positive or negative, many teachers choose to enter the profession either to replicate or to rewrite their learning experiences for the young people with whom they work.

A good example is Maricela Meza Buenrostro, a first-grade teacher in the Los Angeles Unified School District, one of the youngest teachers in the group. Arriving in the United States from Mexico as a fluent Spanish speaker but speaking no English, she nevertheless wanted to succeed in her new country and speak its language. She didn't have the resources at home to help her, but her teachers gave her, she said, a "helping hand that allowed me to be myself and be successful."

> *I owe many of my successes to those teachers who took some time out of their regular day to provide the support that I couldn't find at home—their passion, just doing it voluntarily because they wanted to help, not because there was any compensation. I feel that I'm who I am because I retained my native language and because of those dedicated teachers who always cared about what I was going to become. So I hope I can become that teacher, not just for one student but for every student in my classroom.*

Maricela Meza Buenrostro is currently teaching sixth grade in the Heber Elementary School District. After teaching in Los Angeles for three years, she decided it was time to pay it forward in her community and, as a result, she moved back to her hometown. She continues to strengthen her teaching practices by staying current with her students' needs and getting involved in the community. Maricela strives to be the best teacher every day in order to empower all students to take ownership of their academic success. Her positive and enthusiastic attitude brings joy to students' learning and makes every day meaningful.

Maricela's teachers pushed her to be academically successful *while at the same time encouraging her to be herself.* This is just one example of how teachers honor students' language and culture. Rather than pressure students to assimilate by abandoning their identity—including their native language—culturally responsive teachers understand that young people whose language and culture are affirmed tend to be more successful students (Flores-Gonzalez 2002; Valenzuela 1999; Irizarry 2007, 2011a). These teachers heed the advice of Margaret Gibson (1988), who many years ago urged "accommodation without assimilation," suggesting that students who maintained their language and culture were more likely to be more academically successful and emotionally healthier than those who are pressured toward what Alejandro Portes and Rubén Rumbaut (2006) have called "premature assimilation."

Angela Fajardo is a native of Granada, Nicaragua. Arriving in Los Angeles in 1983, she graduated from Garfield High School, where Jaime Escalante (of "Stand and Deliver" fame) was one of her teachers. She attended Loyola Marymount University, earning a bachelor's degree in Spanish and a master's degree in bilingual/bicultural education. Angela taught math and science at Lenox Middle School for nine years, mathematics and Spanish at Animo Jackie Robinson Charter High School for three years, and was also a clinical faculty member at Loyola Marymount University in teacher preparation. She was an associate principal at R. K. Lloyde High School, a continuation and credit recovery school, and Lawndale High School, both in the Centinela Valley Union High School District. She has served on the Lennox, California, school board for the past six years as president and vice-president, and she worked diligently with staff to create a common vision and mission with strategic priorities to enhance quality education in the Lennox School District. She is the proud mother of a ten-year-old daughter, Regina, who attends the Lennox School District's dual language program at Moffett Elementary School. She has also worked with NALEO as a participant in multiple board member institutes and is part of the High School Equity Task Force. Angela is currently serving a second term as a board member of the California Latino School Boards Association. Currently the principal at Crozier Middle School in the Inglewood School District, Angela is a passionate advocate for high standards and quality education for inner-city children and English language learners.

Another LMU teacher who cited her childhood experience as a reason for becoming a teacher never intended to be a teacher, although she has been one for thirteen years. Angela Fajardo arrived in the United States from Nicaragua at the age of ten knowing no English. She ended up at LMU only because her sister was studying education and encouraged her to take a class. Angela took a course in second language acquisition "that explained to me how I learned English." The personal experience she had as an immigrant became the foundation for how she teaches emergent bilingual students:

> *It was this great aha moment. I said, "Oh, my God! I can do this! I can help other students who are learning English go through this process. I can do something that will be good for the community that looks like me." So that was the catalyst, it was that course that really opened my eyes.*

Angela still calls herself an English language learner because she continues to have questions "like asking is it *on* or *in*?" Connecting her personal experience as an immigrant with her students, who are so much like her, has kept her in the profession.

A deeply personal connection motivated Griselda Benítez, a nineteen-year veteran of the public schools, to become a teacher. Her grandmother, who was a great source of inspiration, had been a teacher in Mexico:

> *I always go back to her words. She said, "Hay maestras por vocación y hay maestras por equivocación." Loosely translated, although without the rhyme, it means, "There are teachers who have a vocation and teachers who are there by mistake." I always think of that and I say, "I'm not here por equivocación. Estoy aquí por vocación. I'm not here by mistake. I'm here because of vocation."*

As she spoke about her grandmother, Griselda's voice trembled, but when she repeated her grandmother's words, besides comforting her, the rest of the group laughed knowingly.

Currently an educator in the dual language enrichment program in the Montebello Unified School District, **Griselda Benítez** has worked in bilingual/bicultural education for over twenty years. She received her undergraduate degree from Loyola Marymount University, where she also earned a master's degree in biliteracy, leadership, and intercultural education, as well as an administrative credential. An advocate for multilingual/multicultural education, Griselda serves on the board of Scholarships for Scholars of Montebello, which raises scholarship funds primarily for, but not limited to, undocumented students seeking higher education. She enjoys traveling to distant lands.

Making a Difference for Emergent Bilingual Students

A great deal of the LMU teachers' conversation focused on their wanting to make a difference in their students' lives as a motivation for becoming teachers. A comment made by María Guerrero, a ten-year veteran of the public schools, was typical: "Well, it sounds corny, but I became a teacher to work in the community and make a difference and motivate students, especially those coming from a community of color and working-

María Guerrero is currently a sixth-grade teacher at Lennox Middle School, in California. She takes pride in working in Lennox, an underserved area of Los Angeles County. Lennox epitomizes the heart of the immigrant experience, and the middle school's mission is to educate the children of immigrants. María has been teaching at Lennox for the past seventeen years. During her tenure, she has taught English language arts and development, mathematics, science, and social studies. She also has provided instruction in Spanish to newcomer students in mathematics and science. In addition to teaching multiple subjects, María has also served as a schoolwide leader. In 2005, she was one of the founders of the Lennox Educational Advancement Foundation, spearheading the organizing committee that established the foundation. She also served as its Executive Director in its formative years, working to deepen existing partnerships with various stakeholders, including The Boeing Company, Northrop Grumman Corporation, Raytheon Company, LACOE Foundation, El Clasificado Publications, and Loyola Marymount University. She has served on the school site council, the organizing committee for the Mujeres in Action (Women in Action) Conference, a youth conference for middle school girls, and she has moderated the Girls Only Club. She has a bachelor's degree in history and Chicano/a studies, a master's degree in biliteracy, leadership, and interculturalism, an administrative credential from Loyola Marymount University, and a multiple subject teaching credential and BCLAD certificate from the state of California.

class families, to continue their education." Several of the teachers were the children of immigrants who had not had the privilege of a formal education; most were the first in their generation to attend college or even to graduate from high school. Their parents, in spite of their own lack of formal education, had urged their children to study and get a good education so that their lot in life would be easier than their own.

Leticia Ornelas has been in the profession for twenty years, all of them in various schools in the Montebello Unified School District. As a high school student, she volunteered in an elementary bilingual classroom as part of a program for low-income children. "I enjoyed it and I said, 'Oh, I'm pretty good at this!'" Motivated to become a bilingual teacher, Leticia pursued her dream. While still in high school, she took a summer job as an aide in a bilingual classroom. After high school she enrolled in a college teacher preparation program. Since then, she has taught at three different schools in the Montebello Unified School District.

Making a difference in the lives of students motivated Maricela Meza Buenrostro as well. In high school she had flirted with the idea of becoming a lawyer, "but I couldn't do that. I couldn't because my passion was in teaching and laying down the path for many other bilingual students to be able to embrace who they are not just as English learners but as speakers of Spanish or any bilingual student."

Maricela spoke at length about the value of forging strong relationships with her students. Yet before beginning her first teaching job, she kept getting advice that felt contrary to her values and dispositions. "I had a lot of teachers, veteran teachers, telling me, 'You have to be strict the first month because otherwise

Leticia Ornelas was born in Juárez, Mexico, and came to the United States at the age of two. She attended English-only classrooms in the Montebello Unified School District. Spanish dominant, she remembers struggling with the English language, working twice as hard as her English-speaking peers to keep up. This experience led her to become a bilingual educator. Leticia began her career in traditional bilingual late-exit transition programs and later moved to a dual immersion program. She taught in a kindergarten bilingual classroom in the Little Lake City School District in 1989–90 and transferred the following year to the Montebello Unified School District, where she has been teaching for twenty-three years. By the time she earned her Bilingual Cross-Culture Credential, she was a reading teacher, working part of the school day as a Spanish bilingual kindergarten teacher and the other half as a Reading Recovery teacher for Spanish-speaking students. Later, as a dual-immersion maintenance Spanish teacher, she taught grades K–3. She believed so strongly in bilingualism and biliteracy that when her only daughter entered kindergarten she enrolled her in the program. Unfortunately, the program was phased out because of misconceptions about bilingual education in the political climate of the time and the passage of California's Proposition 227. Currently a first-grade transition bilingual teacher, she also promotes the benefits of bilingual education in discussions with families in the community.

they stomp all over you. They'll make your life miserable if you don't have a stern face every day, no smiling.'" This advice made her anxious and unable to sleep at night before the first day of school because being stern and unsmiling, especially with first graders, wasn't natural to her. Just like Angeles Pérez, the bilingual teacher highlighted in Chapter 3 who refused to not smile until after Christmas, when Maricela went into her classroom her first day on the job, she wisely put aside the advice she had been given:

> *The day came. I saw my students, and everything those teachers told me, I just put to the side. I was myself, I smiled at them. I tend to be very caring and loving. They're first graders so a lot of them came very scared and intimidated because it was a new school. I knew that it was going to be important to build that relationship where they feel safe, where I'm not the mean, grumpy teacher who is going to be upset and yelling the whole day, every day.*

Teachers connect with students in many ways. Jennifer Fleming, a substitute teacher for the LA Unified School District, explained that she doesn't have the same kind of relationship she used to have with students when she was full-time. But it's still very important to her to establish relationships with students. For one thing, she sees relationships as a way to manage behavior in the classroom. She does a lot of subbing at the school where she used to teach and recognizes the siblings of some of the children she taught in the past:

> *Sometimes when I see the students coming in, I'll say, "You look familiar, you look like so-and-so's brother." That stops the kids in their tracks, and whatever they thought maybe they would do in class that day suddenly evaporates because the connection is there. I know a lot of the teachers at the school and when they see me with the teachers, that also establishes a relationship that I'm not just someone passing through.*

Katie Shibata, who had been teaching for five years, spoke about her first year in the classroom, in a Minneapolis high school, teaching immigrants from Somalia. Many of them had never been in a classroom and several suffered from post-traumatic stress disorder (PTSD). Even holding a pencil for some of these students, most of whom were nineteen or twenty years old, was a challenge, learning English even more so. Katie taught these students for three years, in an accelerated diploma program, and spoke at their graduation: "It was a tremendous honor to speak at that graduation ceremony, to watch thirteen students who had overcome a great challenge walk down that aisle." Some of them went

An educator for approximately sixteen years, **Jennifer Fleming** started her teaching career informally by helping her mother, an elementary school teacher, in her classroom. After graduating with a Bachelor of Arts degree from the University of Oregon, she formally started her own teaching career by teaching English as a second language in Japan for three years. Jennifer received her teaching credential in 2004 while teaching social studies to middle school students in the Los Angeles Unified School District. After seven years, with a Master of Education degree from Loyola Marymount University, she taught at a charter school. In 2011, Jennifer was promoted from her teaching position to assistant principal at Century Academy for Excellence Charter Middle School, in Inglewood, California. She is currently in her second year as assistant principal.

 **Katie Shibata** designs and implements educational programs in areas from the Midwest to the West Coast. Areas of expertise include school leadership, English language development, curriculum design, and teacher and staff coaching. She holds teaching credentials in Minnesota and California, and she has a master's degree in biliteracy, leadership, and intercultural education and a California administration credential. She has been a director in schools for Somalian refugees and a department chair in private international language schools. After teaching in high school classrooms for nine years, Katie moved into higher education. She recently joined the team at the International English Language Testing System (IELTS) and is now the recognition manager. As an experienced educational professional in English language development and intercultural education, she is excited by the opportunity to work at IELTS USA and is thrilled to be part of a company that shares her professional values.

on to study at the University of Minnesota. "Those students will be the most successful, both in their hearts and externally." Katie felt particularly thankful to have been able to help them: "It forever affects me as a teacher and always makes me step back and realize how lucky I was to be a part of that for those students."

Leticia Ornelas had a lot to say about forging strong bonds with students, one way being to "loop" with them (teach them for two successive years). Disappointed that her school no longer expects teachers to make home visits, she continues to do so. She also strengthens her relationship by having "lotion day" every Friday. She explained:

> *My skin gets dry, so I put lotion on, and because kids notice everything you do, one day they said, "You know, you don't share your lotion with us." I said, " 'Oh, no! You didn't notice that!' So I said, 'You want some of my lotion?' " and they said, "Yeah!" So I gave it to a little girl, and now I have this long line of students every Friday.*

She also instituted "Lotion Day" with a smaller group of English language development students she teaches who, when they found out about it asked "How come you don't have 'Lotion Day' with us?" As a result, Leticia started the practice with them too. She said, "students really, really connect to you with little, minute things. If I take my vitamins, they want vitamins!" Since this activity is different from what Leticia called "the testing and being quiet and stern" mode, she and her students connect in this way because, as she said, "they know I'm real. I tell them, 'You use so much of my lotion, so don't bring me chocolates—bring me lotion!' " Given the proscription against hugging, kissing, and other

Gabriela Olmedo is a proud mother, a dedicated wife, and a thriving first-grade teacher at a Catholic elementary school. Her family is her first priority because she says nothing compares with a loving and caring family. Her husband and daughter are the loves of her life. She thanks God each day for all the blessings she has and is able to give. Teaching is one of Gaby's biggest passions. Her mission is to be the best teacher she can possibly be: "It is up to me to provide my students with learning experiences that will guide them to be good citizens and become the best at all they do. My goal is to make information understandable and, most important, attainable to all. I set very high expectations for my students. I believe they can become excellent students and achieve success through their learning." An alumna of Loyola Marymount University, where she received a liberal arts bachelor's degree with a Spanish minor and a bilingual multiple subject teaching credential, she also attended LMU for graduate studies, earning a Master of Arts in biliteracy leadership and intercultural education, as well as an administrative credential.

contact with students, Leticia mentioned another benefit of the practice: "Applying the lotion involves touch, something you're not supposed to do with students; it's a form of contact."

Students have more serious problems than dry skin, of course. Speaking about the uncertainty that some of her students face on a daily basis, Gabriela Olmedo brought up a student who, when she stressed how important doing well on a test was to getting his high school diploma, said, "Can you assure me that I'm going to be alive tomorrow? You don't know. You don't know what I'm feeling. My friend got shot on my way to school and he was in uniform and he was not in a gang and you cannot assure me." This young African American was one of the school's best football players and had a better chance than most of getting a scholarship, but given the lure of gangs, the extent of crime in his neighborhood, and the lack of the kinds of supports available to middle-class students, the future seemed gloomy to him.

María Guerrero, who teaches sixth grade, greets her students at the door each morning. "I'm big on, 'Look at me, say good morning.' I also have students share what's on their minds during Community Circle, generally first thing in the day. This year it's been awesome. They ask for it." She also teaches her students a new word each day, not necessarily words that are part of the curriculum. A recent word was "mindfulness, you know, what it means to be that." To her, these activities are

> *the glue that keeps the teaching going because if a kid feels safe in your class, they're going to ask for help. There's not going to be these walls going up that prevent them from asking for help. There's a back and forth and I totally agree, it's the human element in teaching. You cannot divorce that. It has to be a base in the classroom.*

Griselda Benítez said that in spite of current mandates and restrictions on what teachers can do, she plans to continue holding a Community Circle whether it's sanctioned by the school or not: "I don't want to give it up because I know it's good for the students, I've seen the effects. It doesn't matter what the administrator might say; I'm keeping it going."

Carmen Alcazar, a teacher at the same school, agreed. "There comes a time when we have to put the other stuff aside. We're not dealing with numbers, we're dealing with people, no matter their ages."

Carmen Alcazar has been teaching for eighteen years in the Montebello Unified School District's dual language enrichment program; her three sons all attended district schools.

Griselda's students have gone directly into Carmen's class for the past eight or nine years, and she sees firsthand the effect of the relationships Griselda has developed with them: "Those first months when they come into my room, they're like, 'Where's Community Circle?' It's not an every day thing for me, but I have one from time to time."

It isn't only elementary school children who need care and support. Angela Fajardo's high school students still need her, although in other ways than younger students might. Her classroom "resonates with the importance of building relationships with students." Her students are always hungry, so she has a refrigerator (stocked with food) and a microwave in her classroom. About one class she said: "This was my prep for the California exit exam. These were juniors who had not passed the exam yet. So I was, 'What do I have to do for you to learn this?' and they said, 'Feed us, just feed us!' "

The metaphor of food as intellectual sustenance is not lost on Angela and the other teachers who recognize that what they do to show their commitment to their students is about nurturing and feeding their souls, their intellects, and even their bodies.

Affirming Family and Community Resources

Building a strong relationship with students entails more than smiling at them, giving them lotion, or feeding them. It also requires reaching out to and getting to know the students' families, as well as becoming part of the community in other ways. Leticia Ornelas spoke about the responsibility of Latino/a teachers to speak up when other staff members complain or speak negatively about the students and their families: "That's *us*! That was *us*! That's the way that we grew up!" She doesn't remember her own parents ever going to any meetings or understanding the reasons for doing so. Yet this didn't mean they didn't value education. To refute the conventional wisdom that Latinos/as in particular don't care about education, Angela Fajardo brought up the many sacrifices parents and other family members make for their children: "Our students' parents work in hotels; they work at the airport. They have night shifts. How can you tell me these parents don't care when they are working all hours for their children?"

In many ways the LMU teachers have become members of their students' family. Gabriela Olmedo said some of her students call her *Tía* and others call her Mom. "To me, that's the relationship we have, and I'm very much like a mother because I'm on them and they're [sarcastically], 'I love you too' when I'm really upset at them, and that's not what I want to hear." She sometimes wishes she had a counseling credential, because there are times when she is her students' only counselor. Wistfully, she said, "It's this human condition that touches you; it breaks you."

Connecting with students is inevitably about connecting with, and affirming, their family as well. When Carmen Alcazar had to be out of town for a couple of days for a conference, one of her students confided that he was feeling anxious because she was leaving. She confessed that she was anxious too, because she's hadn't flown since 9/11.

> *He's a Spanish learner, and in his best Spanish he said, "I'm going to lend you a little charm bracelet with all the saints. My dad gave it to me but I'm going to lend it to you." That meant so much to me because I was already nervous and worried. It speaks to the relationships that are formed and how comfortable the students feel. He was feeling my anxiousness and trying to make me feel better, that little gesture—no, it wasn't a little gesture, it was a* big *gesture. I emailed his mom when I was in Sacramento. I told her, "Your son just totally blew me away, he lent me this charm bracelet and now I can't take it off because it's going to bring me back home."*

A teacher at Lennox Middle School, María Guerrero told a story of how she used to teach math and science in Spanish to the "newcomer kids," that is, those new to the country. She had a very difficult child who she found out was being abused by his father. The family moved back to Mexico, and she hadn't heard from Roberto again until that year. Now seventeen, he showed up at the school's office one day asking to see Ms. Guerrero. When the secretary called to ask whether it was okay, María said, "You've got to be kidding me! Send him my way!" When he arrived, she broke down:

> *I couldn't help myself, I just started to cry because I thought of them going back to Mexico. They weren't documented and I knew that the family was disintegrating. I told him, "We worried and prayed for your family. We thought of you and what you were going through."*

Roberto is working at a butcher shop in town now and comes to visit María sometimes on Mondays, his day off. He's become a sort of older brother to her students: "I have a tough group of boys this year, I tend to get the tough boys, and he was one of them and now he's hanging out in my class." Even though María and her colleagues were not able to help this family resolve their problems, Roberto remembered what they did for him. María said:

> *To me, those are the ultimate compliments. It's not what another adult tells me. It's when the kids say, "Thank you, Ms. Guerrero" and seven, eight years later, there's Roberto hanging out on a Monday afternoon so it makes me realize the importance of the human element. So essential.*

Well aware of their students' realities and the challenges they face daily, these teachers try to involve, include, and welcome families into their schools in many ways. To forestall misbehavior, Jennifer Fleming reminds students that their parents came here for a better education for their children. She'll ask, "How are you honoring your parents when you're at school? What is it that your parents want for you?" When she had her own classroom, she had her students do an oral history project about their parents: "That was powerful, for the child to know that their parents took that much risk just for their children's education."

Angela Fajardo was proud that as a middle school teacher she had taught a number of students who are now teachers. One of them teaches in the classroom next to her daughter's; another is a high school Spanish teacher. But the student who gives her the greatest pride is a young woman who was run over by a truck during her junior year and almost died. Angela taught the girl at home. When she recovered ("miraculously"), the girl returned to school, took her AP exams, and passed them all with flying colors. She's currently a student at Berkeley, but because she's undocumented and is prohibited from receiving financial aid, Angela's school has put on a number of fundraisers for her.

> *It's a privilege for me to work with the whole family in trying to support her. I have no doubt she's going to be an MD, a surgeon, like she wants to be. I'm so lucky to have crossed paths with students like her, because they're bright and they made it. I wonder about the ones who didn't.*

"The ones who didn't make it" was a theme that came up indirectly in our conversation. What was also evident through the teachers' comments is that many "didn't make it" because of current policies at the state and national levels that get in the way of student learning and success. This leads us to the next theme that emerged through the conversation with the LMU teachers: their frustration and disillusionment with public education today.

Disillusionment with the Current State of Public Education

These teachers let it be known that many students don't make it because current policies at the state and national level get in the way of their learning and success. In a nation of immigrants, teaching emergent bilingual students is an especially awesome responsibility. Yet state and national policies have not always been developed with an eye toward benefiting these students: struggles over desegregation, challenges to a standard curriculum that excludes many, and battles about bilingual education have left a trail of unfulfilled promises and educational failure in their wake. The title of a recent book, *Additive Schooling in Subtractive Times* (Bartlett & García 2011), captures this dilemma perfectly. Based on an ethnographic study of Luperón High School, in Washington Heights, on Manhattan's Upper West Side, the book chronicles the tremendous but unexpected success of this high school. What made the school an example of *additive schooling* were the expectations of an energetic and dedicated staff and community who honored the language and culture of the largely Dominican student body as a way to promote academic learning and success. The *subtractive* elements were the city, state, and national mandates and other policies that made doing so almost impossible. It's an apt description of the work of bilingual and ESL teachers everywhere in the nation.

In spite of their obvious enthusiasm for and commitment to teaching, the LMU teachers expressed frustration and disillusionment with the current state of public education. María Guerrero contrasted the idealism with which she had begun teaching a decade ago with the increasing demands on teachers to raise students' test scores. In an era of rigid accountability and overreliance on tests, "it seems we're so far removed from the idealism. We're being pushed to be technicians and to produce robots, just to keep pace, with no regard for the human element." She mentioned that in the past she had Math Nights for parents, teaching them specific games they could play with their children to help them develop math strategies. The parents had different levels of education and varying abilities, but most had not had much formal education. Math night "is not so much about the math; it's about getting them comfortable in the school," an important role for teachers of immigrant students. But because of recent mandates and other restrictions, María can no longer hold Math Nights.

Challenges the teachers face include the bureaucratization of teaching, the pressures brought about by high-stakes testing and other mandates, and the pall these conditions have cast over the profession. A number of the teachers broke down when they described dealing with these challenges. Although María Guerrero was grateful she and her colleagues shared a similar philosophy of teaching, strong relationships with their students, and connections with the community, she felt the year had not been a positive one for her. She was just *functioning*, not thriving. It was no longer enough to close her door; she had to speak out more than ever. She described what the current context is doing to her spirit:

> *I don't want my spirit to be* que me desanimen *[demotivated]; that's how I felt last week. I felt I was being suffocated; I felt I was being policed; I felt I was being checked in on. And I'm like, "Oh, no, I don't operate that way!" I need to maintain my voice, and keep saying what I've always said. And I think the moment that I allow "them"—whoever "them" is—to squash my spirit and put it in a box, that's the moment—I won't say I'll never be a teacher, but I checked myself this weekend and I said, "No, it's my spirit, I have to be who I am, and I have to say what I have to say when I have to say it." Because I do have a voice and I do have power. I don't want my spirit to be squashed.*

Griselda Benítez echoed this sentiment, saying her priority is to develop strong relationships with students, yet the pressure from the school to control "by the minute, by the hour, do this or do that" was constraining her efforts. For Angela Fajardo, who works at a charter school, the pressure was not as great as for her colleagues who work in regular public schools. Although she too was "stressed out," she still felt she had more autonomy than most of her LMU colleagues. Angela's greatest challenge was balancing the mandates while maintaining some level of autonomy. Katie Shibata, who teaches ESL in a private school, felt fortunate that she had a great deal of autonomy. When she was hired, the ESL program was "an empty canvas" that she could fill. As a fairly new teacher in a school with few mandates Katie is "becoming what I want to become instead of sucking up my passion."

Maricela Meza Buenrostro, another fairly new teacher, described herself as not yet thriving ("I'm still just surviving") but credited her master's program at Loyola Marymount University with motivating her to continue. She said it had changed her life. Before entering the profession, Maricela thought that she would spend three years or so in the classroom and then become an administrator. Once she started teaching, she quickly changed her mind, deciding that the real power was in the classroom. She is passionate about teaching and vehement that she won't be broken by "the system." She's determined that her ideals will never be compromised or taken away from her: "Right now, with all this bureaucracy that's going on, that's what they try to hit, your passion for what you're doing, the real reasons that you're in the profession." She acknowledged her peers, who had inspired her so greatly: "I hope one day I can look back and know that because of the words I heard from all these wonderful, experienced, and dedicated teachers, that passion has persisted through twenty, fifty years of teaching."

Conclusion: Teaching Is Honoring Students' Identities and Believing in Their Futures

The teachers I interviewed at Loyola Marymount University are impressive not only for their passion and commitment but also for their perseverance and insights. They realize they have multiple roles to play: they not only "represent" (in the colloquial meaning of that phrase) their profession but also are mentors, family members, and counselors for their students. Many other teachers play these roles as well, especially those who teach the most vulnerable populations, but bilingual and ESL teachers also often teach parents and colleagues. They help parents and family members navigate an often unknown and perplexing system so that their children will have a better chance at obtaining a good education. They are frequently asked to translate, mediate meetings with parents, and make phone calls to families in their home language. They clue in colleagues about the challenges facing students who are trying to learn a second language, attempting to understand another culture, figuring out who they are as they negotiate their own identities, and on top of all that, facing the trauma of immigration, war, or other calamities.

All the LMU teachers I spoke with were willing to do these things in spite of the added burden. Attending to the needs of their students, helping students' families and their own colleagues become partners in this endeavor, and trying to maintain a sense of integrity and motivation in the face of mandates and a high-stakes testing climate are not easy tasks. Although it took its toll on these teachers, they were nevertheless dedicated to the profession and their students.

Heeding the wisdom of these teachers would change the nature of teaching and learning in our nation in stunning ways. They recognize—because of their relationships with their students and their students' families and often because of their own autobiography—that language and culture are assets not to be wasted or disparaged. Unfortunately, many emergent bilinguals languish in classrooms where the strengths they bring to their learning are either overlooked or rejected outright, either through the elimination of bilingual education (in California and several other states) or because of the tendency to see emergent bilingual students as deficient simply because they have not yet mastered the English language. Imagine if all teachers and all schools recognized what these teachers already know: that no language is inferior, that no culture is "a culture of poverty," and that students' identities and experiences are rich resources on which to build.

The LMU teachers also insist on the significance of family and community strengths. Rather than viewing their students' families as uneducated and disinterested in education, they recognize that education is a strong value in the Latino/a and immigrant communities. These families understand only too well that education is the only way their children may have a chance at a better life than their own. Until all teachers and schools recognize this truth, the American dream will continue to be an elusive one for the emergent bilingual and immigrant children in our schools.

NOTES

Bartlett, L. & García, O. 2011.
Bustos Flores, B., Hernandez Sheets, R., & Riojas Clark, E. 2010.
Flores-Gonzalez, N. 2002.
Freeman, D. E. & Freeman, Y. S. 2011.
Freeman, Y. S., Freeman, D. E., & Ramirez, R., eds. 2008.
García, O., Kleifgen, J., & Falchi, L. 2008.
Gibson, M. 1988.

Irizarry, J. G. 2011.
Nieto, S. 2003.
Palmer, P. J. 1998.
Portes, A. & Rumbaut, R. 2006.
U.S. Census Bureau. 2010a.
U.S. Census Bureau. 2010b.
Valenzuela, A. 1999.

Chapter 7

Teaching to Nurture Students' Dreams

Teaching is not just knowing one's subject matter or how to teach it, as important as these elements are. In addition to content and pedagogy, teaching is getting to know one's students: who they are, what they know and need to know, their dreams and hopes, their struggles and frustrations, their strengths and talents. It is also nurturing students' dreams and helping them create a vision for their future. The three teachers profiled in this chapter understand this reality.

Yolanda Harris, a teaching assistant in Rochester, New York, challenges societal preconceptions about her students by forging strong relationships with them and encouraging them to develop their confidence. María Ramírez Acevedo, a Head Start Program teacher for Milwaukee public schools, refuses to accept stereotypes and predictions about her young students, most of whom are Latinos/as and African Americans and many of whom have special needs. For John Gundereson, who teaches in a largely affluent community in southern California, challenging conventions means promoting creativity and character in an age of high-stakes assessment.

Yolanda Harris

A teaching assistant for eleven years, Yolanda Harris was working at Charlotte High School, in Rochester, New York, at the time of her interview. Several teachers in the district recommended Yolanda as exemplifying the kinds of attitudes and practices I was researching. Yolanda had an associate's degree from a local community college and was completing course work at Nazareth College in Rochester to become a fully licensed teacher. She also worked part-time as a hairdresser, a job she had held since graduating from high school. She has since completed her bachelor's degree and is now pursuing graduate studies.

After graduating from high school, **Yolanda Harris** never planned to go back to school; she became a hairdresser. But a few years later, a friend inspired her to follow her example and become an assistant teacher. With great trepidation, Yolanda enrolled in her local community college. She did well, graduated in short order, and continued her education at Nazareth College, in Rochester, New York. There she received a degree in English literature with an extension in adolescent education, as well as certification to teach students with disabilities in grades 7–12. Currently teaching English part time to seventh and eighth graders with special needs, she is in the process of applying to graduate school. After I sent her a draft of this chapter, she sent me a note: "I want you to know that reading your email and draft was a bright light peering through what started off as a cloudy Monday. After reading not only my story but the stories of John and María, I found myself both laughing and shedding tears about how much I have grown both personally and professionally, about my 'boys,' and about the many students I have managed to make an impression on over the years. My hope is that things will get better because others start to see what we see in our children."

Yolanda began her career at Charlotte High School as a teaching assistant in a Special Education classroom, working with only boys, all Latinos and African Americans. "The teachers and the other students didn't think too highly of the students I worked with." Labeled ED (emotionally disturbed), they were, according to received wisdom, "the troubled kids, the kids that are not going to go anywhere in life, the kids that are going to end up in jail or dead." But Yolanda had a special way with "my boys," as she called them, and she worked with the same group throughout their three years in the school. She was assigned another group the next three years. Charlotte High School had been labeled an "underperforming school" and was being restructured. All staff members had to undergo a new interview if they wanted to retain their position. Part of the school was going to be made exclusively a boys' school. Although Yolanda had her choice of schools to which she could apply after she finished her undergraduate degree at the end of the semester, she decided she wanted to return to Charlotte: She explained that despite the challenges, "I *like* working with the boys."

Since her own experience as a high school student had been difficult, Yolanda hadn't gone on to college. "I said high school was it for me. If I made it through, I was never *ever* going back to school. It was too nerve-racking." She took a job as a teaching assistant only because a friend of hers encouraged her to do it with her. Although she knew that to get ahead she would have to continue her education, the idea of returning to school did not appeal. Nevertheless, fifteen years after graduating from high school, she enrolled at the local community college. To her surprise, her placement test grades were quite good. "It must have been all the years I have worked in the classroom. I was learning with the students." She raced through community college in two years, doing very well, while continuing to work full-time. At the time of her interview she had almost completed her university studies and was still working part-time.

A mother of two boys and recently a baby girl, working full-time at the school and part-time at the beauty salon, and also going to school, she has made many sacrifices in her quest to become a teacher. She likes being in a school, explaining: "It keeps me alive as a person. I love to see students who feel like I felt, 'I can't do it, I can't do it, I can't do it,' and then have that moment when they see that they *can* do it, there is no better feeling."

Born in Vega Alta, Puerto Rico, to Dominga Ramírez-Murphy and Eugenio Ramírez-Quiñonez, **María Ramírez Acevedo** currently lives in Milwaukee, Wisconsin with her husband Dr. José M. Acevedo, a recently retired administrator at South Division High School, and her thirteen-year-old son, Armando R. Acevedo, who is attending Marquette University High School. This is her sixteenth year working for the Milwaukee Public Schools, eleven years as an early childhood–special education teacher at Forest Home Avenue School and for the past five years at Albert E. Kagel School as a Head Start teacher. The youngest of eight, María was inspired to become a teacher by the example of four of her siblings, who also worked for Milwaukee Public Schools (and are now recent retirees). A niece and a nephew currently work for Milwaukee Public Schools ("the more the merrier!"). María has always taught with passion and is eager and willing to go the extra mile so that her students can make academic gains. María views early childhood education as "a window of opportunity" not only for children with special educational needs but for all children in need of opportunities to catch up with their typically developing peers. She recognizes that this task cannot be achieved alone; all parties involved—the district, the school, the teachers, other school affiliated professionals, the community, and the parents—must have open, collaborative discussions for this to be accomplished.

María Ramírez Acevedo

Maria Ramírez Acevedo works in a Head Start Program at Albert E. Kagel Elementary School, in Milwaukee, Wisconsin. Although María had been teaching in a bilingual Spanish classroom throughout most of her thirteen-year career, the year I interviewed her was her first in a monolingual English classroom with Latino/a and African American children. Nevertheless, because about half the children are Spanish dominant, she is, in effect, still teaching in a dual language way, at least informally. Before starting at Kagel, she had been an early childhood special education teacher at Forest Home Avenue School, also in Milwaukee.

María comes from a family of teachers: her husband, now an administrator, began as a teacher; four siblings and a niece and nephew are also teachers. She resisted entering the teaching profession ("I didn't want to be another teacher in the family!"), choosing to follow a different path, first in marketing and sales and then managing a hospital's health promotion program. But finally she succumbed: "I guess it's in the genes. If my siblings could do it, then I could too!" Her first job, at Forest Home Avenue School, was with speech-delayed young children, a perfect fit given her undergraduate studies in interpersonal communication, Spanish, and speech pathology. She also came to the profession with varied life experiences that helped her adjust quite readily. Her students had a wide range of disabilities: autism, Down syndrome, ADD (Attentive Deficient Disorder), ADHD (Attention Deficit Hyperactivity Disorder), CD (cognitively delayed), SDD (significantly developmentally delayed), as well as hearing, visual, physical, and speech and language impairments. However:

> *This was all normal to me and although the children were all at different academically challenged levels, I knew they all had something positive to contribute. I also knew that my co-workers and I could make a difference in their lives through the use of specialized teaching strategies along with adaptations and modifications to the curriculum that would help the children make positive gains towards their IEP (Individualized Education Plan) goals. We encouraged them to do their best and praised them often for their efforts and hard work.*

John Gunderson, who has taught at Dana Hills High School, in Dana Point, California, since 1991, loves what he does and is amazed that he has been teaching for over twenty years. He has spent his entire adult life at the school where he teaches. He attended Dana Hills as a student and after graduation, he started coaching the DHHS soccer team while attending college. He student taught at DHHS and has never left. He believes being a lifelong member of the community enhances his teaching and is proud to be part of Dana Hills, which he considers to be a unique and nurturing educational environment. John received his Ph.D. from Claremont Graduate University in 2003 and, in addition to teaching at Dana Hills High School, he is also an adjunct professor at Chapman University, where he teaches classes in the master's and credential programs. He loves working with preservice teachers and fellow professionals. A social science teacher, John has taught U.S. and world history and psychology. He feels very fortunate to be able to teach psychology, a course in which students are encouraged to think about their lives. John believes strongly that passionate relational teaching grounded in theory and philosophy can transform lives. For him, great teaching is much more than just covering curriculum: it is connecting with other human beings and working together toward a common goal. He says this is one of the greatest gifts we receive as educators. John's greatest joy in life are his 9-year-old twin sons, Dan and Jack, who mean the world to him. He is so proud of them and they are what make everything he does worthwhile.

John Gunderson

The town of Dana Point is a mostly affluent community in Orange County, California. The demographics of Dana Hills High reflect the town's profile: 78 percent White, 20 percent Latino/a, and 2 percent "other," with a number of English learners, largely Latino/a, most of whom live in the less affluent part of town.

John Gunderson has taught at Dana Hills High his whole career. His father, a teacher, did not encourage John to follow in his footsteps ("My dad was like, 'Oh, you don't want to be a *teacher!*' "), and John did not seriously consider teaching until after graduating from college. Then, as a former soccer player, he thought first about coaching: "I've always been the leader in teaching people stuff and coaching and playing sports. But I'd never realized how much teaching was a part of me until I started doing it." When he found his way into teaching, John realized it was what he was meant to be doing:

> *I realized the second I walked into my first classroom that it was the best decision I'd ever made! I was like, 'I'm going to teach for the rest of my life!' I felt alive; it was me. I was lucky I made that decision at twenty-two. I felt I was lucky because some of my friends have searched to find their calling, and I found mine at a very young age.*

That was nineteen years ago, and John is still at Dana Hills High. Teaching is at the heart of his identity: "I can't think of myself as ever doing anything else. That's definitely a core part of me."

John is also an adjunct professor at Chapman University, in Orange, California. He makes sure to push his preservice and practicing teachers to think about their philosophy of education, about the learning theories that form the basis for their teaching practices, and about their own identity:

> *I think the identity question is essential. We need to focus on identity. Instead, teacher education programs think it's too "touchy feely" to talk about identity, because that's not about the standards and what you know. It's hard to transcend the space between the content and the students without being a human being; that's where identity is so important. We have to know ourselves to really know our content and give it to our students.*

Teaching mostly White preservice teachers in his university courses, John finds the issue of race especially tricky to address. He began using *Other People's Children*, by Lisa Delpit (2006), which critiques how White teachers often refuse to take race and identity into account when teaching Black children. Although he considers it a very effective teaching tool, he realizes that many young White preservice teachers might feel attacked by the book, so he gives them ample time to digest it and talk about it. His own response when he first read the book was quite different: "My reaction was, 'How many kids have I hurt?' I didn't take it as a personal attack. So many of the people in my classes take it as a personal attack: 'I'm not racist!' "

John finds teaching both high school students and preservice teachers a fortuitous combination; each informs the other. His teaching at both levels has been enriched by the synergy.

Common Values in Diverse Settings

Although Yolanda, María, and John teach in settings that are different in many ways, they share some common values about teaching and, indeed, about life. They view teaching as a life of service. They also believe in the power of connecting with students as a way to challenge societal and school-based conventions and perceptions that get in the way of learning.

A Life of Service

Originally from Puerto Rico, María Ramírez Acevedo has spent most of her life in Milwaukee. She identifies strongly as a Puerto Rican woman and made it a point, when she was a little girl, never to forget her Spanish because she wanted to be able to speak with her parents and other Spanish-speaking members of her community. She feels children need to be proud of who they are and where they come from, and she tries to create a culturally rich environment for learning. She sees herself as a member of a larger community and teaching as a call to service:

> *My mother was a woman of great faith and very giving to those in need. This is certainly a character trait that she instilled in me and I'm very grateful. I've always been willing to help those in need, going the extra mile if need be, and always wanting to give something back to my community. The teaching profession was a way I could make a positive contribution, not only to Spanish-dominant children with significant academic and language delays, but to other children who are faced with equally challenging situations.*

She knew the Milwaukee public schools were where she would most likely teach.

Another way María serves her community is by connecting with her students' parents and families. Because the Head Start Program requires at least two home visits to every family, she has a better opportunity to get to know the families than other teachers might. She sees which families have the means to support their child, which ones have a more difficult time, and some of the obstacles that get in the way:

> *Whether it's a dual- or single-parent household, a lot more parents are working these days, so they may not be able to provide the academic support that a teacher would like to see. I keep an open mind about things, listen to their needs and try my best to provide families with simple games anyone can play that reinforce the skills students need to work on.*

For María, the key to serving families is communication and empowerment. When teaching children with special needs, she explains a student's IEP (Individualized Educational Plan) so that parents have a thorough understanding of their child's academic strengths and weaknesses, what goals are going to be addressed, and how long the services will be provided. For María, the key is to keep parents informed and provide them with the necessary tools to support their child's academic performance.

María had once been offered a promotion that would have taken her out of the classroom, but she decided not to take it, because she knew she would miss the day-to-day interactions with her young charges. "I'd rather be a teacher. There are so many things that happen in that classroom that give you such joy." Her passion for teaching keeps her in the profession: "That passion comes across whenever I talk about the kids, whenever I talk about their progress. And they can feel it. They can feel your passion, they learn from it."

For Yolanda Harris, service means working to improve her students' lives as well as her community. Creating an orderly, rigorous, and caring learning environment is one way she can protect her students' dreams and advocate for their future. While student teaching, Yolanda became more aware than ever of the difference school policies and practices can make, even when students are of the same race, ethnicity, and social class. In both schools in which she student taught, rules and standards were the same throughout the school. Students were not hanging out in the hall or cutting class or "cursing adults out and fighting and just being ugly to one another." Administrators supported the teachers in numerous ways, and teachers worked well together. These conditions combined to create schools that were organized for learning. The experience reinforced for her that "This is what matters. This is how urban students can be successful."

For John Gunderson, service is epitomized in how he views education. He is adamant that education is about improving the human condition, not just getting high test scores. He makes these values evident in his classroom from day one; he spends the first few class periods getting to know his students and letting them know who he is, where he comes from, and what he values. "I'm not afraid to be real or vulnerable. I share my life with my students and, as a result, we can relate on a personal level to whatever it is we're talking about."

Teaching, for John, is making the human beings in front of him feel comfortable enough to want to learn, to see how the curriculum is connected to their lives. When that happens "any barrier can be moved and any test scores can get raised." His goal is to try to bring humanity into his teaching, "not make them better test takers so they can play Jeopardy later in life, but make them thinkers who can really make a difference. I don't want my kids to grow up to be good test takers; I want them to be human."

Connecting with Students Through Shared Identities and Experiences

Sharing race, ethnicity, social class, and other identities and experiences with students can help build strong relationships. Research has found that a higher number of teachers of color in a school can promote the achievement of students of color (Dee 2000; Clewell et al. 2001). In a paper on the role of HBCUs (Historically Black Colleges and Universities) in preparing teachers for the nation's schools, Jacqueline Jordan Irvine and Leslie Fenwick (2009) reviewed extensive literature on the positive impact teachers of color can have on the learning of students of color as well as White students. They write, "Teachers of color do more than teach content. They dispel myths of racial inferiority and incompetence and serve as surrogate parents, guides, and mentors to their students" (p. 5). It does not necessarily follow that sharing identities and experiences with students is either a requirement for strong relationships or an assurance that such relationships will follow. It is an advantage, not a guarantee, one that needs to be nurtured. However, all teachers regardless of background have both the ability and the responsibility to build strong relationships with their students.

Yolanda and María's ethnic identities and lived experiences help them connect with their students, but it is not simply shared identities that help teachers form strong bonds with their students. For instance, John, María, and Yolanda all live in the same community that their students do. It is not unusual for them to run into their students outside school. María's extended family also lives in the community. They run into María's students' parents at, for example, El Rey Super Mercado, the largest Latino/a food market in the city. Working at the hair salon part-time has helped Yolanda strengthen her relationships, not only with her colleagues who are clients, but also with the mothers, grandmothers, aunts, and sisters of her students. Her students tend to be more respectful with her as a result.

John Gunderson grew up and went to school in the community in which he teaches and shares a sense of place with his students and their families. He feels fortunate that he teaches courses in psychology because this gives him the opportunity to focus on students' identities and their humanity. Fundamental to his philosophy is that teaching is about relationships:

> *It's not about knowing how to do a lesson plan. It's about knowing how to create an environment to foster humanity, to foster human relationships. When you do that, the content will be so much easier to transmit because you're in a conversation with people, telling a story.*

In his psychology classes, John has been able to create "a little island that focuses on kids' lives." Nevertheless, he feels the pressure to teach an AP class instead of the general psychology class he teaches because some students have told him this would help raise their GPA and improve their chance to get into a good college. But for him, his psychology classes are what education should be: a gathering of students of various backgrounds, different academic levels, and varied interests where they are encouraged to think creatively and critically about exciting subject matter. John creates a sense of community by building relationships:

> *The crux of it for me is finding that the relationship with your kids and your classroom is more important than any other template, because when you find that relationship and create that climate of trust and understanding, it's about that relationship. We're trying to find and discover together how we can relate to whatever the curriculum is.*

At the end of the first semester, John's high school students write a paper about their life in which they examine the most important events that have shaped who they are. He also asks them to think about what they hope to be doing when they're thirty-five. Then they create a "playlist of their lives" that are representative of who they are or want to become. John spends about six weeks grading these papers, and speaks with each student individually on the day of the final exam. The task is time-consuming and draining (he has between 160 and 200 students), but it's worth it:

> *I don't get people ten years later telling me "that test you wrote on standards changed my life." But I do get an email about once a month from a former student telling me "I read that paper again" or "that really made a difference in my life" or "I hope you're still doing that." This experience of talking about life in the context of school really transforms my classes.*

By sharing and talking about their lives, the class becomes a family: "We really know and understand each other. I hope this is something they realize for the rest of their lives."

María Ramírez Acevedo's identity as a Puerto Rican woman from urban Milwaukee who came from humble beginnings helps her relate to her students personally. Her culture remains a very significant part of her life: "I identify myself with the Puerto Rican culture: the music, the dance, the food, the language. I can still recall my experiences growing up, and I share those memories with my students." She feels it's important for children to know who they are and recounted how her previous school had a rich cultural environment: "You walked through the hallways and felt so proud of the ethnic backgrounds represented. Teachers put together cultural programs about Puerto Ricans, Mexicans, African Americans, and others."

Knowing oneself is a key ingredient in being able to connect with one's students. María makes it clear that she is part of their community. She is critical of people who disparage others who are different from them whether in ability, race, ethnicity, social class, or anything else: "Sometimes I hear people say 'those people' and exclude themselves. I've been there, so I'm always inclusive instead of exclusive. I also try my best to keep an open mind and give others the benefit of the doubt before passing judgment."

Yolanda Harris builds her relationships with students by expecting a lot from them, in terms of both their behavior and their work. She lets them know how other people view them and how their actions play into that image. She tells them, "If you keep acting like that, you are making yourself look bad, you are making your family look bad, you are making me look bad." At the same time, she relates personally to their experiences: "One of the things I tell them during the tough times is, 'Hey, I'm from the same streets you're from! I am here to tell you there is a better way, but you have to believe that for yourself.'" She wants her students to know that she is not "the bad guy":

> *You need to have an* understanding *of what's going on in their lives, what is important to them. They need to have some sense of their value, that you're not just this person they have to spend six hours a day with but who could care less about them, you know? They want to know that you appreciate them being there.*

Yolanda knows that she is more than a teacher to her students. They feel comfortable with her and know that if they have a problem, she will listen and try to help them work it out. She brings in food and shares it: "I tell them, 'I believe you should be able to eat while you're learning. It will help you.'" She doesn't take personally anything negative the students might say to her:

> *I want to model that you don't have to hold on to whatever is going on with you. It's okay. This is a safe place for you to release the beast. Get it off so that you can move on.*

This kind of selfless empathy endears Yolanda to her students.

Shared experiences affect not just relationships but also curriculum. When her students complained about having to learn about the Civil War, something they felt had little relevance to their lives, Yolanda researched the connections Rochester, New York, had to the Civil War. She found that the local hospital, right across the street from the school, was where wounded soldiers were brought to convalesce after some local Civil War battles. Students were skeptical until she showed them an old photograph and they were able to compare it with the hospital as it is today. She also found that Rochester had been a stop on the Underground Railroad. "Now we had fun learning about the Civil War. 'You're on the property! You're on the premises.' Every day they were ready."

Not all of Yolanda's stories have happy endings. Five of her students have died, three of them murdered. Several others are in prison for murder. Precisely because of this reality, Yolanda keeps at it: "The people I work with inspire me, teach me ways that I can first learn about myself and then help a student learn."

Questioning Conventions

John, María, and Yolanda all challenge conventional thinking and preconceptions about their students. For María, having high expectations for her students, especially young children with special needs, is fundamental. Seeing students' progress is what makes the hard work worthwhile:

> *They're all unique. They all have something that they can contribute to and learn from one another. Every child is as important as every other. When three-year-olds still in diapers with significant academic and speech and language delays make progress toward talking and doing things for themselves, parents are disappointed when I tell them I will no longer be their teacher. My response is, "Your child has grown and has made a significant amount of progress. He is ready to move on, something that we are all proud of."*

For Yolanda, who teaches African American and Latino males, a major concern is counteracting the negative messages they hear in school, the community, and the media about young men of color. She consistently gives her students positive messages about themselves and their community because it helps build their confidence and also is a way to counteract some of the negative messages with which they are bombarded on a daily basis:

> *I am constantly telling them, "Don't believe them! You can do it! Believe that I work for you and that I am here for you and that I want you to feel good about yourself." Because a lot of the students don't feel good about themselves; they chalk themselves off as a failure because they listen to the negativity. They've heard so much negativity from those who should believe in them that they start believing it themselves.*

Yolanda talked about an eighth grader in a special education class when she was student teaching the previous semester. He only came to school every twenty days or so—he was on probation and had to be in school at least one day in twenty or his mother had to appear in court. "I told him, 'I want you here *every day*, get your butt out the bed,' and he looked at me like 'This lady is crazy!'" To her surprise, however, he showed up the next day and the next and the next. He still didn't do any work, but at least he came. The day before her professor was coming to observe her, she gave the class a heads-up. "*Your* professor?" he asked. "*You* go to school?" She told him she would look bad if he was just sitting there, not doing anything. "I asked, 'You going to do something?' and he said, 'Yeah, I'm going to do something,' and I said, 'Well, you've got to start getting prepared today so here, do some work!'" He quickly finished it, and she gave him more. The next day both the professor and the young man showed up. "And he worked for me just beautifully."

One day he had trouble completing a class assignment about battles during the Civil War, and Yolanda realized he was a struggling reader:

> *So I said, "I tell you what, hold on 'til everybody goes, and then I'm going to be your partner." After everyone left he was nervous and said, "No, I changed my mind," but I told him, "Come on!" I read the names of the battles for him while he located the places on a map. When we finished, I said, "You've completed the assignment! I don't know about you but I feel real good. How do you feel?" And he said, "I'm all right, I'm all right, I'm all right."*

That whole semester, a security guard at the school tried to convince Yolanda that for her own safety she shouldn't let the student into her classroom. The other students also criticized her: "Why you always baby him? You know that boy, he nothing but a thug!" Yolanda was furious. "I said, 'What?! A thug!? Are you crazy? He is in *eighth grade*! He isn't a thug yet, but he's in training.' The world might be training him to do whatever, but I am training him too. And it is his decision which way he wants to go. Obviously he wants to be here." Near the end of the semester, the classroom teacher told Yolanda that the work the boy had done for her was the only work he had done all year. After Yolanda left, he went back to his usual one in twenty days, but Yolanda saw firsthand that one teacher *can* make an enormous difference, a truth reinforced by this experience.

Teachers also challenge conventional wisdom by questioning school policies and practices. John Gunderson thinks about the current push for accountability and standardization a great deal. Although he has many criticisms of high-stakes tests and the dismantling of public education, he has no problem with high standards, in fact strives for them in everything he does: "Any teacher worth his weight has standards and accountability, because you're not just going in there and faking it." The problem is how to make those standards meaningful to students' lives and dreams, especially high school students on the brink of adulthood.

Although he can still teach the courses that matter to him in a school system that has not yet succumbed completely to the testing frenzy, John has many criticisms of education today, particularly standardization. He worries about the impact of these values on students:

> *We're robbing education of its humanity by trying to make everybody a test score, trying to make people fit into boxes. You're this AYP number, or you're that number on the test, or you're less than proficient, or you're more than proficient, instead of looking at the kid as a student and as a human being and as someone who wants to learn.*

John thinks the focus on standards, rather than helping, is limiting teachers' ability to create curriculum and relate it to students' lives. "The standardization movement is turning teaching into a delivery system of facts to be measured."

John also challenges conventions by including issues of inequality in his curriculum. He wants to make certain his students confront issues of racism, privilege, and power, topics he feels everyone needs to grapple with:

> *I love that in every class I teach I do a unit on prejudice and racism to try to get the students to be aware of the power of our own biases and how we use them to judge people and how horrible it is. How can you* not *talk about racism and prejudice in psychology? It's a huge construct.*

John shows his students the famous *Blue Eyes/Brown Eyes* videos of teacher Jane Elliott, as well as other material that gets them thinking about how easy it is to create and perpetuate a climate of prejudice. "I just love the way they react, because they're so surprised. My goal is always to get them to think, to be provocative enough to make them challenge their comfort zones, to make them feel, to react." (See www.janeelliott.com for more information on both Jane Elliott and her experiment.) Having the courage to confront biases is an essential skill for living in a multicultural and democratic society and an especially important quality in teachers who claim to be in favor of equality and fair play. "If you say that you stand up for diversity and then let people say racist comments in your class, you have no credibility."

Conclusion: Teaching Is Challenging the Status Quo

John Gunderson, María Ramírez Acevedo, and Yolanda Harris all help nurture students' dreams by challenging the status quo, although they do so in different ways. Whether by speaking out against the excesses of the high-stakes era or challenging limiting notions about students based on their identities or abilities, these teachers understand that all students need support and encouragement to reach their potential. While conventional wisdom might hold that students living in poverty cannot match the achievement of middle-class children, or that students of color are doomed to failure, these teachers make it clear that no such barriers should or can exist if we are really to put into practice the American creed of equality and fair play. Teachers cannot, of course, do it alone. On the contrary, it will take an overhaul of our entire public educational system to reach this goal. In the meantime, teachers can continue to push, individually and collectively, to make changes in their classrooms and their schools.

Education is increasingly viewed as a functionalist endeavor that primarily prepares students to do well on tests; instead, it is necessary to reignite the vision of education as an ennobling endeavor. While the standardization movement has had a chilling effect on what a public education means, in the recent past teachers have begun to organize against this narrow view of education. John, Yolanda, and María reject limited views of education and of their students, joining the other teachers featured in this book in understanding the far broader purpose of public education in a democratic society: to help prepare moral human beings and productive citizens.

NOTES

Clewell, B. C., Puma, M., & McKay, S. A. 2001.
Dee, T. S. 2000.
Delpit, L. 2006.
Irvine, J. J. & Fenwick, L. T. 2009.

Chapter 8

Teaching as Social Justice and Advocacy

There is no template for social justice teaching: no checklist, no rubric, no single model, no one "best practice." Teachers who create empowering and multicultural curricula, teachers who embrace a culturally responsive pedagogy, teachers active in their local union, teachers who organize families in their communities, teachers who show they care about their students, teachers who demonstrate in the streets for public education, all these and more fit under the social justice umbrella. However, even though it means different things to different people, in general teachers understand social justice as *advocacy*. Teaching as advocacy means looking out for students' best interests, challenging placement or curricular decisions that put young people in jeopardy of academic failure, learning about students' identities and using this knowledge in the curriculum, respecting students' families and communities, and learning another language, among many other perspectives and actions.

In Chapter 2, social justice was defined as including four essential components:

1. Challenging misconceptions, untruths, and stereotypes.
2. Providing all students with the necessary material and emotional resources to learn.
3. Drawing on students' talents and strengths to enhance their education.
4. Creating a learning environment that promotes critical thinking and supports agency for social change.

This chapter presents concrete examples of social justice teaching in real classrooms. María Federico Brummer, Geoffrey Winikur, and Hyung Nam, each in different ways, embody what it means to be a social justice educator. We begin with the thoughts of other teachers interviewed for this project because, in one way or another, they all spoke about social justice as a primary focus of their work.

Social Justice Education: Different Contexts, Diverse Strategies

Teaching from a social justice perspective may mean standing up for the most marginalized students. Amber Bechard, a middle school teacher in a suburb of Chicago, has seen herself as a social justice educator since she first decided to become a teacher, when she was in high school. She knew *who* she wanted to teach, if not *what* she wanted to teach: "I started to feel the need to champion the underrepresented and decided I wanted to be not only a teacher but a special ed teacher because if I really loved the learning process, then I needed to take it to those for whom it's hardest."

Being a social justice educator also means fighting injustice whenever and wherever one finds it. One year the students of Carmen Tisdale, a third-grade teacher in an all-Black school in South Carolina, were inadvertently excluded from a summer school program because admission was first come, first served and nobody had told her. Carmen was furious and reacted, she said, like "a Black Momma":

> *I went right to the principal and told her, "Know that I will always fight for my children. You can do anything you want to me, but if you want a fight, mess with my children." That's a Black woman. That's a Black Momma. You want to fight? You mess with her children. So she let my students in and didn't really mess with me anymore.*

Adam Heenan, a high school social studies teacher in Chicago, defines himself first and foremost as an activist teacher. He has given a great deal of thought to why he teaches: it's a question of "for what am I teaching? There's a million ways to get to the *what* do you want to teach, but to identify the *for what* do you teach is an activist stance. You have to be willing to say, 'I am willing to fight for that, I am willing to stand up for that.'"

Adam is an activist educator for many reasons, not the least of which is his concern that his students are not always well served by policy decisions. Frustrated with this era of standardized education, Adam feels that students are often guinea pigs for disastrous and unproven policies. He is critical of such programs as Teach for America that place untested and quickly trained teachers in urban schools of high need. Rather than firing all the teachers of a school declared to be "underperforming," he suggests that a better policy would be to require new teachers to commit to more than two years of teaching. Although he is quite involved in the Chicago Teachers Union, Adam made it clear that his first priority is to remain in the classroom: "I keep telling people that I couldn't be a major activist if I wasn't teaching every day; teaching makes the fight worth it."

Advocacy as a way to fight injustice is also the stance of Griselda Benítez, a nineteen-year veteran teacher of emergent bilingual students in California. Speaking movingly about the values and commitments that keep her in the profession, she cited one of her heroes, Paulo Freire, who embodied what it meant to struggle for positive change in schools and beyond:

> *I look back also to Freire and how he mentioned teaching as a political or revolutionary act; that's also what keeps me going, seeing it as an act of social justice, being part of that, being part of helping to create some sort of change, not just being a cog in a money-making machine.*

John Nguyen, a social studies teacher at Hillhouse High School, in New Haven, Connecticut, was attracted to social studies because it's a subject that includes almost every other field and because it relates to people's lives. Even more than teaching history and social studies, which he loves, John says that building trust with his students is his first priority. He explained: "My classroom is more based on discussion and finding out, exploring the outer limits of what we think the world should be, and exposing some of the myths my students believe, because in many cases they haven't been outside New Haven."

He and his students discuss everything in his largely African American classes, including race, racism, and disparities in wealth and how these things are related to one's quality of life. The murder of Annie Le, a Yale graduate student, was all over the media for weeks at the time of John's interview, and he and his students had discussed the case at length. They talked about whose life is more valuable, a "Yalie's" or a Hilltown student's:

> *Morally, everyone is going to say it's the same, but I posed the question as, "What would the average person in Connecticut think? Let's talk about the reasons why; let's talk about disparities in wealth." And they understood. They could tell from the degree of newspaper coverage. One of my students said, "Six days of this" as he waved the newspaper at me, "if this was me, it would've been a little blurb." They realize that and they're still talking about that. It wasn't a mean conversation. It was a thoughtful conversation that carried over to the other classes.*

Social justice teachers are as concerned about the dignity of teachers as they are about the lives of their students. Many are involved in organizations that respect teachers' intelligence, professionalism, and intellectual ability. Adam Heenan is heavily invested in a National Foundation for Educational Research project called Teacher Voice: "If I weren't involved in this movement for promoting teachers' voices, I would feel helpless, I would feel part of the problem."

Understanding the history of teacher advocacy and self-determination is also part of being a social justice educator. Adam often wears a t-shirt proudly emblazoned with the words I AM A TEACHER:

> *It speaks to the professionalism of what we do, it speaks to the historical civil rights struggle, the African Americans in Memphis, the people wearing the "I am a man" billboards. It's a reclaiming of identity in fact and dignity.*

Adam also has a tattoo on each arm: one is *tolme*, which is Greek for *audacity*, the other is *topino titta*, which is Greek for *humility*. The terms honor a statement made by his teacher Bill Ayers when Adam was a student at the University of Illinois, Chicago: "Good teaching requires audacity but demands humility."

Stories of Social Justice Teachers

Geoffrey Winikur, Hyung Nam, and María Federico Brummer, each in his or her own way, epitomize what it means to be a social justice educator. All three teach in high schools: Geoffrey, a white male, is an English teacher in Philadelphia; Hyung Nam, who identifies as Asian American, is a social studies teacher in Portland, Oregon; and María Federico Brummer, a Chicana, was a social studies teacher in the beleaguered, and ultimately dismantled, MAS (Mexican American Studies) program at Tucson High School. Each centers his or her teaching around social justice. All three have an unswerving dedication to their students' well-being, to curricular integrity, and to the teaching profession.

Geoffrey Winikur, an English teacher at Parkway Northwest High School, is himself a product of the Philadelphia School District. From the beginning, he has taken an inquiry stance in his English classroom in order to foment rigorous, collaborative learning. Through his decade-plus leadership as a summer institute facilitator in the Philadelphia Writing Project, he has been able to reflect on his own practice and help provide high-quality professional development centered on literacy and culture to many teachers in the Philadelphia School District. Borrowing a term from Freire, Geoffrey calls himself a teacher-learner; he has a "critical curiosity" for the subject he teaches and a deep and abiding interest in African history, literature, and art. For Geoffrey, teaching English is about providing his high school students with the critical thinking skills necessary to create a community of scholars in his classroom who can then pursue a college education successfully. The way he works *with* his students, families, and colleagues places him "in the mix." He is married to Cheryl, also a teacher. They have three sons: Isaiah, Manny, and Asa.

Geoffrey Winikur

Currently an English teacher at Parkway Northwest High School for Peace and Social Justice, in Philadelphia, Geoffrey Winikur has been a teacher since 1993, at Parkway since 2005. His original goal was to be a college professor of English literature, but after realizing in his second year of graduate school that "I was pretty miserable," he decided instead to follow in his parents' footsteps, both of whom were high school teachers. When it came time to do classroom observations as part of his teacher preparation program, his mother told him about a couple of fantastic teachers, Bob Fecho and Marcia Pincus, whom she knew through the Philadelphia Writing Project and who were teaching at Gratz High School. "After one day I was like, this is it! This is what I want to do." He was later hired at Gratz and got to see "firsthand what excellent teaching was. I felt like I got the best education for free." Geoffrey has followed his mother's lead and is a member of the Philadelphia Writing Project, as are quite a number of other teachers in the school. The courses he teaches focus on literature, writing, and film.

Geoffrey's students are mostly lower middle class, primarily African American and Afro-Caribbean. Parkway is also known as a safe school and attracts LGBT students and other young people who might not fit into one of the bigger schools in the city. The curriculum is more attuned to the realities of urban students and students of diverse backgrounds. Parkway has been enormously successful compared with many other urban schools populated primarily by students of color. Geoffrey knew of only three or four students who had not graduated on time and said 99 percent of Parkway graduates go on to some sort of postsecondary education.

Geoffrey is unswerving in his commitment to being a social justice educator, one reason being the inequality and injustice he sees in public education and society in general. He also sees how students' identities are often made invisible or disparaged in school, and he understands how curriculum can counteract these things. He believes it is crucial to talk to students about identity, something that is frowned on in other classrooms and other schools.

Identity is a significant issue for Geoffrey not only because of the students he teaches and the focus of the school and his subject area but also because he's a member of a biracial family—his wife is African American and his two children identify as biracial. He's also Jewish, although not religious in any real way. Geoffrey believes it's important to be transparent about race and privilege. When issues of diversity come up in his classes, he feels comfortable discussing them.

A learner at heart, Geoffrey loves the give-and-take of teaching and says he learns from both his students and his colleagues. Self-initiated professional development is a vital part of learning for him, and he's taken a course offered by the National Endowment for the Humanities and has co-facilitated the Philadelphia Writing Project for several years. This work "has been a gift" because it has given him the opportunity to learn with and from colleagues. He has also mentored novice teachers.

María Federico Brummer

María Federico Brummer, whose family has been in the United States for four generations, was born and raised in Tucson, Arizona. She graduated from the Tucson high school where she currently teaches. Volunteering in her *Tia's* (aunt's) elementary school classroom and helping set it up each summer inspired María to become a teacher. Although she decided she didn't have the creativity to teach at the elementary level ("to have to cut those little circles and that kind of thing," she said, laughing), she followed in her aunt's footsteps because of "just the type of teacher she is; that motivated me and I knew by twelve years old that I wanted to become a teacher." María has been teaching since 1998. Her aunt, who is still teaching as well, has been María's greatest mentor.

The Mexican American Studies program at Tucson High (which María was part of at the time of our interview and which has since been dismantled) was reportedly the only high school ethnic studies program in the United States. The teachers and staff members of the program defined it as "critically compassionate pedagogy" (Cammarota & Romero 2006). Students' academic skills flourished as a result of the curriculum, pedagogy, and relationships with the program's instructors. Many of the students went on to postsecondary education. A much larger percentage of students in the program graduated than those who were not in the program. In a 2012 study of the program that included cohorts from 2008–2011, the peak years of MAS enrollment, graduation rates were impressive: MAS students were 51 percent more likely to graduate than their non-MAS peers. "These results suggest that there is a consistent, significant, positive relationship between MAS participation and student academic performance" (Cabrera et al. 2012, p. 9).

Despite its success, the program became the rallying cry for conservative politicians, who defined it as "divisive," "un-American," and even "subversive." In explaining the roots of the MAS program, Curtis Acosta, a former teacher in the program, and Asiya Mir (a former student who is Pakistani American, thus refuting the claim that only Mexican American students benefited from the program), write:

> MAS was born from generations of systemic failure in educating Chican@/Latin@ students in the Tucson Unified School District and the dogged determination of our elders and the rest of our community to ensure an equal educational experience for our youth. Our classes were products of the Chican@ Movement in the 1960s and a further grass-roots effort in the 1990s to build an educational experience for our youth founded on the premise that the experiences, history, literature, and art of Chican@s/Latin@s were a necessary and valid area for rigorous academic exploration (Acosta & Mir 2011, p. 16).

(As of this writing, based on an investigation of the U.S. Department of Justice into Special Master Willis Hawley's committee proposal, a new comprehensive multicultural program is planned for the near future.)

María was a Project Specialist with the MAS program. She also taught an elective course, American History from Chicano Perspectives, mostly to eleventh graders. The majority of students who registered for the course were Chicanos/as, since 90 of the school's student body were Mexican American. While some of them were very motivated to learn more about their heritage, others took the course out of curiosity and to hang out with friends. Nevertheless, the class became a place not only where they learned history and where the identities of the Chicano/a students were made visible and affirmed but also where they learned to think critically. White students and students of other backgrounds were encouraged to take the course as well, and some of them were the biggest supporters of the program when it was under attack.

María Federico Brummer believes that it's an honor to be an educator, a profession that allows her to create with beautiful young people every day. She made the decision early in life to become a secondary social studies teacher because, as a student in Tucson, Arizona, where she was born, raised, and feels deeply rooted, she noted that the subject was taught almost exclusively by European American males. She began teaching at Hohokam Middle School in 1998; there, collaborating with the Tucson Unified School District's Mexican American/Raza studies department and the Pascua Yaqui Tribe, she had the opportunity to develop a Chicano/a and Yaqui studies curriculum. This experience was a turning point. In 2005, she began a new journey as a critically conscious educator. She became a project specialist for the Tucson Unified School District's Mexican American/Raza studies department, the product of student and community struggle. From 2006 until 2012, she was honored to be an educator in the only K–12 Chicano/a Studies department in the nation within a public school district. The program was eliminated with the implementation of the HB 2281 (now ARS §§ 15-111 and 15-112), Arizona's anti–ethnic studies law. In October 2010, she was one of eleven TUSD Mexican American Studies educators who filed suit in the United States District Court against Arizona's Superintendent of Public Instruction and the State Board of Education. Later, two TUSD students joined as plaintiffs. Today they continue the struggle to overturn this law.

In college, María majored in Chicano/a studies, and before beginning to teach at Tucson High, she was already involved with the Raza Cities Team, a group of Tucson educators who met once a month to share their experiences and generate support for ethnic studies. About being a teacher in the ethnic studies program she said:

> *I'm in my dream position. I felt that this was, in my heart, the best possible teaching position that I could ever have. Going through my teaching program, I never thought I could be in this space, so it's a great honor that I am teaching here. It's also a huge responsibility. We're continuing the work of the movement and we can't go back.*

Teaching was hard at the beginning. It was new and challenging, and she had much to learn; she often remained at school until 6 p.m. She still works late on many nights, but for different reasons: "I'm there till six o'clock but it's because I'm so engaged in what the kids are doing. Sometimes they're there helping me. They guide my instruction a lot of times." Her students (and former students, many of whom visit frequently) give her feedback that has helped her improve her craft. Also, because they become mentors for current students, the role of the alumni has been crucial for the program.

Initially the attacks on the program were from outside politicians, including State Schools Superintendent Tom Horne. Later there were also internal attacks; two members of the district school board were determined to eliminate the program, and the school district's central office began dismantling it. All but two of María's MAS courses were taken away from her. In addition, her supervisor was no longer the Director of the MAS program, but instead an assistant principal who had never been involved with the program.

Within two years, the situation had worsened dramatically. In January 2012, after the Arizona legislature had passed HB 2281/ARS 15-112, all the Mexican American courses were eliminated from the school district and the Ethnic Studies Program was dismantled. Certain books were banned—*Pedagogy of the Oppressed* by Paulo Freire, and *The Tempest* by William Shakespeare, among others—even though they are regularly used in other schools around the nation. Some teachers formerly in the program were reassigned to other schools. Although María kept her position at Tucson High, she is now teaching only general education American government classes. The teachers are under constant surveillance, as she explained:

> *Our lesson plans have to be approved and we were provided "training" from administration and other teachers on how to "tease out" any MAS curriculum. All teaching materials and books used in our MAS curriculum were removed from the classrooms. This was devastating to our students, our community, and our teachers.*

The former teachers and students in the Ethnic Studies Program have filed a lawsuit against the state and are awaiting a judgment from the federal district court judge. The Office for Civil Rights has visited Tucson High to investigate complaints about the program's elimination. The case has received national attention; many educators and civil rights organizations around the country support the students, teachers, and administrators of the MAS program.

Hyung Nam

A quintessential social justice educator, Hyung Nam currently teaches history, political science, economics, global studies, and the occasional guitar class. He has been teaching for thirteen years, first for two years in an alternative school and since then at Wilson High School, both in Portland, Oregon. Wilson is much less socioeconomically diverse than Hyung would like. It is one of the two wealthiest schools in the city. Nonetheless, it does have some racial and ethnic diversity, with a fairly good number of immigrants and English language learners, mostly Latinos/as and Somalians.

Hyung's philosophy of teaching developed from his background, his previous studies, his experiences, his identity, and his time in the profession. As an undergraduate he studied philosophy and critical theory, which helped him, he says, "lose the arrogance of thinking that one way of seeing or understanding the world is the only possible way, and recognize that there are many different ways of naming and understanding the world." This understanding helps him see that, given their varied experiences and diverse backgrounds, his students have different ideas and perspectives that need to be acknowledged.

Shortly after Hyung began teaching, one of his colleagues told him about the grassroots organization Rethinking Schools (see www.rethinkingschools.org). Started twenty-five years ago by classroom teachers in Milwaukee, Wisconsin, Rethinking Schools is still largely controlled by teachers. According to its webpage, Rethinking Schools

> began as a local effort to address problems such as basal readers, standardized testing, and textbook-dominated curriculum. Since its founding, it has grown into a nationally prominent publisher of educational materials, with subscribers in all 50 states, all 10 Canadian provinces, and many other countries. While the scope and influence of Rethinking Schools has changed, its basic orientation has not. Most importantly, it remains firmly committed to equity and to the vision that public education is central to the creation of a humane, caring, multiracial democracy.

Hyung Nam is an immigrant from South Korea. After graduating from college, working for Greenpeace, and doing a year of volunteer work in India, he wanted to find work back in Portland, Oregon, that would make a positive difference in the lives of young people. He started working in social services with homeless and runaway youth and decided that educating young people to be critical agents for change, not only in their own lives but in the broader society, would make a more profound difference than just helping them manage their immediate life crises. Because of his passion to make a difference, his experience with youths placed at risk because of social and economic inequality, and his own interests in critical thinking and social studies, he became an educational assistant and then was hired to teach at an alternative school for immigrant and refugee youth. Without graduate school preparation and certification, he felt unqualified. Discovering Rethinking Schools publications and the Portland Area Rethinking Schools educator group inspired him and helped him envision becoming a teacher for social justice. His association with Rethinking Schools also helped integrate his interest in critical social theory and his desire to make a palpable difference in young peoples' lives. It especially helped him realize the importance of reforming public schools from within and defending this core of the public sphere from further erosion and annihilation. This led to graduate school at Lewis and Clark College. As a social studies teacher, he has been a member of local teacher groups, including Portland Area Rethinking Schools and Portland Area Social Equality Educators, as well as an organizer for the Northwest Teaching for Social Justice Conference.

Hyung was immediately hooked on the philosophy of the organization and the materials it publishes ("I was struggling and also teaching at a school with very few resources; I was seeking out curriculum from everywhere, especially critical curriculum") and discovered that two of the founders, Bill Bigelow and Linda Christensen, were then teaching in Portland.

Hyung's relationship with RS has had a profound influence both on his teaching and his life. But for Rethinking Schools, he would probably have given up as a teacher early in his career:

> *Having colleagues share ideas and resources and learn from one another really made me feel I could teach. It was my first experience in an autonomous study group where we were there not because we were in school and we were trying to get credit for anything, but purely out of the desire to understand and share ideas and collaborate. It was amazing. It profoundly changed me.*

Social Justice in Practice

Although many schools profess to be grounded in social justice education, there are few concrete examples of what this means. In what follows, we focus on several key components of social justice teaching, with examples of each from our focus teachers. The components are:

- social justice and curriculum
- social justice and pedagogy
- social justice and relationships
- social justice and courage.

Social Justice and Curriculum

Social justice teaching requires curriculum that gives voice to stories, histories, and perspectives that were not absent in history but are still largely missing from the traditional curriculum. Social justice educators seek out—and vet—other sources of information and use that information to make the curriculum more truthful, honest, and complete. (Helpful books on how to make history more engaging and relevant are Howard Zinn's classic *A People's History of the United States,* latest edition 2010, and James Loewen's *Teaching What Really Happened: How to Avoid the Tyranny of Textbooks and Get Students Excited About Doing History,* 2009.) Social justice education is about making the curriculum more critical and honest in social studies, English, science, math, the arts—all subjects.

Using the curriculum to embody social justice means challenging conventional wisdom, from asking "Who *said* Columbus 'discovered' America?" to "Why are all the artists we learn about in the History of Art class White males?" (for material related to these and many other silenced topics, see the resource section at the end of the book). Mary Cowhey (2006), for example, challenges even her first and second graders to ask such questions, proving that even young children are capable of beginning the process of learning to think critically. Similarly, Vivian Vasquez (2006) taught children as young as four and five years old to think inclusively and critically.

Challenging conventional wisdom is a way to get students to engage in critical discourse, bring up topics not generally sanctioned in schools, become comfortable addressing matters missing in the curriculum, and learn that they have the responsibility to make the world a better place. Young people also need to learn that they have rights that need to be exercised if change is to happen; this too is an essential ingredient of social justice teaching.

Given the nature of the school where Geoffrey Winikur teaches, it is not surprising that social justice plays a central role in the curriculum. Parkway Northwest High School for Peace and Social Justice is a small special-admit school of 285 students with an innovative curriculum. All ninth graders take Multicultural Ethics and Leadership and Social Development. The school also has a Service Learning Center, staffed by a full-time teacher, through which students are engaged in community service. Teachers create courses as they see the need. For example, when teachers noticed that the twelfth graders lacked research skills, they developed a course in which ninth graders research interdisciplinary social justice issues. The resulting projects are presented to the whole school in "teach-ins."

Geoffrey's entire curriculum consists of social justice issues—topics that interest him and that benefit the students. His own research has focused on African literature and film, and on the transAtlantic slave trade. He has pursued professional development opportunities on these topics from the National Endowment for the Humanities (NEH) and other places. Specific examples of his curriculum have included studies of the Belgian Congo; Gandhi's teachings of peace; products originating from sugar, cocoa, and coffee; sweatshops; and African art.

He rejects the use of textbooks, preferring instead to have students read novels and poems, view films, and consult other primary sources:

> When I tell them that we're not going to use the textbook, there's a big exhale. Then when I tell them that I'm going to teach them how to read these other sources, not just that we're going to read them, they like that. When they are allowed to talk and express themselves, they really like that. They can do it. They just need a context.

The curriculum is also a major way through which Hyung enacts social justice. Although the students at Wilson don't "need" him as much as less wealthy students might, he says that they do need someone who will make them think critically about social studies and about life in general:

> *They need teachers who can expand their horizons and connect them to inspiring people from history and in the world who have confronted the kinds of problems that societies have struggled with over time in many different places, show them that although people do not always succeed, they can work together collectively, they can be problem solvers, they can be agents for positive change.*

Through this kind of curriculum students learn that life is complicated, that there are no easy answers like those on the multiple choice tests they have been forced to take since elementary school.

Because he teaches in a fairly conservative community, Hyung encounters his share of conflicts. Nearly every year, he's called on by the administration to explain his rationale for teaching some controversial issue or other. He credits supportive colleagues (particularly his Rethinking Schools network) and his vice principal with helping him overcome these obstacles:

> *Sometimes I think if I were alone and isolated it would be too much for me, but knowing other teachers who have gone through it, and knowing that people throughout history who have been agitators and have challenged and questioned the dominant society have gone through it, I kind of thrive on it.*

A social justice curriculum formed the heart of María Brummer's Mexican American Studies program. When I first interviewed her, she described a project in which students researched their families and communities, interviewed family members, and wrote "eloquent pieces." The students also wrote about their school experiences, pieces that yielded much more relevant information than that contained in their cumulative folders. The research on their families gave the students' perspectives of who they are, "the total package," because as María said, "I need to know about their families. I need to know where they're coming from. I need to know what their goals are in life."

Social Justice and Pedagogy

Pedagogy is much more than particular strategies or tricks of the trade ("magic bullets") that motivate students. What makes pedagogy socially just is the *ideology* and *purpose* behind it—what a teacher believes the students are capable of learning, what he or she thinks a student deserves, the ends the teacher and students hope to accomplish.

Although it's not the only method they use, a good number of the teachers I interviewed mentioned dialogue as indispensable in creating a social justice classroom. Many students are unaccustomed to dialogical teaching, particularly in this era of No Child Left Behind, Race to the Top, and other mandates. In the face of pressures to "teach to the test," many students, as well as their teachers, have developed a short-answer mentality. Dialogue is a two-way street and differs markedly from what happens in many classrooms. Dialogue allows all parties to benefit from the exchange. Ira Shor, in a book with Paulo Freire (1987), explained it this way: "The students are not a flotilla of boats trying to reach the teacher who is finished and waiting on the shore. The teacher is also one of the boats" (p. 50).

For Hyung Nam, dialogue is essential if students are to become aware of life outside their limited experiences. He wants his students to learn more than the curriculum. His pedagogy is directed toward opening his students' eyes to reality. He especially wants them to understand that people are agents who can change things: "People are constantly struggling to problem-solve and no matter what kind of context and limited situations we're faced with and embedded in, we can problem-solve together to try to create a better world."

Through his pedagogy, Hyung has helped his students understand some complicated ideas. Using data based on the 2010 Census Report, he showed them that income inequality has increased tremendously in the past three decades; among industrialized Western countries, the United States now has the most unequal incomes. He also used research by G. William Domhoff, a sociologist at UC Santa Cruz, who wrote *Who Rules America?* (2009), to underscore the power and wealth disparities in the United States: one percent of Americans own 34.6 percent of the wealth in the nation, the remaining 19 percent in the top quintile own 50.5 percent, and the other 80 percent own 15 percent. He went on:

> *I have them imagine that there are a hundred people and a hundred sandwiches that represent the population of and the wealth in the United States. Imagine one person stuffing his face with thirty-four sandwiches, most going to waste. Another nineteen share fifty sandwiches, a little bit more than two each. But eighty people struggle over the crumbs of fifteen sandwiches. In that way, I hope to get them to see inequality.*

Pedagogy like this can create a cognitive dissonance because as Hyung explains, many of his students, particularly those from more privileged backgrounds, have been taught to believe in a meritocracy, where one is rewarded simply for one's efforts, not for one's station in life.

Hyung also wants his students to think in more complicated ways than they usually do. He wants them to lose the habit of always looking for the "right answer":

> *I tell them there are good answers and not so good answers and that a good answer is an answer that is convincing, that includes evidence to support the conclusion, and that that's the best we can have until someone else has a better answer.*

Geoffrey Winikur, who teaches English language and literature, uses a similar approach:

> *I teach in a dialogical way. I try to build from the students' strengths, and I try to build a community of student voice. I want students talking, I want them writing, I want them disagreeing, I want them writing a lot. That leads to a bit noisier, a little bit less traditional-looking classroom.*

A demanding teacher, Geoffrey uses some college-level (even graduate-level) books in his English classes. He wants his students to learn to read difficult books in challenging ways. This is "always a reward," whether he has them read *Fences, Catcher in the Rye, Things Fall Apart*, or *The Things They Carried*. Another innovation in Geoffrey's pedagogy is making student work—in writing (journals, poetry, other forms) or through dialogue—part of the essential text; he says it's a "powerful way of teaching." One of his IEP ninth graders had a severe spelling problem but wrote an amazing memoir: "I read it four times. I felt like I was in the presence of a genius." When he spoke with his student about it, she dismissed his praise ("Oh, I just wrote it"). He said, "I'm a fairly decent reader. I've read enough literature to know good literature when I see it, and I'm thinking, 'Am I making this up?' It doesn't feel like it—but she doesn't see it."

Geoffrey ascribes the lack of confidence students sometimes have about their abilities to the demands of No Child Left Behind, which leaves little time for creative work. Although a lot of his students claim they cannot write poetry, Geoffrey tells them, "Well, you know what? You haven't been taught how to write poetry, so you might think you can't." When they became more confident, they began writing poetry.

The results of Geoffrey's pedagogy have been worth the hard work: "By reading the kind of books we read, the students feel validated as intellectuals." A student once told him that he was the first teacher that ever made her feel like a student. "That was the nicest compliment I've ever heard. It made not only my day but my entire teaching career."

Social Justice and Relationships

At its core teaching is a social activity. Showing students—especially students whose experiences with schooling have been neither positive nor productive—that they are cared about is a crucial element in student learning. All student/teacher relationships are of necessity different, depending on the teacher, the students, and the context. Some teachers form relationships that resemble family ties, others base their connection with students on the curriculum. There is never just one factor but a combination of factors that help teachers and students forge strong connections.

Angela Valenzuela (1999) found that some Mexican American teachers were especially effective because they treated their students as extended family, bringing them snacks or attending out-of-school events in which the students participated. María Brummer too sees her students as family members: "They kind of relate it to my being their *Tía* [aunt]. They know that I'm there for them and they know that I'm pushing them as far as they possibly can go and I'll be there for them forever."

To promote the feeling of family, María has *encuentros,* or familial gatherings, with the students and their families: "Our students' parents are giving us their prize possessions and we have to get the most for them." In these *encuentros,* the students showcase their work, sharing with their families the pride they feel in having completed rigorous assignments. María also invites students to her home, something most students have not previously experienced:

> *Every year, I have students ask, "Are we allowed to go to your house?" All this time they've never been in their teachers' homes! I tell them, "Well, why wouldn't you be allowed to? What's going to happen? You're welcome into my home just as much as I hope I am welcome into your home."*

Families are related forever, and María tells them, "I'm going to be your teacher for the rest of your lives if you want me to be."

Geoffrey Winikur connects with his students both academically and personally. He feels honesty and transparency are important in any relationship, that forming strong bonds with students is not possible without these qualities:

> *I feel my relationship with students has to be based on love. That means sometimes it's very joyful and sometimes it's not. I try to treat them as I would my own kids—sometimes they need a hug and sometimes they need a knock upside the head, so to speak.*

Forming close relationships with students helps Geoffrey connect with them academically, because only then can trust develop. This is why it is easier for him than it might be for other teachers to broach difficult and sensitive topics: "I feel it's really important to be honest with kids. Showing them that I will talk about anything at all in an academic context has been big for me and for them." Geoffrey talks to his students about identity, race, and privilege, discussions that are frowned on in other schools and classrooms. His identity as a member of a biracial family "helps me navigate certain issues, things that I've learned from my wife and what it means to have biracial kids. It can be helpful and I think the students like knowing about a teacher's family."

Social Justice and Courage

Teaching for social justice sometimes means taking unpopular stands that challenge the status quo. To alter the curriculum to be more inclusive, advocate for more rigorous courses, change not only *what* one teaches but also *how* one teaches, challenge taken-for-granted policies and practices, one must be courageous—particularly in schools without supportive colleagues or administrators.

María Brummer certainly had to summon up her courage during and after the turbulent period in which the Mexican American Studies program at Tucson High was eliminated, but there was no choice as far as she was concerned. Given what it had taken to establish the program, all concerned—teachers, administrators, students, families—had to defend it. As she said, "Our classrooms are sacred. We struggled for them and we're going to honor those who were in that struggle so that we could be here." Being one of the eleven educators who filed a lawsuit challenging HB 2281/ARS 15-112 helped María define her identity more clearly: "I'm an educator activist who has the responsibility to continue fighting for an equitable education for all our students and our community."

Geoffrey has advocated courageously for the integrity of his curriculum. Parkway was a more tradi-tional school when he first began teaching there, and he was at odds with some of the other teachers. His being White while his students and many of the other teachers were Black made his curriculum suspect. The principal observed his class on African literature and film more frequently than any of his other classes: "I read into that that there were some questions about what, why, and how I was teach-ing that class, although the kids tended to like it." When the class became a humanities elective and its content changed, Geoffrey incorporated the original content into his regular English classes. Those classes are now interdisciplinary: they are also more interesting for the students and generate a great deal of collaboration among the teachers.

Because of his pedagogy and curriculum, Hyung Nam has had his share of discord. He spoke at length about some of the obstacles that get in the way of social justice teaching, particularly in a fairly conservative community. During his first year of teaching, a very bright student, previously home schooled, took two classes with him—Global Studies and U.S. History. A Christian, she was "someone with a genuine heart who felt compassion and cared about people." She was initially drawn to his social justice curriculum—excited by these ideas and outraged at past injustices. But in the middle of the year, after talking with her grandfather, she decided that many ideas she was encountering in Hyung's classes were "communist." For the remainder of the year, she used what Hyung called her "amazing intelligence" to resist his curriculum. "At the end of the year, I received a four-page letter from her father accusing me of 'being anti-capitalist, anti-American, anti-White, anti-Christian, anti-nonenvironmentalist, anti-consumerist' and telling me that if I don't like it in this country, why don't I go back to Korea."

In spite of the conflict that social justice curriculum and pedagogy can generate, Hyung is ada-mant about being a social justice educator. He will continue doing what he does, because he knows introducing his students to a critical perspective makes a difference, even though "some parents and students are going to have a hard time with that." He asserted, "I see that part of my job is to agitate. I think about the kind of society that we have with all the problems and potential. As a teacher, I can make people think and question things."

Conclusion: Teaching Is Advocacy

The corporatist focus on education has largely removed the moral dimensions of teaching and learning from existing notions of school reform. Achieving AYP, rating teachers based on their students' test scores, and "racing to the top" have become the major goals of public education, while its broader purposes—traditionally defined as preparing young people for informed, moral, meaningful, and productive lives in a democratic society—have become obscured. The focus has shifted to careerist and competitive goals, as if preparing for a job and being "first in the world" are all that schools are good for.

At the same time, although they are the ones most affected by the changing educational landscape, students and families have been largely silenced in the ongoing debates about how to improve public schools. Their participation is conspicuously absent from most of the numerous commissions, panels, and "white papers" on public education. This is particularly true of the most marginalized students and their families. Witness the dismantling of the MAS Program at Tucson High, a decision made by those wielding the most power and against the wishes of the students, families, teachers, and even the administrators of the school.

What teachers have to say about the current state of education is also obscured. Their voices are missing not only from the national debate but also from policy and practice decisions, even within their own schools. Pressures to "teach to the test," growing accountability demands that take a great deal of time from the curriculum but may result in little learning, and an increasingly prescribed curriculum all make teachers' jobs today problematic and, many times, unsatisfying. Teachers such as María Federico Brummer, Geoffrey Winikur, and Hyung Nam remind us that teaching is always about advocacy: advocacy for students' lives and learning, advocacy for the integrity of the content they teach, and advocacy for the professionalization of teaching.

NOTES

Acosta, C. & Mir, A. 2012. 15–26.
Cabrera, N. L., Millen, J. F., & Marx, R. W. 2012.
Cammarota, J. & Romero, A. 2006. 305–312.
Cowhey, M. 2006.
Domhoff, G. W. 2009.

Loewen, J. 2009.
Shor, I. & Freire, P. 1987.
Valenzuela, A. 1999.
Vasquez, V. 2004.
Zinn, H. 2010.

Part III

Lessons Learned

What have we learned about being an effective teacher of students of diverse backgrounds? Chapter 9 expands on the themes introduced in Chapters 3 through 8, which range from understanding teaching as love to becoming advocates for students. Chapter 10 discusses some of the dispositions needed by teachers to be effective with all students and gives examples of how these values are enacted in the classroom. Chapter 11 tackles the question of how teachers thrive and provides four recommendations for how to do so derived from these teachers' stories and from my own many years as a teacher and teacher educator. That teachers *do* thrive, in spite of the obstacles that get in their way, is a testament to their resilience, even their stubbornness.

Chapter 9

Teaching Students of Diverse Backgrounds

What Does It Take?

The teachers we've met in this book are thriving in spite of the many obstacles that can stand in their way. While policymakers—through commissions, reports, and conferences—may debate the relative advantages and disadvantages of particular policies that have a direct impact on teachers and their students, teachers rarely have the opportunity to engage in such high-level conversations. Yet they have a great deal to teach us about what works, what's important, and what needs to change in education.

To expand on some of their ideas, we return to the themes in the concluding segments in Chapters 3 to 8:

- Teaching is an act of love.
- Teaching is an ethical endeavor.
- Teachers thrive when they keep learning.
- Teaching is honoring students' identities and believing in their futures.
- Teaching is challenging the status quo.
- Teaching is advocacy.

This chapter elaborates on these themes.

Teaching Is an Act of Love

In Chapter 3, Angeles Pérez and Roger Wallace spoke about their vocation as an act of love, and the other teachers echoed this sentiment during their interviews. Teaching is *who they are*, not just *what they do*. John Gunderson had not set out to be a teacher but fit into the role as easily as fitting his hand into a glove: "I just felt alive, it was me," is how he described it. In spite of what he called "this behavioristic mill" of the high-stakes testing culture, John said, "I love what I do and I love getting kids to think. I look forward to work every morning." When asked what made teaching most rewarding, John said, "Knowing that they want to be in my class."

When I speak about loving one's students, I'm not referring to maudlin, sentimentalized love but rather *critical* love (Nieto 2010)—believing in students, pushing and cajoling them, being both nurturing and demanding, and working tirelessly on their behalf. It also means being steadfast. For John Gunderson, teaching doesn't finish "when the bell rings." María Federico Brummer takes it even further, telling her students she will be there with them "forever." Angeles Pérez's sense of effectiveness as a teacher is tied to the relationships she has with her students. She was more thrilled for her student who won the spelling bee than he was. "I'm their biggest fan so when they succeed, I feel like I'm succeeding."

Loving one's students is also feeling both *solidarity* with and *empathy* for them. A number of years ago I edited a book of essays written by teachers (Nieto 2005b) in which they demonstrated how they related to students' experiences and lives even if markedly different from their own. Empathy "is produced within networks of power relations" (Ullman & Hecsh 2012, p. 624). Teachers cannot negate their own identity and power when interacting with students, but they *can* attempt to understand their identity as intertwined with those of the students they teach. In their study of preservice teachers, Ullman and Hecsh found that although preservice teachers of color were more likely to have a sociocultural consciousness—an awareness and understanding of their students' realities—the vast majority of teachers of all backgrounds did not come to the classroom with these understandings. Rather, they developed them by working with young people who had difficult lives and by analyzing the structural and historical contexts that explained how these lives had come to be.

No matter one's own identity, loving one's students is not always easy. I once asked Angel, my husband, who was a wonderful middle and high school teacher, whether he loved his students. "Of course!" he responded without hesitation, adding, "How can you teach if you don't love your students?" Then he laughed. "Of course, I don't always love them when they're all *together*!" That's a reality all teachers understand. Carmen Tisdale spoke about loving students unconditionally in spite of everything. She also made it clear that loving one's students is standing up for them: "I've done a lot of fighting," she said. Remember her powerful words: "You can do anything you want to me, but if you want to fight, mess with my children."

Loving one's students also requires the humility to recognize that one does not always have the only, right, answer. Roger Wallace said, "That's how I became a teacher: love of children, the love of exchange of ideas, the love that my perspective wasn't the only one, that there are a lot of others." Just as important, loving one's students is not letting preconceived notions about students get in the way of teaching. These preconceptions—whether based on students' race, language, accent, social status, ability, or other differences; the advice or warnings of other teachers; or a student's cumulative record—can become self-fulfilling prophecies. Instead we must look beyond all these things and think of each student as a *possibility*. Roger Wallace's admonition to "put your stuff away!" is one of the wisest pieces of advice in this book. If all teachers put their "stuff" away, there would be more engaged students, more exciting learning, and more joyful schools.

Teaching Is an Ethical Endeavor

Teaching is a moral endeavor in many ways, including modeling ethical behavior. Almost all the teachers I interviewed discussed how they attempt to be authentic with their students. Amber Bechard said, "I'm not a different person when I go to school. I don't walk in the classroom and put on a teaching persona." When teachers are authentic, students pick up other essential messages as well: the importance of being truthful, the fact that teachers do not know everything, the need for personal connection. Hyung Nam still feels uneasy when he can't answer every student question on the spot saying: "If I don't have an answer they're going to see me as being incompetent, that I should know these answers." Nevertheless, he's come to realize that "it's so important for us to show them we are learners and that there are no simple answers in the world anyway."

Preparing students to be moral human beings is a theme that ran through all the interviews. Carmen Tisdale said teaching for her is primarily about preparing good people, while at the same time giving students the hope of having options in life. She wants her students to dream, to hope, and to imagine other possibilities. Adam Heenan had been taught by his mother from an early age always to think of other people, not just himself, and he decided when he was in high school that he wanted to be a teacher. For Adam, teaching is a way to serve his community. Similarly, although she had decided as a young girl not to follow in the footsteps of her parents who were teachers, after hearing Jonathan Kozol speak about his book *Savage Inequalities* (1991) about the dismal conditions of education for vulnerable students, Alicia López decided that teaching was the most important thing she could do with her life. She recalled: "I thought, 'I want to do something to help people.'" Once she started she "was hooked, even though it was so hard."

Most of these teachers made it clear that the goal of teaching is to prepare young people to make ethical life choices, not simply get high scores on tests. María Guerrero, who became a teacher to help working-class families like hers, found it was becoming more difficult than ever to do so in the current sociopolitical context. In spite of this context, many of the teachers mentioned that teaching students to think, to question, to challenge, to rethink, and to understand their own responsibility to help improve the world was why they remained in the profession.

Being a social justice educator is very important to Hyung Nam; he wants his students to understand larger social issues and how they affect their lives. In that way, they can learn to think beyond their own limited perspectives and become empowered, productive citizens in a democratic society. Katie Shibata, who is currently an ESL teacher in California but who began teaching Somalian high school immigrants in Minnesota, was forever changed by the experience: when they arrived at the high school, many did not even know how to hold a pencil, yet a few years later some of them were graduating from college.

Teaching is also ethical in terms of how one prepares and presents the curriculum. According to Geoffrey Winikur, a "bogus multicultural curriculum" contradicts the goals of teaching students complex and nuanced concepts and ideas. For Geoffrey, "if you have diverse schools, you can't have standardized scores and you can't have a watered-down curriculum where you just read a story about an Asian family, or a Latino family, or an African family, or an Eastern European family." For Geoffrey, an authentic multicultural curriculum presents students with complex issues and genuine food for thought that can help them ponder real moral issues.

Teachers Thrive When They Keep Learning

All these teachers were, in one way or another, enthusiastic lifelong learners. This was certainly evident with Alicia López and John Nguyen (Chapter 4) but true of the others as well. Roger Wallace joked about how he loves teaching anything and everything: "I even like teaching how to diagram sentences. Now, that's scary!" he said, laughing. Roger also loves learning about sociology, psychology, advanced mathematics—in a word, everything.

Amber Bechard is equally passionate about learning. For her, "there's never enough!" She said she hoped her enthusiasm for learning was obvious to her students, and that they might think, "Look at that passion! You can't *not* catch it!" Amber has not only completed a master's and a doctoral degree but also dedicates each summer to her continued professional learning. She has been awarded a number of Fulbright and Freeman grants, traveling to Mexico, South Africa, China, and Japan and bringing back her newfound knowledge and insights to share with her middle school students. She also earned National Board Certification and has taken a number of seminars to enrich her curriculum. It isn't so much the content of learning that keeps her engaged but rather, she said, "I finally decided after twenty years of teaching that I like the *process* of learning, and teaching others to learn."

One of fifteen children, twelve of whom were older, Amber knew well what to expect in school. Her second-grade teacher didn't know what to do with her because Amber already knew the math curriculum:

> *My second grade teacher said, "I'm going to send you back to first grade, and your*
> *first-grade teacher will use you as a tutor." As a second grader I went into the first-grade*
> *classroom and had my own math group! It was so empowering, it was so much fun. So I*
> *decided that I wanted to be a teacher.*

For Amber, education is also the way out of poverty and hopelessness: "I see education as a path to make your dreams come true. You can be anything you want to be. You can go wherever you want to go, whether it's in a book, whether it's in a school." It's why she is so passionate about teaching and learning. Amber is eternally grateful to her first teachers, saying: "I'm a teacher still because of what my first- and second-grade teachers did for me. I think that's what made me fall in love with it. It becomes who you are, and I think that's why I'll never tire of it." But learning is not just something that she does to keep ahead of her students. Amber simply loves to learn: "Just as much as I want my kids to learn, to devour literature, to read a book or to learn to speak, or debate, or to think, I also want to continue to learn those things."

Geoffrey Winikur too spoke about teaching as being above all a love of learning. He keeps very busy as a learner and thrives on his varied learning experiences. But he learns just as much from his students: "I love culture, I love art, and I love history even though I'm not formally trained in studying history. I love that I can learn with my students about Caribbean culture, or whatever their culture may be, or religion even." Geoffrey was quick to equate teaching and learning with happiness: "Anytime we have really powerful dialogue about a book or a film, that to me is joy because I'm learning more from the kids than they're learning from me." At the same time, Geoffrey is a demanding teacher, selecting texts that are "pretty substantial," ones commonly read in college or even graduate school, in an urban school and with students who are not often offered this kind of curriculum.

A learner at heart, Geoffrey loves the give-and-take of teaching, learning from both his students and his colleagues. Self-initiated professional development is a vital part of learning for him: he's taken courses offered by the National Endowment for the Humanities and is an ongoing member of the Philadelphia Writing Project, which he has co-facilitated for several years. This work, he says, "has been a gift." He has also mentored novice teachers, work that he says helps change the culture of the school and is another way for him to keep learning. Geoffrey says:

> *The NEH courses were really important and the work with the Writing Project. I also*
> *do some work with Teach for America. I really like working with my colleagues; we*
> *engage strongly with one another. I love the adult relationships in teaching. And I like*
> *kids. I like teaching kids and I love watching kids learn, you know, "the light in their*
> *eyes" [Nieto 2010]. When I read those words, I was like, "Yes, I know exactly what that*
> *means." I love that stuff.*

But learning is not just what happens through the curriculum. John Nguyen does not relegate learning to a particular lesson or unit. He cherishes those moments that although not part of the curriculum, take off from it: "My favorite lessons now are the ones that are not content related." Although he knows his responsibility is to make sure everyone is on task, he insisted, "You have your moments away from it, and I think you should build these moments into the curriculum."

As a high school student in Chicago, Adam Heenan won a coveted Golden Apple Award (www .goldenapple.org), given to one hundred students in Illinois each year. While paying for a good part of a college education, Golden Apple Awards come with the stipulation that awardees teach in a "school of need" for five years. That "clicked": he had never considered teaching anywhere *but* such a school (he'd attended one himself). For Adam, lifelong learning is the kind of learning that benefits not only him but also his students. He said that teachers need to be resourceful, to find out everything they can about what the community has to offer, that this is a sacred responsibility: "It is the number one thing that you can be as a teacher for your kids: a pipeline to other opportunities outside the classroom." This pipeline can and often does offer students options they might not otherwise have. It gives them cultural and social capital that those from under-resourced communities usually don't have access to (Stanton-Salazar 2001).

Teaching Is Honoring Students' Identities and Believing in Their Futures

Although conventional wisdom and generations of practice have defined assimilating students into mainstream American life and culture as a primary role of teachers, the teachers in this book see their role differently. Of course, they recognize that no matter what subject they happen to teach, they have a responsibility to teach their students English—and to teach it well so students become fluent Standard English speakers able to participate fully in U.S. life. In addition, they know they have a responsibility to open up opportunities and options for their students by exposing them to U.S. life, history, and contemporary culture. At the same time, these teachers do not accept that their students must divest themselves of who they are in order to succeed in the United States. On the contrary, they welcome their students' identities into the classroom, encouraging them to retain their native or community language and to maintain ties to their families and communities, knowing that these ties will in the end prove immensely important to their students' emotional and psychological well-being. They are an anchor that will keep students grounded, a truth eloquently expressed in a recent inspiring book of the voices of immigrant youths (Sadowski 2013).

Teachers' actions, even if they are subconscious, reflect how they value or do not value their students' cultures and identities. Elsewhere I have made several practical recommendations about how teachers can honor students' identities: learn another language; become "students of their students";

make a sincere effort to get to know the families of their students; become involved in the community in which they teach; and use students' real names and learn to say them correctly (Nieto 2012). The last suggestion, as innocuous as it may seem, is violated every time a teacher changes a student's name from María to Mary or mispronounces a student's name. It is an example of cultural disrespect. Actions like these have been called *microaggressions*, "subtle daily insults that as a form of racism, support a racial and cultural hierarchy of minority inferiority" (Kohli & Solórzano 2012, p. 441). In their research on the K–12 memories of people now mostly in their twenties and thirties, Rita Kohli and Daniel Solórzano documented painful memories of shame, embarrassment, and humiliation when teachers mispronounced or changed students' names or other students laughed at and mimicked them. Some students went through their entire K-12 schooling with a name different from the one they had been given at birth or voluntarily changed their name to avoid humiliation. One student refused to go on stage to receive a prestigious award because she knew her name would be mispronounced.

Examples of how teachers manage this delicate balance are clear in the words of these teachers. For many, their own identity is a way for them to understand the significance of culture and language for their students. Maricela Meza Buenrostro talked about her own experience as a second language learner. She was fortunate to find teachers who affirmed her identity while teaching her English. Angela Fajardo knew firsthand how difficult it was to learn English, and that experience motivated her to become a teacher. She calls herself an English language learner still; connecting her personal experience as an immigrant with her students inspires her.

Carmen Tisdale, an African American teacher of African American students, takes her responsibility to affirm her students' identities very seriously. It is her way of counteracting the negative messages they hear. Yolanda Harris, also African American, has been particularly effective with African American and Latino males, many of whom have special needs. Feeling abandoned by many of their teachers over the years, these young men respond positively to Yolanda for a variety of reasons: their shared identity as urban people of color, the community in which they all live, Yolanda's being a mother of boys, and her uncompromising demands in the classroom.

Alicia López's identity as Puerto Rican and Spanish helps her understand students of diverse backgrounds, both immigrant and nonimmigrant. "I think it's also very important for my students to know": it shows her White middle-class students a different model of what it means to be Latina and is an affirmation for her Latino/a and immigrant students of who they are. For Angeles Pérez, being a role model and mentor to her fourth graders, all of whom are also Latinos/as, is especially significant. She wants them to see a successful Latina because "it shows them that they can be that way." Several of her fourth graders have decided that they want to become teachers too.

Honoring culture and language are just as important for teachers whose identity is different from the identities' of their students. John Nguyen, who emigrated from Vietnam with his family at an early age, decided to become a teacher in New Haven, where most of his students are African American, because he felt he could have more of an impact there than in a wealthy suburb. John is a student of his students, learning as much as he can about them yet always feeling there's more to know. He wants to know "where they live" and someday would love to spend an entire twenty-four hours shadowing a student, seeing what his classes are like, following him from home to school, going with him to work, and so on. He said that in this way, he would have a better idea of what it's like to walk in his students' shoes.

When Amber Bechard took a class in multicultural education before moving to Chicago, she found that what she learned was relevant as well for the privileged and overwhelmingly White kindergarten students she was then teaching. Being exposed to issues of diversity, race, privilege, and power expanded Amber's world and taught her that issues of identity were significant for all of her students. She has made it a point ever since to have open discussions about identity, encouraging students to speak about who they are and why it's important to them. "I want everybody in my classroom to feel okay however they decide to identify themselves." Sometimes some of her White students—a distinct minority in her current school—confess that they feel they don't have a culture. She pushes them to understand that everyone has a culture: "They do have an identity. I don't want them to feel invisible. They get to be who they are too. And that is just as valuable."

Teaching students of diverse backgrounds is what Geoffrey Winikur wanted to do. "If you like diversity, then you're going to love working with diverse students." Building on his interest in African literature and culture, he created a curriculum that benefited his students as well as himself.

Teaching Is Challenging the Status Quo

Standing up for children and for what is right may mean challenging the status quo. It takes courage to do this. We've seen numerous examples of courage in the words and experiences of the teachers in this book. Their courage is evident in small ways (Angeles Pérez and Maricela Meza Buenrostro rejected the advice of veteran teachers to "not smile until Christmas") and large (María Federico Brummer and other Tucson High teachers defined their Mexican American Studies program as a "sacred space" for which they were ready to fight in whatever way they could).

Courage can be demonstrated in everyday interactions as well as in one's very philosophy of teaching, a philosophy that might contradict conventional wisdom, "the way things are done." Amber Bechard says, "I don't see my role as a teacher to deposit knowledge into a kid. I see my role as a teacher to facilitate that student's learning for himself or herself." These teachers speak up when they feel they have to defend their students, their curriculum, their pedagogy, and their profession. Sometimes this gets them in hot water but they do it nevertheless. According to Adam Heenan, "My family tells me I am just not prudent in the things I am saying. Sometimes I don't keep my mouth shut, I get involved too much, but that was what I was brought up to do." Griselda Benítez challenges the status quo by continuing her Community Circle activity in spite of high-stakes tests and similar mandates that make such practices less common and, in some schools, no longer permitted.

The pressure to have students do well on standardized tests was the elephant in the room during many of the interviews. Teachers often felt stifled, particularly those who worked in under-resourced schools. Nevertheless, most also felt up to the challenge. Amber Bechard doesn't let tests get in the way of her job, even though they are always in the background. Angeles Pérez decided early on that she would not "teach to the test," certain that her students would do well on them—and she was right.

John Gunderson, openly critical of the current high-stakes environment, bemoaned the fact that schools have become "this behavioristic mill that's churning out what you have to do instead of focusing on learning and making kids see the relevancy of education in their lives." Rather than fall in line with this kind of thinking, he's worked hard to "find a little island and create a class that focuses on kids' lives." It's relationships that matter, not templates or models or rubrics. "The crux of it for me is finding that the relationship with your kids and your classroom is more important than any other template." Given all the demands on teachers today, María Guerrero said she felt suffocated. Nevertheless, she was eloquent in refusing to give up her values and commitment, believing that it's more important to stay true to herself and to retain her spirit.

Another way to challenge the status quo is through the curriculum. Hyung Nam feels that his students need him "to expand their horizons," and he uses the curriculum to do it. Because they aren't used to his problem-posing and dialogical approach, his students have a hard time when there's not a "right answer" and exams aren't multiple choice. They do, however, learn how to learn in this way and most of them appreciate being exposed to content that isn't taught in other classes For example, Hyung mentioned that, given the learning environment he creates in the class, students feel free to discuss issues they might not address in other classes. When they discussed health care reform, for instance, one of Hyung's students talked about the struggles her family had gone through. The same had happened when they discussed family members' unemployment stemming from the depressed economy. That they feel comfortable contributing to these discussions like this is a testament to Hyung's curriculum.

John Nguyen was attracted to social studies in the first place because it relates to people's lives. It also gives him the opportunity to discuss meaningful topics with his students—discussions in which they may question the current state of affairs. He considers himself a teacher with a social justice perspective, and his classes discuss issues often considered taboo in school. Knowing that many of his students have difficult and sometimes tragic lives, John tries both to teach them to be critical thinkers and to encourage them to continue their education. He realizes this is a tough sell for some of his students and that it's important to understand the circumstances in which they're living. At the beginning of the academic year, he shares his story as a member of an immigrant family and asks them to write their personal stories:

> *Some students will write long stories. Invariably, all of them will have a death of someone close in there. This year they were so emotional. I read so many; it was heart wrenching. Just to know that there were so many deaths that they had to go through, so many drug problems.*

Because of the stories his students have shared, John has come to admire their resilience and courage more than ever, saying, "It's pretty impressive. It's understandable if they have a bad day, or a couple of bad days."

John knows his teaching can have an impact on his students' lives: "You never know what the effect is until they come back. They'll remember some of the stuff that I taught them, and I'm shocked because I forgot that I taught that."

Teaching Is Advocacy

These teachers recognize that teaching is advocacy. The decisions they make—curricular, pedagogical, other—are primarily for the benefit of their students. Advocacy can be as simple as listening to one's students. John Nguyen recalled asking his students why they liked him. When they responded, "Well, you listen to us," John was appalled that some teachers won't even bother to listen to their students: "It's so *basic*. To hear them say they don't have people who listen to them blows my mind." For Gabriela Olmedo, advocacy means, among other things, having a refrigerator, microwave, and food in her classroom to feed students who are frequently hungry. For John Gunderson, advocacy is being fully present in class: "When I'm with you," he tells his students, "you get all of me, and in return I expect you to be here too."

Advocacy also involves cultivating relationships and giving students hope and another vision for the future. María Guerrero talked about the need for classrooms to "resonate with the importance of building relationships. It's the human element in teaching. You cannot divorce that. It has to be a base in the classroom." Angeles Pérez is the consummate advocate. She needed to learn how to handle a student who always "put up his walls." Rather than humiliate him when he didn't do his homework or call on him and put him on the spot, she made sure to recognize him in other ways. Showing immense wisdom for a second-year teacher, Angeles said, "Each kid, he really has his own individual thing that you've got to know." Carmen Tisdale also advocates for her students by getting to know them individually. About a child in her classroom, she said, "It's my place to show him that you can be more and that you need to be more."

Gabriela Olmedo told the poignant story of trying to convince a student about the importance of an education even though he confronted her with his reality: gangs, friends getting shot, and other tremendous obstacles in his life. But teachers who are advocates continue to push hope in spite of these obstacles, not with naiveté but with the understanding that their students, even the most vulnerable, need to hear other scripts for how their lives might go.

Advocacy is also helping students grow and flourish. Roger Wallace used the metaphor of teacher as gardener: "You're planting seeds, and a sower of seeds really does not want to see the seedling come up too soon. They have very little root so they might blow away. We also know that oftentimes the seeds can't find a place to root because the ground is too rocky. So my job then becomes to help the children move the rocks."

Roger's advocacy takes many forms: he gives his students his home and cell phone numbers and encourages them to call him whenever they need to; he meets frequently with parents whenever and wherever it's comfortable for them, even at the laundromat. He tries to understand each child on his or her terms. "Being in my class is not about the capitol of Idaho is Boise or the Atlantic Ocean is contained in part by the Gulf Stream." Instead, his students learn what kind of learners they are, how best they learn and under what conditions. Teaching students of different ethnicities, races, and social classes, he recognizes that some children have more resources and opportunities than others, and he tries to even the playing field:

> *They don't pass two vocabulary tests and see if I don't show up at their house and say, "Where do you study for your vocabulary? How do you study? Let's go to your room and organize." I don't know how many teachers go to their kid's houses but I do. Some parents say, "Now, don't you be coming over here," but that's very rare.*

For María Federico Brummer, advocacy takes on a collective meaning that encompasses the welfare and future of her students and their community. Recalling the civil rights and Chicano Power movements, she and her colleagues in the Mexican American Studies Program felt that advocacy went beyond individual students and included the entire community: "We're continuing the work of the movement." Many of the Loyola Marymount University teachers in Los Angeles also spoke of teaching as advocacy for their students and their students' communities. Several recalled their own experiences as children feeling lost and alone with nobody to turn to. It is no wonder that they take their responsibility as advocates very seriously.

Conclusion: Teachers Make a Difference

Although teachers would certainly benefit from better pay and improved working conditions, providing monetary and other incentives based on students' test scores is not the answer. Merit pay and higher salaries haven't made a big difference in teacher satisfaction. A survey of over two hundred New York City public schools at which incentives were tried (Fryer 2011) found no evidence that they increased student performance, attendance, or graduation rates, nor did they change teacher or student behavior. If anything, researcher Roland Fryer suggests that teacher incentives might even *decrease* student achievement, especially in larger schools.

There are many caring and committed teachers in our nation's schools but they are often invisible. It is to our detriment as a society for them to remain so. Having highlighted these teachers' stories, their hopes, and their experiences, I hope that others—teachers, administrators, families, policymakers, the general public—will see the tremendous difference teachers can make in the education and future of our children, particularly if they are given the chance to do so unencumbered by rigid accountability schemes that rob teachers of their creativity and joy.

NOTES

Barron, J. 2009.
Fryer, R. G. 2011.
Kohli, R. & Solórzano, D. E. 2012. 441–262.
Kozol, J. 1991.
Nieto. S., ed. 2005b.

Nieto, S. 2010.
Nieto, S. 2012. 48–62
Sadowski, M. 2013.
Stanton-Salazar, R. D. 2001.
Ullman, C. & Hecsh, J. 2012. 603–629.

Chapter 10

From Dispositions to Actions

Becoming Culturally Responsive Teachers

The teachers you've met in the preceding chapters exemplify what it means to be *culturally responsive*. This term is often thrown around carelessly these days, as if saying it will make it happen. Because of the plethora of related terms, it is sometimes hard to get a firm hold on what being culturally responsive encompasses.

In education literature, terms such as *culturally responsive* (Gay 2010), *culturally relevant* (Ladson-Billings 1995), and *cultural competence* (National Association of Social Workers 2001) are often used interchangeably (although the latter is used more often in relation to social work and medical care). While they are somewhat different in meaning, they convey the same message: *if teachers are to be effective with students of diverse backgrounds, they must be knowledgeable about, and attuned to, their students' backgrounds, cultures, and experiences and know how to incorporate them into their curriculum and pedagogy.* Each term is a bit different from the others. *Culturally competent* refers to a teacher's knowledge about their students' cultures and experiences; *culturally responsive* focuses on a teacher's ability to behave in ways that respect and honor students' cultures and experiences; and *culturally relevant* generally refers to how the curriculum and pedagogy enacted by the teacher are meaningful for their students.

Other terms have entered the conversation since Gloria Ladson-Billings first coined the term *culturally relevant pedagogy* in 1995. Carmen Rolón (Nieto & Rolón 1997) used the term *centering pedagogies* to suggest that curriculum and pedagogy should be centered on the life experiences and backgrounds of students, while also recognizing that identities are multiple and in constant flux. Similarly, Jason Irizarry (2007) came up with the term *culturally connected* to describe teachers who, regardless of their own backgrounds, find ways to learn about their students' daily realities, including how they identify, the language or discourse they use, and their community experiences. More recently, Django Paris (2012) has developed the notion of a *culturally sustaining pedagogy*, arguing that this term more directly supports the value of ensuring our multicultural, multiracial, and multiethnic future. Paris finds this particularly important given the contradiction that currently characterizes our society: a growing diversity but increasingly restrictive linguistic and cultural attitudes, practices, and legislation.

Whatever the term used, there is growing research that supports this kind of teaching and reinforces the idea that teachers need to learn who their students are, respect and affirm their identities, and form close bonds with them in order to best teach them (Irvine & Hawley 2011). Here, I generally use the term *culturally responsive* since it is the most widely used, but I include under it the insights inherent in the other terms.

Enacting Values in the Classroom

It is one thing to articulate certain values but quite another to enact those values in the classroom. When particular beliefs and values are expressed but not implemented, they become little more than a mantra ("all children can learn" comes to mind). The values that the teachers in this book reflect are neither templates nor recipes for success. Rather, they are dispositions—inherent qualities of mind and character—that guide a person's behavior and actions. More specifically, dispositions

> refer to a teacher stance, a way of orienting oneself to the work and responsibilities of teachers. . . . Those responsibilities are ultimately about moral practice, in which the teacher mobilizes her knowledge and skills in behalf of the learners entrusted to her care (Diez & Murrell 2010, p. 9).

Moving from *dispositions to actions*, teachers become *culturally responsive*.

The teachers featured in this book try to live their values daily: they do not simply say what they believe but attempt to carry out those beliefs in their classroom. What are those values? I think we would agree that all teachers worth their salt love their students and the subject matter they teach; are passionate about teaching; persevere in the face of seemingly intractable obstacles; are humble about their own limitations; and, given all the demands made of them, have a great sense of humor! This is a tall order for a profession that often pays new teachers embarrassingly low salaries yet expects them to know everything, put in long hours, buy supplies with their own money, continue their professional development—often on their own time and dime—and be teacher, parent, counselor, nurse, and confidante all in one. But this is what we expect of all good teachers. What makes being a teacher of students of diverse backgrounds different? In some ways, this is a moot question: today, *all* teachers are, or soon will be, teachers of students of students who differ from one another in terms of race, culture, language, and immigrant status. Also, it is no longer just urban areas that are characterized by racial and ethnic diversity. Children of color, immigrants, and students for whom English is a second language can now be found in every suburb, every small town, every isolated hamlet in our nation.

However, diversity is more than race, culture, language, and immigrant status. We need to expand the notion of diversity as it is generally understood. The children in our classrooms and schools, regardless of how similar they may look on the outside, are diverse in ways that may not be apparent—social class, ability, family structure, sexual orientation, the language spoken at home, among others. The dispositions I consider here are important for *all* teachers because even if they do not teach students of color or immigrants, their students nevertheless reflect a tremendous number of other differences.

Dispositions and practices of teachers of students of diverse backgrounds include:

- engaging in critical self-reflection
- valuing language and culture
- insisting on high-quality, excellent work from all students
- honoring families
- exemplifying a commitment to lifelong learning.

Engaging in Critical Self-Reflection

Culturally responsive teachers realize that before they can understand their students in all their complexity, they need to figure out who they themselves are and where and how they fit into the picture. This requires critical self-reflection about issues that are easy for teachers to avoid because they are difficult to face. It means critically examining one's values, assumptions, and biases, particularly when these get in the way of teaching a diverse group of students effectively. It means seriously assessing one's talents and also one's limitations. It means understanding one's privileges and how those privileges may obstruct one's understanding of those who are different. Ronald Glass and Pia Wong (2009) call confronting dominant ideologies about their students' identities and traditional expectations *engaged pedagogy*. They explain: "To practice engaged pedagogy means to dream big, to act both strategically and focused on making an immediate difference, and to never cease our own critical self-reflection and professional development" (p. 244).

John Gunderson has given a great deal of thought to what it takes to be a reflective practitioner with regard to issues of diversity. Teaching at the university level has taught him a lot about confronting these topics. When he read Lisa Delpit's book *Other People's Children* (2006) for the first time, rather than getting upset or angry, he thought, "Oh, my God! How many kids have I hurt?" He sees the book as a powerful teaching tool and assigns it to his university students. Having had little experience with diversity, however, the majority of his university students often feel attacked for being White. John focuses on how his students, all of whom are or will soon be teachers, can work through those feelings and come to understand that being a culturally responsive teacher means putting aside their own feelings of guilt in order to understand their students. It also means, for him, being responsive to *all* his students, including White students.

Roger Wallace also exemplifies what it means to reflect critically. A veteran teacher, he has learned to accept students on their terms while also opening them up to many opportunities. For Roger, helping students become all they can be means teaching them *as they are* rather than trying to change them. He challenges the notion that some children are not ready to learn if they don't exhibit certain behavior or haven't had particular experiences. Roger's advice—"if you want to be a successful teacher of kids of diverse backgrounds, *put your stuff away*"—is an important insight about putting aside one's preconceptions in order to be effective with students different from oneself.

Valuing Language and Culture

Culturally responsive teachers view their students' personal backgrounds and voices as a rich resource for curriculum. This is not simply because it may make students "feel good" about who they are (although this can be vital), but because their languages and cultures are valuable in their own right. All teachers use culture in their lessons (through their curriculum and pedagogy, as well as their relationships with students and their cultural references) but if they're from the majority culture, they may be unaware of it. It is like fish in the fishbowl, who may not realize they're in the water—it's just their environment. Culturally responsive teaching also acknowledges students whose language and culture are often invisible in the curriculum. Culturally responsive teachers recognize that it is one of their responsibilities to make their students' language and culture visible, accepted, and honored.

Culturally responsive teaching is thus *purposeful* and has specific goals: to affirm who students are in order to have them connect with school, accept and relish who they are, and succeed academically. Maricela Meza Buenrostro is a good example of a teacher whose experience as an immigrant helped her become culturally responsive. Although she wanted to succeed in her new country with a new language when arriving in the United States from Mexico as a child, she lacked the linguistic or material resources at home to help her. Her teachers gave her those resources, helped her learn English and adapt to her new environment. They showed they cared, and because of them she is now a teacher. They inspired her to "become *that* teacher" for her own students.

Can teachers who do not share their students' language and culture become "*that* teacher" for their students? They not only *can* but *must*. It *is* possible to become culturally responsive educators, but it takes the will and humility to learn who our students are and to respect their identities. Amber Bechard appeared at my door one day about a dozen years ago pleading with me to allow her into my oversubscribed course in multicultural curriculum development. Her husband's company had relocated him to Chicago and she knew she'd be teaching students of diverse backgrounds and didn't know where to begin.

Amber was an excellent student and is an exceptional teacher, whether teaching kindergarten in an affluent and mostly White private school, as she was at the time, or teaching language arts in a middle school with tremendous diversity, as she is now. What she didn't realize but soon learned was that it wasn't *only* teachers working in urban areas who needed multicultural education, but *all* teachers working with all kinds of students. She became not only knowledgeable about multicultural education but also an extraordinarily enthusiastic proponent of its value for all students, regardless of background, and has since completed a doctoral degree in the subject. She put this philosophy into practice immediately in her all-White kindergarten class by having the children paint the color of their skin, a lesson she picked up from my friend and colleague Patty Bode (2005). The lesson opened the way for Amber and her students to start a conversation about race: "They had to mix paint colors and they started saying, 'You know, we're not really all the same color, are we? We're all different colors.' "

The course in multicultural education exposed Amber to "this concept of affirming each person where they are, and who they are, and getting to know students as individuals and families as individuals, and bringing these conversations up in the classroom." Armed with her new knowledge, Amber felt ready to tackle issues of diversity in her new school in an urbanized suburb. The course she had taken with me, in which we discussed issues of race, power, privilege, and difference (which are often taboo or at least discouraged in school), had given her permission to broach these issues in her own classroom: "Being comfortable enough to do that is very important."

Valuing culture and language is an important way for teachers to find out about their students. Amber wants to know everything she can about her students so that she can not only develop strong and trusting relationships with them but also help make school more relevant in their lives. She wants to find out who they are, what's important to them, and the hopes they have for the future. She wants to find out, she said: "What do you dream? What do you want to learn?"

Insisting on High-Quality, Excellent Work from All Students

Insisting on high-quality work is an indisputable message that teachers care about their students and believe they are capable and worthy. This combination of high standards and caring is too often missing from the standards movement, an important lesson we can learn from Geoffrey Winikur.

Geoffrey has incorporated his interest in African literature and culture into the English and humanities courses he teachers (most of them are interdisciplinary). A demanding teacher, Geoffrey never uses textbooks (students sigh with relief when he tells them that) but instead selects books that are challenging and respectful of their intelligence. Perhaps because Geoffrey has been so involved with the Philadelphia Writing Project, where teachers are treated as intellectuals rather than as functionaries, he also sees his students as intellectuals. He tells them he's not just going to assign difficult books but is also going to teach them *how* to read them.

Geoffrey is also close to his students. He is one of those teachers defined by Judith Kleinfeld (1975) as *warm demanders*. While communicating personal warmth, these teachers also practice "active demandingness," insisting that students perform at high levels. They are unrelenting in their demands while also nurturing and loving. A team of researchers in a study of thirty-one highly effective teachers in nine urban schools characterized as "low performing" found similar results (Poplin et al. 2011). What surprised the researchers was how strict most of the highly effective teachers were. Their teaching was described as structured, intense (instruction was always going on), and traditional. At the same time, they formed close and respectful relationships with their students. While realistic about the challenges facing many of their students, the teachers did not use the students' backgrounds as a rationale for not expecting the most from them.

Researchers Jacqueline Irvine and James Fraser (1998, p. 56) provide an example of how a "warm demander" might speak to a student who is inattentive or lazy: "That's enough of your nonsense, Darius. Your story does not make sense. I told you time and time again that you must stick to the theme I gave you. Now sit down." This kind of talk is not often viewed as a positive thing, presumably because it might seem abrasive. But when it is done with care and knowledge of the students being addressed, it sends the undeniable message that the teacher both cares about them and expects a lot from them.

In her all-Black classroom, Carmen Tisdale enacts this kind of "demandingness" with her students, who are not intimidated by her "Black Momma" stance and instead recognize it as expecting the best from them because she loves them. Geoffrey Winikur is also a warm demander. While he feels that his relationship with his students is based on love and he tries to think of them as his own children, this means, as he said, "sometimes they need a hug and sometimes they need a knock upside the head."

The proof is in the results. Geoffrey's students, and in fact the students in his school as a whole, have done extremely well in terms of graduation rates and achievement, surpassing all expectations for students of color in urban schools.

Honoring Families

Although many teachers work hard at forming relationships with their students, they may not extend the same effort toward getting to know their students' families. Bill Dunn, a former student of mine, was a teacher at a high school that had changed dramatically over a twenty-year period from having a small minority of Puerto Rican students to having a majority. One semester, Bill decided to "come out of the closet as a Spanish speaker" when he realized that he understood a good deal of the Spanish his students were speaking. He kept a journal of his foray into learning the language and learned other valuable lessons along the way: why his students were often tired and restless in class (learning a second language is exhausting); why they made the kinds of grammatical mistakes they made (learning Spanish syntax and vocabulary was difficult and confusing); and why he withdrew into what Stephen Krashen (1982) calls "the silent period" after a few weeks (his brain wanted to shut down with so much information coming in). He also found that one of the benefits of learning Spanish was learning about, and learning to honor, his students' families. In his journal, Bill wrote:

There are things about Puerto Rican people and culture that I admire very much. I would also have to admit that I did not always admire these things because I did not understand them at first. This is a good lesson not only for second-language learning but for any situation where different cultures come in contact (Dunn 2010, p. 174).

Family means many things to culturally responsive teachers: it means regularly communicating with the families of their students, respecting them, and learning from them. One way teachers do this is by reaching out to parents who might not be able to attend meetings and other school activities, as Carmen Tisdale did to a parent who had never come into the school. As a consequence, a strong bond was created between teacher and parent. Angeles Pérez, to encourage the fathers of her students to attend Dad's Night, ran out to greet parents as they picked up their children and even offered them rides to the event. Three hundred fathers showed up, a remarkable result, particularly in a school where all the parents are Hispanic and little parent involvement is expected.

It also means creating a sense of family in the classroom. In addition to honoring students' languages and cultures, the teachers I interviewed at Loyola Marymount University insist that all families and communities have strengths. Rather than believing that their students' families, most of whom are Mexican and Central American, are uncaring about education, they realize the parents know that education is the best hope for their children to have a more positive life than they themselves have.

For Griselda Benítez, establishing relationships with students is a matter of building trust through communication. She makes sure to have activities such as Community Circle as a regular part of the day (even though the school's administrators discourage it), because it is a way for students to share their feelings and let her know what's going on with their lives and in their communities.

Exemplifying a Commitment to Lifelong Learning

Learning is an indispensable part of being a teacher. This means redefining teaching as an intellectual activity and teachers as intellectuals, something that is far from the case in most schools today. At the beginning of his career, John Nguyen had a hard time, particularly with discipline. But John persevered and has become an excellent and award-winning teacher who is an inspiration to both his students and his colleagues.

An incredibly enthusiastic learner, John has sought out the kinds of experiences and knowledge, from community service to internships to international travel, that help him be a better teacher. After eleven years of teaching, John still thinks of himself as a student and continues to learn all he can and bring this knowledge back to his students. He believes strongly that learning can happen anywhere. His best years in college "were the ones away from it." He received academic credit for doing an internship with the National Council for the Social Studies in Washington, D.C., as well as for going to Vietnam with his geography professor. He studied in London, afterward traveling throughout Europe for several months. Even then, teaching was foremost in his mind: "I knew that wherever I went, I was going to teach, and I just learned as much as I could in order to bring it back into the classroom."

Whether pursuing self-initiated professional development, continuing their education in a master's or doctoral program, attending conferences, obtaining National Board certification, providing workshops for their peers, writing grants to attend seminars in distant places, or in countless other ways, these teachers have persuasively demonstrated that learning does not stop when one becomes a teacher. On the contrary, that's when it truly begins.

Conclusion: Living the Values of Social Justice

Lofty goals and values are one thing, but attempting to live a life committed to those goals and values is quite another. The teachers featured in this book work hard to live their values, not just articulate them. Many assessments mention dispositions, but there are no conventional ways to measure them. Probably the best way to determine whether teachers believe what they say is to listen to them express their hopes and expectations about teaching and watch how they enact these hopes and expectations in their work. I feel privileged to have heard the words of these teachers and discovered them to be heartfelt expressions of their daily commitments.

There are many problems with how teachers have traditionally been evaluated. Simply observing a teacher for a prearranged and inauthentic half-hour a couple of times a year will not do; likewise, value-added measures are both highly suspect and inaccurate measures of what teachers do. It is time we recognize that some of the most consequential aspects of teaching cannot be measured in the same old ways we're used to and look for more genuine ways of evaluating what teachers do every day.

NOTES

Bode, P. 2005. 49–57.
Delpit, L. 2006.
Diez, M. E. & Murrell, P. E., Jr. 2010. 7–26.
Dunn, B. 2010. 169–175.
Gay, G. 2010.
Glass, R. D. & Wong, P. L. 2009. 229–246.
Irizarry, J.G. 2007. 1–7.
Irvine, J. J., & Fraser, J. W. 1998. 56.
Irvine, J. J. & Hawley, W. D. 2011. 2–5.

Kleinfeld, J. 1975. 301–344.
Krashen, S. 1982.
Ladson-Billings, G. 1995. 465–491.
National Association of Social Workers. 2001.
Nieto, S. 2010.
Nieto, S. & Rolón, C. 1997. 93–128.
Paris, D. 2012. 93–97.
Poplin, M., Rivera, J., Durish, D., Hoff, L., Kawell, S., Pawlak, P., Hinman, N. S., Strauss, L. & Veney, C. 2011. 39–43.

Chapter 11

From Surviving to Thriving

The Role of Hope in Teaching

Being an effective teacher of students of diverse backgrounds takes a great deal of hard work and dedication. It means being a learner not only of content and pedagogy but also of students. It takes keeping abreast of one's profession and the latest research, technologies, and innovations. It often means getting to school early—sometimes earlier than sunrise—and once in a while staying until the sun has set. It means shedding more than a tear or two and also finding inexpressible joy in the everyday happenings of the classroom. Above all, teaching well takes hope, without which we cannot function, either as educators or as human beings.

But hope is not always easy to maintain, and even teachers who prevail are sometimes disillusioned to the point of wanting to give up. What is needed, according to Robert Bullough (2011), is a culture of hope and happiness to replace the culture of stress and despair so common in the teaching profession today. Although hope and happiness are rarely if ever mentioned when school reform is discussed, Bullough insists:

> *We need critical hope the way a fish needs unpolluted water.*
>
> —Paulo Freire (1994, p. 8)

> Efforts to create greater effectiveness among teachers, more learning among students, and higher performing schools that ignore the hope and happiness of children and teachers will inevitably fail. Worse, they will be harmful (p. 17).

To build hope and happiness he says, "necessitates work conditions that enhance agency and pathways and, importantly, encourage engagement and invite and inspire self-transcendence" (p. 27).

Such exalted language is nonexistent in discussions of school reform, yet the conditions that Bullough describes are as important for students as they are for teachers.

My original purpose in doing the research for this book was to learn how thriving teachers, particularly teachers who work with students of diverse backgrounds, grow in the profession. As I interviewed the teachers and analyzed what they were saying, it became clear that the book would have to focus not only on teachers' resilience but also on how they develop the knowledge, skills, aptitudes, and behavior of culturally responsive teachers. For teachers who work with students of diverse backgrounds, thriving and finding joy in teaching them go hand in hand. This chapter looks at how the teachers I interviewed manage to do both. This is particularly crucial at present because (1) our nation's schools are becoming more diverse than they have ever been and (2) teachers are our greatest national resource, yet we are losing them by the tens of thousands to other professions because of the current context of public education. Nearly all the teachers I spoke with expressed frustration with the current instrumentalist and test-based notions of teaching, bemoaning the fact that something important is missing in education if that's all there is. Because I am often asked for advice, especially for new or struggling teachers, I end the chapter with four specific recommendations for teachers who want to thrive in the classroom, and who also want to do well with their students of diverse backgrounds.

What Does It Mean to Thrive?

Teaching is difficult, but like anything worth the pain and frustration involved, it can bring untold benefits. Although I set out to interview teachers who are flourishing, I was not so naïve as to think I would find teachers who are blissfully and innocently happy or ignorant of the state of education today. I was looking for teachers who understand the pitfalls of the profession while also believing in the nobility of its outcomes. Thriving should be seen as a continuum, with teachers falling somewhere between joy and quiet fulfillment and going through sometimes frustrating and difficult periods. Insecurity and anxiety accompany a teacher's daily life. Even seasoned teachers who believe they have understood the mysteries of the craft or have learned enough or "get it" find there is always uncertainty and apprehension about their ability and even their purpose.

Thriving Despite Anxiety, Insecurity, and Frustration

The teachers I interviewed almost to a person expressed anxiety and insecurity about teaching. Geoffrey Winikur told me, "I think I am thriving but it doesn't always feel that way," a common feeling among the interviewees. Hyung Nam even suggested he might not be the right teacher to include in this book: "Maybe I'm the wrong person for this. I guess it's hard for me to say that I'm thriving." He had been through a tough couple of years during which he questioned whether he should even be a teacher. Whether it was a midlife crisis or just a difficult point in his career, it was a disquieting time. He said:

> *I was really scared, thinking my whole identity has been, for over a decade, based on being a social justice teacher. That's my primary role in the world and what makes my life meaningful and I was so scared in thinking, "What if I'm not cut out to do this and I can't continue to do this? What am I going to do with myself?"*

Fortunately, the following year was one of Hyung's best, but his experience highlights how vulnerable teachers feel. Hyung characterized himself as not necessarily thriving but rather grateful to be in the profession, saying: "I think I feel inspired and really empowered and honored to be in a role where I can help students to question the world and expand their horizons and to see the possibility that they can be agents to change the world to be a better place. I guess in that sense I could say that I thrive."

Alicia López, even after fifteen years in the classroom, expressed both the joy and the self-doubt that inevitably accompany teaching, saying she didn't feel she was thriving "a hundred percent of the time." Nevertheless, she added, "I usually wake up and feel happy about going to school." She confessed that she still feels a little nervous every day and "the first day of school, forget it!" After thinking about it for a moment, she decided that being nervous is about caring for her students and her craft. For María Ramírez Acevedo, thriving is caring about her students' learning and communicating that caring to their parents in positive ways: "That's what thriving is all about," she concluded.

An important piece of advice about thriving comes from Carmen Tisdale, who teaches African American third graders, many of whom already feel defeated. Knowing how easy it is to fall into despair and hopelessness, she warned against letting oneself be dragged down by the negativity one sometimes finds in teachers' conversations. "To thrive you just have to have motivation on the inside and you need to align yourself with people who are also happy and who are professionally motivated instead of always down on the kids, always down on what's going on at school."

Diverse Perspectives on Thriving

John Gunderson considers himself to be thriving because he loves his job and his students, and he looks forward to going to work every day. He expects no less from his students. He tells them, "I love my job and if you can't see that, I'm not doing it right. Even if I've had a tough day with my own children or something, I'm not going to come in and give you half of me. When I'm with you, you get all of me and in return I expect you to be here too." Creating a relationship with each of his students for the 180 days they're together is most important for him. He said that thriving depends not just on a teacher's feelings but also on the reaction of students and their parents. It's not just about thriving but about learning: "So, when you ask me if I'm thriving, I hope I am, but I think I am because I try to engage kids in something that is meaningful every day." John's classes aren't over when the bell rings. "I want them to go home and talk about it with their parents. I want them to talk about it with their friends. I always tell parents at Back to School Night, 'If you haven't heard about my class yet, I'm not doing my job.'" This, John insists, is what thriving is about: not only individual teachers and students, but whether education as a whole is thriving.

For Adam Heenan, thriving is not just succeeding as a teacher but "enjoying every day and really reaching out and getting the teachable moments regularly." He knows when his lessons are going to be excellent and he can figure out how the students will react, but he also knows that not every lesson will be stellar. Even in those cases, he is confident that "I know how I can bounce back after lessons bomb." Geoffrey Winikur has very clear ideas about what it means to thrive: "If you want to have talented teachers thrive, it's really important for the teachers to have a lot of freedom in the classroom and that does not mean a lazy kind of freedom." For Geoffrey, autonomy, creativity, innovative curricula, and professional development all create the climate for thriving.

Thriving as Learning and Renewal

Amber Bechard had few reservations about whether she is thriving or not. For her, to thrive means to continue to learn, something she does with passion every day. "I keep learning too, and I think that is a part of what thriving is: to continue to learn." Angeles Pérez, a fourth-grade bilingual teacher in her second year of teaching, beams when she talks about her students. It is clear that they are the reason this young novice teacher is thriving. Her students are her buddies, she says, and at the end of each day, she leaves with a hug from each of them. According to Angeles, thriving as a teacher goes beyond students scoring well on tests. Although the students she taught her first year did very well on the state test, seeing them learn to accept who they are and be happy with themselves is her greatest achievement.

Roger Wallace thrives by keeping teaching new. When students ask him which has been his favorite class during his thirty-seven years of teaching, he tells them that because every group of students is unique, every class is his favorite. He gives his all to each student he has taught over his long career. He pushes for excellence by listening to and learning from his students. The bottom line: Roger thrives by creating more empowered learners.

Bringing Feeling Back into the Teaching Profession

Teaching is a caring profession, but the focus on accountability and standardization in recent years has somehow managed to drain all the emotion out of it. We speak now of templates and standards, of rubrics and AYP; we've diminished or completely obliterated any sense of feeling. Nevertheless, the teachers interviewed for this book made it abundantly clear that caring, love, and other emotions are a significant part of teaching. Whether they teach young children or high school students, these teachers (and many like them) are intimately involved in their students' lives, thinking, hoping, and worrying about them every day.

Here's an example from a veteran teacher who was not one of those I interviewed for this book but who also has significant insights about teaching as a caring profession. Berta Berriz (2000), currently co-lead teacher of the lower school in the Boston Teachers' Union School, a public school managed by the local teachers' union, describes how Ramona, one of the third-grade teachers, welcomes her students on the first day of class. "Ramona hugs each one as they enter and says, 'Tu eres mío [you are mine].' This cultural gesture communicates to the children that they belong and that they are wanted" (p. 78). Berta explains the meaning of this gesture:

> With these three little words, we affirm our love, support and protection. This is a promise to all our students—they are ours, we are theirs. Once each child has received this ritual embrace, we are ready to begin the process of building our relationship as a learning community (Berriz 2012).

Berta relates personally to her students because she was one of them. As an immigrant, she still feels like the little third grader who arrived in this country from Cuba over fifty years ago. She has experienced their confusion, anger, and embarrassment: "I understand, firsthand, how the imposition of a different language and culture can profoundly affect a young child's identity formation, self-esteem, and capacity for learning." Although being an immigrant undoubtedly affected Berta and how she interacts with her students, this kind of personal connection can happen not only with teachers who have lived lives similar to those of their students but also with those who develop a deep sense of empathy for their students regardless of their own identities and experiences.

Teaching can take a toll on teachers. Not just a job, not even just a profession, teaching is personal and emotional work, sometimes life-changing and life-saving and always consequential. This became very clear as I interviewed the teachers. Griselda Benítez broke down when talking about the importance of continuing to hold Community Circles with her students. Adam Heenan, speaking about what makes teaching worthwhile, also became emotional. He explained that teaching is about being part of the solution for his students and it extends beyond the school day:

> *It is so hard, it is so worth it. They deserve better, and I would be part of the problem if I wasn't speaking up. This is the "for what do I teach?" Geez, I don't think it ends outside my classroom, it is their lives.*

The teachers interviewed for this book teach students who are vulnerable in different ways, and they are aware of both the demands and the benefits of doing what they do. For some of them, thriving is primarily about having the autonomy to be creative and independent as they plan their curriculum and hone their pedagogy. For others, it is mostly about creating a learning environment that is equal parts caring and demanding. Some define thriving as having their students thrive. For others, thriving is about helping students become critical learners who can make a difference in the world. For most, it is a combination of all these things.

One essential ingredient in thriving is feeling empowered. According to researchers Steven Zemelman and Harry Ross (2009), empowerment for teachers includes a sense that they are doing significant work, that they are being treated like professionals, that they have the time and space to collaborate with and learn from colleagues, and that they are in control of their professional lives. (Their book proposes and discusses in depth thirteen steps that lead to teacher empowerment.) Empowerment, however, is elusive for teachers who teach under unfavorable conditions.

Although most teachers want to thrive and remain in the profession, whether as classroom teachers or in another capacity, staying can be difficult when the context is contentious, as it has been for the past several years. New teachers especially have a hard time learning all they need to know about the content they must teach and the pedagogy they should use. They must also meet new mandates, see that their students do well on the high-stakes tests that are increasingly part of the educational land-scape, keep up with the latest technology, keep abreast of the newest research in the profession, and learn to work with families, among other demands. Teachers cannot do it alone; they need all the help they can get from all of us.

Four Pieces of Advice

In my travels around the country, I am often asked what advice I would give teachers to help them face the many challenges of teaching, particularly in their first years. I offer the same advice to both new and veteran teachers, because I know that whatever the stage of their career, all teachers need support to keep going. Below are four pieces of advice that span a teacher's professional life. My research for this book has reaffirmed my belief that these recommendations are both sound and timely.

Learn About Yourself

Teachers must first of all know themselves. This is true for teachers no matter the background of their students, but for teachers who are different from the majority of their students in race, ethnic-ity, language, social class, and/or other ways (and in any combination), it is vital that they spend time thinking about who they are and how their identities, experiences, values, and biases can help or hinder their work with students. The critical self-reflections of many of the teachers in this book are compelling examples of what it means to learn about oneself. For example, an important goal for John Nguyen as a teacher is to remember where he came from so that he can understand the chal-lenging lives of his students.

Sometimes the hardest work we can do as human beings is precisely this: to confront ourselves un-flinchingly and honestly in order to improve. Teachers need to evaluate not only their knowledge of subject matter and pedagogy, as important and necessary as these are, but also their knowledge about and interactions with students, especially those with diverse backgrounds. Although learning about one's strengths and talents, shortcomings and flaws, vices and virtues, may be hard work, it is also enormously empowering. It means asking hard questions in good conscience about one's privilege and power, and about how one uses these in the context of teaching and learning. It means asking how one's biases—hidden or overt—might influence relationships with students and their families. It might mean reassessing who one is in the context of teaching and how one's experiences might have a negative impact on one's choices of curriculum, pedagogy, and philosophy of education. Although difficult and exhausting, this deep introspection can be the key to becoming a better teacher and even a better person.

Learn About Your Students

Learning about their students is unquestionably one of the most important endeavors teachers undertake. This is not simply knowing on what grade level students are reading or who their previous teacher was. It also means learning more about their school experiences and knowing how each one best learns. Teachers also need to know how to reach their students and what their hopes and dreams are. They need to learn the sociocultural realities of their students and the sociopolitical conditions in which they live: who they live with, what language or languages they speak, how they identify culturally. It is also enormously helpful to learn about the history, cultural traditions, and values of students' communities. Finally, although students are cultural beings with important family and ethnic connections, teachers must also recognize them as unique and valuable individuals in their own right. This kind of learning leads to empathy and respect, critical ingredients of care. No "bogus curriculum," as Geoffrey Winikur said, will accomplish these things. Learning about one's students means rejecting taken-for-granted assumptions about culture and difference.

There are many ways to learn about one's students, and probably the best and most natural is through daily interactions with them. Community Circle gets young children talking about what's happening in their lives. "Advisory Groups"—a feature becoming more common in middle schools—can help students check in daily with a small group of their peers and an advisor. Amber Bechard greets her middle school students on the first day of class by telling them, "I value you for who you are and I'm going to make sure everybody else in here values you." In order to value them, she needs to really get to know them, their family culture, and their personal culture. She says, "That starts from the very beginning of the school year, and we become very close as a class and as individuals." In high school one may have to think more creatively, because there is precious little time for fostering relationships, but responding to students' journals or setting up time to socialize and eat with them, as María Guerrero does, are excellent ways to connect with students. The curriculum and pedagogy also offer such opportunities, as we learned from Hyung Nam. Whatever one does, the point is to create possibilities for interactions that will be meaningful for students.

Teaching is not simply imparting knowledge, however. It is a give-and-take, the mutual effort of teachers becoming learners and learners becoming teachers (Freire 1970). Learning about one's students also means learning about their families and communities. After all my years of teaching in elementary and intermediate schools, and as a teacher educator, I am still amazed when I discover that some teachers know very little about the communities in which they teach. They leave promptly at the end of the school day, never venturing beyond the school walls. They know almost nothing about their students' families, and even less about the neighborhood in which the school is located. If they teach in a poor community, they may believe it is a wasteland, with few resources that can both uplift and be a source of pride for the people who live there. They thus ignore the opportunity to explore what is almost certainly a vibrant community with remarkable resources.

One way to learn about students is by becoming part of the community. This does not necessarily mean living in the community, although it can. A simple walk around the community is one of the best professional development activities teachers can undertake. It is a valuable exercise in getting a sense of the landscape, where the public library is and what resources it offers; who the shopkeepers are and the services they offer (the local grocery store is often the hub of the neighborhood, providing residents information as well as food); and the social support networks (community and senior centers, hospitals and clinics, afterschool organizations, and so on). Becoming part of the community also means attending students' birthday parties, *quinceañeras,* and bar mitzvahs, going to their recitals and athletic activities and other community gatherings. Roger Wallace confessed that although he was no fan of ballet, he went to almost all of his students' ballet recitals over the years and because they were his students, he learned to enjoy ballet. This gesture of solidarity was not about him, but about them.

A huge commitment, but one that always pays off, is learning at least one of the languages one's students speak. Doing so opens one's eyes to realities that might be hard to understand without knowing the language. If there are many languages represented in the community, learning a few phrases in each is a great way to welcome the students' families and languages into the classroom.

Cultivate Allies

To thrive and grow, teachers need to develop allies. My many years of working with teachers have shown me that when they develop allies, they remain fresh, committed, hopeful, and caring. Teaching is an incredibly difficult job, and trying to go it alone can be overwhelming, particularly for new teachers, but it's just as true for veterans. Geoffrey Winikur says he loves "the adult conversations in teaching"—those occasions when teachers get to interact, learn together, rethink their practice, and improve their craft. Opportunities for doing this are few, as many of the teachers I interviewed mentioned, yet they crave these opportunities because teaching is not only about imparting knowledge but also about renewal and continued learning.

Almost all the teachers spoke about the importance of developing relationships with other teachers. Doing so not only helped them expand their horizons by learning from their peers but also allowed them to share their expertise with others. Carmen Tisdale spoke about the importance of having a close-knit team of teachers who laugh together, plan collaboratively, and enjoy one another's company. María Ramírez Acevedo also spoke about the importance of having close and supportive relationships with her colleagues, something made easier because she is now working in a small school where there is a lot of sharing. Her school seems, she said, like a family, all members focused on what works best for their students.

John Nguyen was especially appreciative of a colleague he called "The Oracle," his greatest mentor in the school, "because she can always sense how I'm feeling." He has counted on her for advice and encouragement over the years:

> *She'd just look you up and down and she knew if you were feeling bad, she'd tell you the right thing. One time I was called something really awful and she was, "You know, they were just assholes that day." And that's what I wanted to hear. I didn't want to hear "every child can learn" that day. I just wanted to hear that I was having a rough day.*

Because of her mentorship, John has made it his business to be a mentor to other new teachers. He has an "underground network"; many new teachers contact him because they've heard of what he calls his "fake mentoring program."

No one has all the answers and, as Amber Bechard has found, it is when working in collaboration with others that the best teaching and learning takes place. She describes her colleagues as "amazing" and "phenomenal" and she has counted on them—as they have on her—to fill in the gaps of her own knowledge. About the other language arts teacher with whom she works, Amber explains, "I have a passion for culture and diversity. She has this passion for literature and we've just really complemented each other." They also work with the math, science, and social studies teachers on their team, planning lessons and sharing resources. But support from colleagues, although incredibly helpful, is not enough. When asked what would help her continue to thrive, Amber said she wanted administrators to have faith in her as a teacher, as an intellectual, and as a professional, to offer "support and freedom and trust." She wants her principal to see that students are happy and engaged, that families are coming into the school and volunteering, and that she and her colleagues continue to be excited about teaching and learning.

Besides fostering professional learning, allies also help teachers handle the day-to-day challenges of teaching, whether dealing with the latest curriculum, difficult students, or endless mandates from the central office. Teachers also need to commiserate and support one another through personal dilemmas. Alicia López, for instance started a Latino/a Support Group in her school district. Meeting once a month or so, the group shares a drink, a laugh, and some nonschool conversation, reminding themselves that although teaching is their vocation and profession, they have lives outside school that also need to be celebrated, a topic to which we now turn.

Have a Life

Teachers, particularly committed teachers with a social justice perspective, often find they have little time for anything other than their profession: they arrive at school early, leave late, bring students' work home to correct, attend their students' out-of-school activities, participate in workshops and conferences, go to school meetings, and take university courses, thinking and worrying about their students through it all. For new teachers, the problem is even greater: in addition to all the above, they need to become familiar with the curriculum, learn how to pace their lessons, and figure out the rules, expectations, and culture of their school. It is no mystery why teachers from novice to veteran often find they "don't have a life."

The last thing teachers should do is focus solely on teaching: in the end, they will inevitably become disheartened, frustrated, or angry. They may burn out and leave the profession, as so many have in the past couple of decades. While acknowledging that teaching depletes one's resources, the teachers featured in this book also spoke about the need to recharge and find other outlets in their lives. They spoke about relying on their family—spouse, partner, children, parents, friends, neighbors—for support and sustenance. They also mentioned the important role played by professional colleagues who give a pat on the back or offer a shoulder to cry on.

John Nguyen warned that teaching can become an obsession, leading to strained personal and family relationships. As a new teacher, he often turned to "The Oracle," his greatest support. As a more seasoned teacher, he brings other teachers, especially new teachers, to speak with her. He does so because she gives "the best hugs on the face of the earth," always helping to make people feel good. She just seems to know how people are feeling. She also taught him that it was all right to have a "me day" in order to recharge. John in turn makes sure new teachers leave the building at a reasonable time, take time off when they need it, are "humans for once as opposed to always thinking in teacher mode."

Hyung Nam spoke about the exhilaration he felt attending the 2010 Rethinking Schools conference in Portland, Oregon, where I interviewed him. Over seven hundred exuberant social justice teachers attended the conference, leading Hyung to say, "Seeing the excitement and inspiration of so many other teachers who are also in the struggle to defend public education, teacher professionalism, and critical teaching is crucial." Activities not related in any way to teaching are just as important for Hyung, because thriving as a teacher is also about thriving as a person:

> *Everything from my commuting to work by bike as much as possible, seeing a deer off the road, or seeing the moon rise or coming home and doing yoga or going out with colleagues for happy hour. All of those things help me thrive. I'm also a musician and I think everything that makes me love the world and love being alive and want the world to be a better place, all of those things help me thrive.*

These four lessons have been simple yet profound guideposts for me in my own teaching, as well as in my work with teachers, administrators, school librarians, and other educators. I often returned to these lessons when teaching was too difficult, when the conditions in which I taught became overwhelming, or when some of the educators with whom I worked were filled with despair and anger. Remaining hopeful in such contexts is not always easy. But overcoming these obstacles can lead to robust learning for both teachers and their students and also to joy and fulfillment.

Final Thoughts

The issue of whether teachers merely survive or thrive and grow in the classroom and profession is a vital one for our society to address. Given the growing diversity of every kind in our nation's schools and the relatively little experience many teachers have had with diversity, the question of how to thrive becomes even more crucial. If we expect our students to thrive and learn, it's not enough for teachers to merely survive, going from day to day with tired ideas, little energy, and even less support. No, our students deserve teachers who are excited about teaching, passionate about learning, and energized to make a difference in their students' lives. Of course, they cannot be expected to be uniformly or ecstatically happy every day; this is as unrealistic an expectation in any profession as it is in life. Nevertheless, the teachers in this book are proof that thriving in the profession is not only possible but necessary. While no checklist of attitudes, dispositions, behaviors, or actions can define what thriving teachers look like, these teachers offer powerful examples of what it takes to face their profession with courage, their content with enthusiasm, and their students with love.

We end with hope in spite of everything that gets in the way. Given the depressing and demoralizing conditions reviewed in this book, this is a difficult call to make. Yet hope is what keeps us going—teachers, students, teacher educators, all those who care about public education. Greg Michie, in his latest book, *We Don't Need Another Hero* (2012b), echoes my own concerns about the glorification of solitary teachers who are unrealistically portrayed in books and movies as nothing short of miracle workers. But the subtitle of Michie's book brings us back to the real heroes: *Struggle, Hope, and Possibility in the Age of High-Stakes Schooling*. Here we have the real story: it is only through struggle and hope that our teachers and our young people, individually and collectively, can expect schools to be in fact what our ideals so proudly proclaim them to be—equal, equitable, and excellent.

I end with the words of John Gunderson on what teaching means to him. A consummate teacher and learner, John, although pessimistic about the turn public education has taken lately, is nevertheless hopeful about teaching and the power of teachers:

> *I want teachers to hear, when they read this, that what they do is important and it makes a difference. What we do is important, it's valuable and it's not easy, but it's the most rewarding and beautiful thing that you can do for a living. It's part of making the world a better place, making humans want to be better people, and so I hope people realize we might be in a tough environment economically, we might be in a tough profession where people might not give us the respect that I think we deserve, but we're doing it because it's an important position to make society and people better.*

NOTES

Berriz, B. 2000. 71–94.
Berriz, B. 2012.
Bullough, R. V., Jr. 2011. 15–30.
Freire, P. 1970.

Freire, P. 1994.
Michie, G. 2012b.
Zemelman, S. & Ross, H. 2009.

ADDITIONAL RESOURCES

The organizations, networks, and publications listed below, while not exhaustive, can help you thrive as a teacher. While most are national in scope, others are regional or local, and a few have branches in different locations. These resources can help you create classrooms and schools that are affirming, inclusive, and critical.

EdChange

www.edchange.org

EdChange is a team of passionate, experienced, established educators dedicated to equity, diversity, multiculturalism, and social justice. With this shared vision, they collaborate to develop resources, workshops, and projects that contribute to progressive change in ourselves, our schools, and our society.

Educators for Social Responsibility (ESR)

23 Garden Street
Cambridge, MA 02138

Phone: (617) 492-1764 or (800) 370-2515

FAX: (617) 864-5164

www.esrnational.org

email: educators@esrnational.org

ESR works directly with educators to implement systemic practices that create safe, caring, and equitable schools so that all young people succeed in school and life and help shape a safe, democratic, and just world. Founded in 1982, ESR is a national leader in school reform and provides professional development, consultation, and educational resources to adults who teach young people in preschool through high school.

Educators Network for Social Justice

www.ensj.org

ENSJ is a network of practicing educators from Milwaukee area schools that includes preservice teachers, classroom teachers, and postsecondary educators. ENSJ is committed to promoting pro-justice curricula and policies so that all students in the Milwaukee area are better served. ENSJ has monthly meetings, typically on the second Thursday of each month (location varies). Meetings are open to any educator interested in social justice.

Facing History and Ourselves National Foundation, Inc. (FHAO)
Headquarters:
16 Hurd Road
Brookline, MA 02445

Phone: (617) 232-1595 or (800) 856-9039

FAX: (617) 232-0281

www.facing.org

Founded in 1976, FHAO is an international educational and professional development nonprofit organization whose mission is to engage students of diverse backgrounds in an examination of racism, prejudice, and anti-Semitism in order to promote the development of a more humane and informed citizenry. By studying the historical development of the Holocaust and other examples of genocide, FHAO helps students make the essential connection between history and the moral choices they confront in their own lives.

National Center for Fair & Open Testing (FairTest)
FairTest
P.O. Box 300204
Jamaica Plain, MA 02130

Phone: 617-477-9792

www.fairtest.org

FairTest works to end the misuses and flaws of standardized testing and to ensure that evaluation of students, teachers, and schools is fair, open, valid, and educationally beneficial. With a newsletter, periodic press releases, and helpful "Fact Sheets," FairTest informs educators and the general public about current news concerning testing policy and practice.

National Writing Project
National Office: University of California
2105 Bancroft Way, #1042
Berkeley, CA 94720-1042

Phone: 510-642-0963

FAX: 510-642-4545

www.nwp.org

Working in partnership with higher education institutions and communities to develop and sustain leadership for educational improvement, the National Writing Project (NWP) is a network of 200 local sites anchored at colleges and universities and serving teachers in all disciplines and at all levels, early childhood through university. The NWP provides professional development, develops resources, generates research, and acts on knowledge to improve the teaching of writing and learning in schools and communities. The NWP believes that access to high-quality education is a basic right of all learners and a cornerstone of equity.

Network of Teacher Activist Groups (TAG)

www.teacheractivistgroups.org

TAG is a national coalition of grassroots teacher organizing groups. Together, they engage in shared political education and relationship building in order to work for educational justice both nationally and in local communities. TAG believes that education is essential to the preservation of civil and human rights and is a tool of human liberation and that every child has a right to a high-quality, equitably funded, public education.

PBS–ART21

www.pbs.org/art21/learn

Art21's education initiatives have a fundamental belief in the power of art, artists, and ideas to inform the most idealistic tenets of education. Access to the voices of artists through film and online media presents a new paradigm for engaging students in art and art making—as well as teaching in innovative and inspiring ways.

Rethinking Schools

1001 E. Keefe Avenue
Milwaukee, WI 53212

Phone: (414) 964-9646

FAX: (414) 964-7220

Email: office@rethinkingschools.org

www.rethinkingschools.org

A nonprofit independent organization advocating the reform of elementary and secondary public schools with an emphasis on urban schools, Rethinking Schools began in 1986 as a local effort to address problems such as basal readers, standardized testing, and textbook-dominated curriculum. RS remains firmly committed to equity and to the vision that public education is central to the creation of a humane, caring, multiracial democracy. Since its founding, RS has grown into a nationally prominent publisher of educational materials. Their magazine, *Rethinking Schools,* is published by Milwaukee area teachers and educators. In addition, RS publishes numerous and timely books on such topics as high-stakes testing, multicultural education, social justice, and progressive teacher unionism.

Teaching for Change

PO Box 73038
Washington, DC 20056

Phone: (202) 588-7204 or (800) 763-9131

FAX: (202) 238-0109

www.teachingforchange.org

email: info@teachingforchange.org

Teaching for Change is a nonprofit organization that promotes peace, justice, and human rights through critical, antiracist, multicultural education. Through professional development and its publications, TFC provides teachers and parents with the tools to create schools where students learn to read, write, and change the world.

Teacher Leader Network

www.teacherleaders.org

The Teacher Leader Network is the Center for Teaching Quality's virtual home of more than 1,500 accomplished teacher leaders from around the nation. The Center for Teaching Quality is a national nonprofit focused on teacher-led transformation of schools and the profession. CTQ supports the TLN in spreading their expertise beyond the classrooms. They offer a group blog site and can also be found on Twitter (@teachingquality).

Teachers 4 Social Justice

t4sj.org

Teachers 4 Social Justice is a grassroots nonprofit teacher support and development organization in San Francisco. A project of the Community Initiative Fund, its mission is to provide opportunities for self-transformation, leadership, and community building to educators in order to effect meaningful change in the classroom, school, community, and society. T4SJ organizes teachers and community-based educators and implements programs and projects that develop empowering learning environments, provides more equitable access to resources and power, and promotes a just and caring culture. They offer a free annual conference as well as other activities.

Teachers for Social Justice

www.teachersforjustice.org

An organization of teachers, administrators, preservice teachers, and other educators working in public, independent, alternative, and charter schools and universities in the Chicago area, this organization works toward classrooms and schools that are antiracist, multicultural/multilingual, and grounded in the experiences of students. The group meets regularly to share ideas and curriculum, develop collective projects, and support one another in their work. An activist organization, TFSJ forms and supports campaigns to get the voices of educators into the public discussion of school policies.

Teachers Speak Up!

www.teachersspeakup.com

This web-based resource is an outlet for teachers to tell their story to the public and get help in publishing it online. It also offers other resources for teachers and allows them to share strategies.

Teaching Tolerance
A Project of the Southern Poverty Law Center
400 Washington Avenue
Montgomery, AL 36104

Phone: (334) 956-8200

www.teachingtolerance.org

Teaching Tolerance is dedicated to reducing prejudice, improving intergroup relations, and supporting equitable school experiences for our nation's children. Their magazine, *Teaching Tolerance*, provides classroom strategies and curriculum ideas for teachers that focus on diversity and tolerance. They also have a number of teaching and video resources and professional development activities that they provide at no cost to individual teachers, schools, and colleges of education.

Use Your Teacher Voice

www.youtube.com/user/UseYourTeacherVoice

Modeled after the It Gets Better campaign, the goal of the Use Your Teacher Voice project is to create a forum for educators, professors, and preservice teachers to post thirty-second videos about what they believe should be changed in education.

Welcoming Schools

www.welcomingschools.org

Welcoming Schools offers tools, lessons, and resources on embracing family diversity, avoiding gender stereotyping, and ending bullying and name calling in elementary schools. It offers an LGBT inclusive approach that is also inclusive of the many types of diversity found in our communities. It provides materials to create learning environments in which all students are welcomed and respected.

Zinn Education Project

www.zinnedproject.org

Inspired by the work of historian Howard Zinn (1922–2010) and his groundbreaking book, *A People's History of the United States* (first published in 1980), the Zinn Education Project is committed to offering teachers resources to help them bring a people's history to life in the classroom. Offering numerous free, downloadable lesson plans and teaching activities for middle and high school classrooms, the site also lists many recommended books, films, and websites.

REFERENCES

AccountabilityWorks. 2012. *National Costs of Aligning States and Localities to the Common Core Standards*. Pioneer Institute and American Principles Project White Paper 82 (February). Washington, DC: Pacific Research Institute.

Acosta, C. & A. Mir. 2012. "Empowering Young People to Be Critical Thinkers: The Mexican American Studies Program in Tucson." *Voices in Urban Education* 34: 5–26.

American Association of Colleges of Teacher Education. 2009. *Teacher Preparation Makes a Difference*. Washington, DC: AACTE.

Americans for the Arts. 2010. "Arts Education: Creating Student Success in School, Work, and Life." http://artsactionfund.org/news/entry/speak-up-for-the-arts-in-schools.

Annenberg Institute for School Reform. 2010. "Value-Added Teacher Assessments Earn Low Grades from NYU Economist." Press Release, September 16, Providence, RI.

Anyon, J. 2005. *Radical Possibilities: Public Policy, Urban Education, and a New Social Movement*. New York: Routledge.

Apple, M. 2004. *Ideology and Curriculum,* 3rd ed. New York: Routledge.

_____. 2006. *Educating the Right Way: Markets, Standards, God, and Inequality*. New York: Routledge.

Artiles, A. J. 2011. "Toward an Interdisciplinary Understanding of Educational Equity and Difference: The Case of the Racialization of Ability." *Educational Researcher* 40 (9): 431–45.

Au, W. 2009. *Unequal By Design: High-Stakes Testing and the Standardization of Inequality*. New York: Routledge.

Au, W. 2013. "Coring Social Studies Within Corporate Education Reform." *Critical Education* 5 (4): 1–16.

Aud, S., W. Hussar, F. Johnson, G. Kena, E. Roth, E. Manning, X. Wang & J. Zhang. 2012. *The Condition of Education 2012*. NCES 2012-045. Washington, DC: U.S. Department of Education, National Center on Education Statistics. http://nces.ed.gov/pubsearch.

Baker, E. L., P. E. Barton, L. Darling-Hammond, E. Haertel, H. F. Ladd, R. L. Linn, D. Ravitch, R. Rothstein, R. J. Shavelson & L. A. Shepard. 2010. *Problems With the Use of Student Test Scores to Evaluate Teachers*. Washington, DC: Economic Policy Institute.

Ball, D. L. & F. M. Forzani. 2010. "What Does It Take to Make a Teacher?" *Phi Delta Kappan* 92 (2): 8–12.

Barron, J. 2009. "A Promising Life, Ended in a Lab Basement." *New York Times*, September 14. http://www.nytimes.com/2009/09/15/nyregion/15yale.html?_r=0.

Bartlett, L. & O. García. 2011. *Additive Schooling in Subtractive Times: Bilingual Education and Dominican Youth in the Heights*. Nashville, TN: Vanderbilt University Press.

Bartolomé, L. I. 1994. "Beyond the Methods Fetish: Toward a Humanizing Pedagogy." *Harvard Educational Review* 64 (2): 173–95.

Berliner, D. C. 2009. *Poverty and Potential: Out-of-School Factors and School Success*. Boulder & Tempe, CO: Education and the Public Interest Center & Educational Policy Research Unit. http://nepc.colorado.edu/publication/poverty-and-potential.

Berriz, B. 2000. "Raising Children's Cultural Voices: Strategies for Developing Literacy in Two Languages." In *Lifting Every Voice: Pedagogy and Politics of Bilingualism*, edited by Z. F. Beykont, 71–94. Cambridge, MA: Harvard Education Press. Available online at *Rethinking schools.com*.

———. 2012. Personal communication, March 3.

Bigelow, B. & B. Peterson. 2002. *Rethinking Globalization*. Milwaukee: Rethinking Schools.

Bode, P. 2005. "Waiting Tables and Juggling Motherhood: Taking the Road Less Traveled." In *Why We Teach,* edited by S. Nieto, 49–57. New York: Teachers College Press.

Bullough, R. V., Jr. 2011. "Hope, Happiness, Teaching, and Learning." In *New Understandings of Teachers' Work: Emotions and Educational Change*, Professional Learning and Development in Schools and Higher Education 6, edited by C. Day & J. C.-K. Lee, 5–30. Dordrecht, Netherlands: Springer.

Bustos Flores, B., R. Hernandez Sheets & E. Riojas Clark. 2010. *Teacher Preparation for Bilingual Student Populations: Educar para Transformar*. New York: Routledge.

Cabrera, N. L., J. F. Millen & R. W. Marx. 2012. "An Empirical Analysis of the Effects of Mexican American Studies Participation on Student Achievement Within Tucson Unified School District." Report submitted to Willis D. Hawley, Special Master for the Tucson Unified School District Desegregation Case. Tucson: University of Arizona. http://works.bepress.com/nolan_l_cabrera/17.

Camarota, S. A. 2012. *Immigrants in the United States, 2010: A Profile of America's Foreign-Born Population*. Washington, DC: Center for Immigration Studies.

Cammarota, J. & A. Romero. 2006. "A Critically Compassionate Pedagogy for Latino/a Youth." *Latinio/a Studies* 4 (3): 305–12.

Carroll, T. 2009. "The Next Generation of Learning Teams." *Phi Delta Kappan* 91 (2): 8–13.

Center on Education Policy. 2010. *State Test Trends Through 2008–2009*. Part 2, *Slow & Uneven Progress in Narrowing Gaps*. Washington, DC: Center on Education Policy.

Chauncey, C., ed. 2005. *Recruiting, Retaining, and Supporting Highly Qualified Teachers*. Cambridge, MA: Harvard Education Press.

Children's Defense Fund. 2012. *The State of America's Children® Handbook*. Washington, DC: Children's Defense Fund.

Clewell, B. C., M. Puma & S. A. McKay. 2001. *Does It Matter If My Teacher Looks Like Me? The Impact of Teacher Race and Ethnicity on Student Academic Achievement*. New York: Ford Foundation.

Cochran-Smith, M. 2010. "Toward a Theory of Teacher Education for Social Justice." In *The International Handbook of Educational Change,* 2nd ed., edited by A. Hargreaves, A. Lieberman, M. Fullan & A. D. Hopkins, 447. Dordrecht, Netherlands: Springer.

Cochran-Smith, M. & S. Lytle. 2009. *Inquiry as Stance: Practitioner Research in the Next Generation*. New York: Teachers College Press.

Coggshall, J. B., A. Ott & M. Lasagna. 2010. *Retaining Teacher Talent: Convergence and Contradictions in Teachers' Perceptions of Policy Reform Ideas*. Naperville, IL: Learning Point Associates, and New York: Public Agenda.

Corcoran, S. P. 2010. *Can Teachers Be Evaluated by Their Students' Test Scores? Should They Be? The Use of Value-Added Measures of Teacher Effectiveness in Policy and Practice*. Providence, RI: Annenberg Institute for School Reform.

Cowhey, M. 2006. *Black Ants and Buddhists: Thinking Critically and Teaching Differently in the Primary Grades.* Portland, ME: Stenhouse.

Darling-Hammond, L. 2010. *The Flat World of Education: How America's Commitment to Equity Will Determine Our Future.* New York: Teachers College Press.

Darling-Hammond, L., A. Amrein-Beardsley, E. Haertel & J. Rothstein. 2012. "Evaluating Teacher Evaluation," *Kappan* 93 (6): 8–15.

Darling-Hammond, L. & N. Richardson. 2009. *Professional Learning in the Learning Profession: A Status Report on Teacher Development in the United States and Abroad.* Washington, DC: National Staff Development Council.

Dee, T. S. 2000. *Teachers, Race, and Student Achievement in a Randomized Experiment.* Cambridge, MA: National Bureau of Economic Research.

Delpit, L. 2006. *Other People's Children: Culture and Conflict in the Classroom*, 2nd ed. New York: New Press.

Delpit, L. & J. K. Doudy, eds. 2002. *The Skin That We Speak*: Thoughts on Language and Culture in the Classroom. New York: New Press.

DeNavas-Walt, C., B. D. Proctor & J. C. Smith. 2011. *Income, Poverty, and Health Insurance Coverage in the United States: 2010.* U.S. Census Bureau Current Population Reports, P60-239. Washington, DC: U.S. Government Printing Office.

Diez, M. E. & P. E. Murrell, Jr. 2010. "Dispositions in Teacher Education: Starting Points for Consideration." In *Teaching as a Moral Enterprise: Defining, Developing, and Assessing Professional Dispositions in Teacher Education*, edited by P. E. Murrell, M. E. Diez, S. Feiman-Nemser & D. I. Schussler, 7–26. Cambridge, MA: Harvard Education Press.

Domhoff, G. W. 2009. *Who Rules America: Challenges to Corporate and Class Dominance.* New York: McGraw-Hill.

Dunn, B. 2010. "Mi Semestre de Español: A Case Study on the Cultural Dimension of Second-Language Acquisition." In *The Light in Their Eyes: Creating Multicultural Learning Communities*, 10th anniv. ed., by S. Nieto, Multicultural Education Series, 169–75. New York: Teachers College Press.

Elster, A. & J. E. Miller. 2007. *I Still See Her Haunting Eyes: The Holocaust and a Hidden Child Named Aaron.* Peoria, IL: BF Press.

Flores-Gonzalez, N. 2002. *School Kids, Street Kids: Identity and High School Completion Among Latinos.* New York: Teachers College Press.

Freedman, S. W., E. R. Simons, J. S. Kalnin, A. Casareno & M-Class Teams. 1999. *Inside City Schools: Investigating Literacy in Multicultural Classrooms.* New York: Teachers College Press.

Freeman, D. E. & Y. S. Freeman. 2011. *Between Worlds: Access to Second Language Acquisition,* 3rd ed. Portsmouth, NH: Heinemann.

Freeman, Y. S., D. E. Freeman & R. Ramirez, eds. 2008. *Diverse Learners in the Mainstream Classroom: Strategies for Supporting ALL Students Across Content Areas—English Language Learners, Students with Disabilities, Gifted/Talented Students.* Portsmouth, NH: Heinemann.

Freire, P. 1970. *Pedagogy of the Oppressed.* New York: Seabury.

———. 1994. *Pedagogy of Hope: Reliving* Pedagogy of the Oppressed. New York: Continuum.

_____. 1998. *Pedagogy of Freedom: Ethics, Democracy, and Civic Courage.* Lanham, MD: Rowman & Littlefield.

Fryer, R. G. 2011. *Teacher Incentives and Student Achievement: Evidence from New York City Public Schools.* Working Paper 16850. Cambridge, MA: National Bureau of Economic Research.

García, O., J. Kleifgen & L. Falchi. 2008. *From English Language Learners to Emergent Bilinguals.* Equity Matters: Research Review 1. A Research Initiative of the Campaign for Educational Equity. New York: Teachers College, Columbia University.

Garet, M. S., A. C. Porter, L. Desimone, B. F. Birman & K. Y. Suk. 2001. "What Makes Professional Development Effective? Results From a National Sample of Teachers." *American Educational Research Journal* 38 (4): 915–45.

Garland, S. 2011. "High-Stakes Tests and Cheating: An Inevitable Combination?" *The Hechinger Report,* July 6, http://hechingerreport.org/content/high-stakes-tests-and-cheating-an-inevitable -combination_5942/.

Gay, G. 2010. *Culturally Responsive Teaching: Theory, Research, and Practice,* 2nd ed. New York: Teachers College Press.

Gibson, M. 1988. *Accommodation Without Assimilation: Sikh Immigrants in an American High School.* Ithaca, NY: Cornell University Press.

Giroux, H. A. 1988. *Teachers as Intellectuals: Toward a Critical Pedagogy of Learning.* Granby, MA: Bergin & Garvey.

_____. 2010. "Business Culture and the Death of Public Education: The Triumph of Management Over Leadership." *Truthout,* November 12, http://archive.truthout.org/business-culture-and-death -public-education-the-triumph-management-over-leadership65083.

Glass, R. D. & P. L. Wong. 2009. "Making History by Creating New Traditions." In *Prioritizing Urban Children, Teachers, and Schools Through Professional Development Schools,* edited by P. L. Lindquist & R. D. Glass, 229–46. Albany: State University of New York Press.

Glazerman, S., E. Isenberg, S. Dolfin, M. Bleeker, A. Johnson, M. Grider & M. Jacobus. 2010. *Impacts of Comprehensive Teacher Induction: Final Results from a Randomized Controlled Study.* NCEE 2010-4027. Washington, DC: National Center for Education Evaluation and Regional Assistance, Institute of Education Sciences, U.S. Department of Education.

Goodman, J. 2012. *Gold Standards? State Standards Reform and Student Achievement.* Faculty Research Working Paper Series RWP12-031(August). Cambridge, MA: Harvard University Kennedy School.

Goodman, K. S. 1990. "A Declaration of Professional Conscience for Teachers," http://www.rcowen .com/rcoprfdv.htm.

Gorski, P. 2008. "Peddling Poverty for Profit: Elements of Oppression in Ruby Payne's Framework." *Equity & Excellence in Education* 4 (1): 130–48.

Gruenberg, B. 1912. "Some Obstacles to Educational Progress." *American Teacher* I (7): 90.

Haberman, M. 1991. "The Pedagogy of Poverty Versus Good Teaching." *Phi Delta Kapan* 73 (4): 290–94.

_____. 2010. "Consequences of Failing to Address the 'Pedagogy of Poverty.'" *Phi Delta Kappan* 92 (2): 45.

Hanushek, E. A. & S. G. Rivkin. 2010. *Using Value-Added Measures of Teacher Quality.* Brief 9. Washington, DC: National Center for Analysis of Longitudinal Data in Educational Research.

Harry, B. & J. Klingner. 2006. *Why Are So Many Minority Students in Special Education?: Understanding Race and Disability in Schools.* New York: Teachers College Press.

Hill, H. C. 2009. "Fixing Teacher Professional Development." *Phi Delta Kappan* 9 (7): 470–76.

Hinchey, B. 2010. *Getting Teacher Assessment Right: What Policymakers Can Learn from Research.* Boulder, CO: National Education Policy Center.

Irizarry, J. G. 2007. "Ethnic and Urban Intersections in the Classroom: Latino Students, Hybrid Identities, and Culturally Responsive Pedagogy." *Multicultural Perspectives* 9 (3): 1–7.

———. 2010. "Culturally Responsive Pedagogy." In *Classroom Teaching Skills,* 9th ed., edited by J. M. Cooper, 188–214. Boston: Cengage Learning.

———. 2011. *The Latinization of U.S. Schools: Successful Teaching and Learning in Shifting Cultural Contexts.* Boulder, CO: Paradigm.

Irvine, J. J. 2003. *Educating Teachers for Diversity: Seeing With a Cultural Eye.* New York: Teachers College Press.

———. 2010. Foreword to *Culture, Curriculum, and Identity in Education,* 2nd ed., by H. R. Milner IV, xii. New York: Palgrave Macmillan.

Irvine, J. J. & L. T. Fenwick. 2009. *Teachers and Teaching for the New Millennium: The Role of HBCUs.* Washington, DC: U.S. Department of Education and National Board for Professional Teaching Standards.

Irvine, J. J. & J. W. Fraser. 1998. "Warm Demanders." *Education Week* 17 (35): 56.

Irvine, J. J. & W. D. Hawley. 2011. "Culturally Responsive Pedagogy: An Overview of Research on Student Outcomes." Paper presented at the Culturally Responsive Teaching Awards Celebration, Pew Conference Center, Washington, DC, December 9.

Jackson, C. K. & E. Bruegmann. 2009. "Teaching Students and Teaching Each Other: The Importance of Peer Learning for Teachers." *American Economics Journal: Applied Economics* 1 (4): 85–108.

Johnson, J., A. Yarrow, J. Rochkind & A. Ott. 2009. *Teaching for a Living: How Teachers See the Profession Today.* New York: Public Agenda, and Chicago: Learning Points.

Kleinfeld, J. 1975. "Effective Teachers of Eskimo and Indian Students." *School Review* 83: 301–44.

Kohli, R. & D. E. Solórzano. 2012. "Teachers, Please Learn Our Names! Racial Microaggressions and the K–12 Classroom." *Race Ethnicity and Education* 15 (4): 441–62.

Konstantopoulos, S. & V. Chung. 2011. "The Persistence of Teacher Effects in Elementary Grades." *American Educational Research Journal* 48 (2): 361–86.

Kozol, J. 1991. *Savage Inequalities: Children in America's Schools.* New York: Crown.

Krashen, S. 1982. *Principles and Practice in Second Language Acquisition.* New York: Pergamon.

———. 2011. "Broken Schools?" Commencement address at Lewis & Clark's Graduate School of Education and Counseling. http://graduate.lclark.edu/news/story/?id=12363.

Kumashiro, K. K. 2012. *Bad Teacher! How Blaming Teachers Distorts the Bigger Picture.* New York: Teachers College Press.

Ladson-Billings, G. 1995. "Toward a Theory of Culturally Relevant Pedagogy." *American Educational Research Journal* 32: 465–91.

———. 2009. *The Dreamkeepers: Successful Teachers of African American Children,* 2nd ed. San Francisco: Jossey-Bass.

Leana, C. R. 2011. "The Missing Link in School Reform." *Stanford Social Innovation Review* (Fall): 30–35.

Lieberman, A. & L. D. Friedrich. 2010. *How Teachers Become Leaders: Learning from Practice and Research.* New York: Teachers College Press.

Loewen, J. 2009. *Teaching What Really Happened: How to Avoid the Tyranny of Textbooks and Get Students Excited About Doing History.* New York: Teachers College Press.

Long, S., A. Abramson, A. Boone, C. Borchelt, R. Kalish, E. Miller, J. Parks & C. Tisdale. 2006. *Tensions & Triumphs in the Early Years.* Urbana, IL: National Council of Teachers of English.

Maimon, G. 2009. "Practitioner Research as Mediated Emotion." In *Inquiry as Stance: Practitioner Research for the Next Generation*, edited by M. Cochran-Smith & S. Lytle, 213–28. New York: Teachers College Press.

Mathis, W. 2012. *Research-Based Options for Education Policymaking: Teacher Evaluation.* Boulder, CO: National Education Policy Center.

MetLife. 2010. *The MetLife Survey of the American Teacher: Collaborating for Student Success.* New York: MetLife.

MetLife. 2011. *The MetLife Survey of the American Teacher: Preparing Students for College and Careers.* New York: MetLife.

MetLife. 2012. *The MetLife Survey of the American Teacher: Teachers, Parents, and the Economy.* New York: MetLife.

Michie, G. 2012. *We Don't Need Another Hero: Struggle, Hope, and Possibility in the Age of High-Stakes Schooling.* New York: Teachers College Press.

———. 2013. "Back in the Classroom, Testing Is As Bad As I Thought—and Worse." *Huffington Post,* January 14, www.huffingtonpost.com/gregory-michie/standardized-testing_b_2468532.html.

Miner, B. 1998. "Embracing Ebonics and Teaching Standard English: An Interview with Oakland Teacher Carrie Secret." In *The Real Ebonics Debate: Power, Language and the Education of African-American Children*, edited by T. Perry & L. Delpit, 79–88. Boston: Beacon Press.

Moll, L. C. 2010. "Mobilizing Culture, Language, and Educational Practices: Fulfilling the Promises of *Mendez* and *Brown*." Sixth Annual Brown Lecture in Educational Research. *Educational Researcher* 39 (6): 451–60.

Morrell, E. 2008. *Critical Literacy and Urban Youth: Pedagogies of Access, Dissent, and Liberation.* New York: Routledge.

Murrell, P. E. 2001. *The Community Teacher: A New Framework for Effective Urban Teaching.* New York: Teachers College Press.

Murrell, P. E., Jr., M. E. Diez, S. Feiman-Nemser & D. I. Schussler, eds. 2010. *Teaching as a Moral Enterprise: Defining, Developing, and Assessing Professional Dispositions in Teacher Education.* Cambridge, MA: Harvard Education Press.

National Association of Social Workers. 2001. *NASW Standards for Cultural Competence in Social Work Practice.* Washington, DC: NASW.

National Center for Education Statistics. 2011. *Achievement Gaps: How Hispanic and White Students in Public Schools Perform in Mathematics and Reading on the National Assessment of Educational Progress.* Washington, DC: NCES. http://nces.edu.gov/nationsreportcard/studies/gaps/.

National Center for Fair and Open Testing (FairTest). 2012a. "Common Core Assessments: More Tests, but Not Much Better." Fact Sheet. Jamaica Plain, MA: FairTest.

———. 2012b. "How Standardized Testing Damages Education." Fact Sheet. Jamaica Plain, MA: FairTest.

———. 2012c. "What's Wrong With Standardized Tests?" Fact Sheet. Jamaica Plain, MA: FairTest.

———. 2012d. "Why Teacher Evaluation Shouldn't Rest on Student Test Scores." Fact Sheet. Jamaica Plain, MA: FairTest.

National Commission on Excellence in Education. 1983. *Our Nation at Risk: The Imperative for Education Reform.* Washington, DC: US Government Printing Office.

National Commission on Teaching and America's Future. 1996. *What Matters Most: Teaching for America's Future.* New York: NCTAF.

National Council of Teachers of English. 2010. *Teacher Learning Communities: A Policy Research Brief.* Urbana, IL: NCTE.

Newkirk, T. 2013. "Speaking Back to the Common Core." Online postscript to *Holding On to Good Ideas in a Time of Bad Ones* (Heinemann, 2009), http://heinemann.com/shared/onlineresources%5CE02123%5CNewkirk_Speaking_Back_to_the_Common_Core.pdf.

Nichols, S. L. & D. C. Berliner. 2007. *Collateral Damage: How High-Stakes Testing Corrupts America's Schools.* Cambridge, MA: Harvard Education Press.

Nieto, S. 2003. *What Keeps Teachers Going?* New York: Teachers College Press.

———, ed. 2005. *Why We Teach.* New York: Teachers College Press.

———. 2010. *The Light in Their Eyes: Creating Multicultural Learning Environments.* 10th anniv. ed. Multicultural Education Series. New York: Teachers College Press.

———. 2012. "Honoring the Lives of All Children: Identity, Culture, and Language." In *Defending Childhood: Keeping the Promise of Early Education*, edited by B. Falk, 48–62. New York: Teachers College Press.

Nieto, S. & P. Bode. 2012. *Affirming Diversity: The Sociopolitical Context of Multicultural Education.* 6th ed. Boston: Allyn & Bacon.

Nieto, S. & C. Rolón. 1997. "Preparation and Professional Development of Teachers: A Perspective from Two Latinas." In *Critical Knowledge for Diverse Teachers and Learners*, edited by J. Irvine, 93–128. Washington, DC: American Association of Colleges for Teacher Education.

Noddings, N. 1992. *The Challenge to Care in Schools: An Alternative Approach to Education.* New York: Teachers College Press.

Oakes, J. 2005. *Keeping Track: How Schools Structure Inequality.* 2nd ed. New Haven, CT: Yale University Press.

Orfield, G., J. Kucsera & G. Siegel-Hawley. 2012. *E Pluribus . . . Separation: Deepening Double Segregation for More Students.* Los Angeles: The Civil Rights Project/Proyecto Derechos Civiles, University of California, Los Angeles.

Organization for Economic Development and Cooperation. 2011. *Divided We Stand: Why Inequality Keeps Rising.* www.oecd.org/els/social/inequality.

Palmer, P. J. 1998. *The Courage to Teach: Exploring the Inner Landscape of a Teacher's Life.* San Francisco, CA: Jossey-Bass.

Paris, D. 2012. "Culturally Sustaining Pedagogy: A Needed Change in Stance, Terminology, and Practice." *Educational Researcher* 41 (3), 93–97.

Payne, R. 2005. *A Framework for Understanding Poverty*, 4th rev. ed. Highlands, TX: Aha! Process.

E. Pederson, T. A. Faucher & W. W. Eaton. 1978. "A New Perspective on the Effects of First Grade Teachers on Children's Subsequent Status." *Harvard Educational Review* 48: 1–31.

M. Poplin, J. Rivera, D. Durish, L. Hoff, S. Kawell, P. Pawlak, N. S. Hinman, L. Strauss & C. Veney. 2011. "'She's Strict for a Good Reason': Highly Effective Teachers in Low-Performing Urban Schools." *Phi Delta Kappan* 92 (5): 39–43.

Portes, A. & R. Rumbaut. 2006. *Immigrant America: A Portrait*, 3rd ed. Berkeley: University of California Press.

Public Agenda and American Institutes for Research. 2013. *Everyone at the Table: Engaging Teachers in Evaluation Reform.* San Francisco: Jossey-Bass.

Public Education Network. 2004. *Voice of the New Teacher.* Washington, DC: PEN.

Quartz, K. H., B. Olsen, L. Anderson & K. B. Lyons. 2009. *Making a Difference: Developing Meaningful Careers in Education.* Boulder, CO: Paradigm.

Ravitch, D. 2012. *The Death and Life of the Great American School System: How Testing and Choice Are Undermining Education.* New York: Basic Books.

————. 2013, "Why I Oppose Common Core Standards." *Washington Post* Blog, February 26, http://www.washingtonpost.com/blogs/answer-sheet/wp/2013/02/26/why-i-oppose-common-core-standards-ravitch/.

Ready, D. D. & D. L. Wright. 2011. "Accuracy and Inaccuracy in Teachers' Perceptions of Young Children's Cognitive Abilities: The Role of Child Background and Classroom Context." *American Educational Research Journal* 48 (2): 335–60.

Reynolds, A. J., J. A. Temple, B. A. B. White, S.-R. Ou & D. L. Robertson. 2011. "Age 26 Cost-Benefit Analysis of the Child-Parent Center Early Education Program." *Child Development* 82 (1): 379–404.

Richards, J. 2012. "Teacher Stress and Coping Strategies: A National Snapshot." *The Educational Forum* 76 (3): 299–316.

Richardson, J. 2009. "Another Teacher Bites the Dust." Editorial. *Phi Delta Kappan* 91 (2): 4.

Roberts, M. A. 2010. "Toward a Theory of Culturally Relevant Critical Teacher Care: African American Teachers' Definitions and Perceptions of Care for African American Students." *Journal of Moral Education* 39 (4): 449–67.

Rochkind, J., A. Ott, J. Immerwahr, J. Doble & J. Johnson. 2008. *Teaching in Changing Times.* Lessons Learned: New Teachers Talk About Their Jobs, Challenges, and Long-Range Plans, Issue 3. Washington, DC: National Comprehensive Center for Teacher Quality, and New York: Public Agenda.

Rolón-Dow, R. 2005. "Critical Care: A Color(full) Analysis of Care Narratives in the Schooling Experiences of Puerto Rican Girls." *American Educational Research Journal* 42 (1): 77–111.

Ross, S. & J. Agiesta. 2012. "AP Poll: Majority Harbor Prejudice Against Blacks."AP Big Story, October 27, http://bigstory.ap.org/article/ap-poll-majority-harbor-prejudice-against-blacks.

Rothman, R. & L. Darling-Hammond. 2011. *Teacher and School Leader Effectiveness: Lessons Learned from High-Performing Systems.* Issue Brief. Washington, DC: Alliance for Excellent Education.

Rothstein, R. 2004. *Class and Schools: Using Social, Economic, and Educational Reform to Close the Black-White Achievement Gap.* Washington, DC: Economic Policy Institute, and New York: Teachers College Press.

_____. 2010. *How to Fix Our Schools: It's More Complicated, and More Work, Than the Klein-Rhee 'Manifesto' Wants You to Believe.* EPI Issue Brief 286. Washington, DC: Economic Policy Institute.

_____. 2011. "A Dire Prediction: The Achievement Gap Will Grow." The Economic Policy Institute Blog, September 12, http://www.epi.org/blog/dire-prediction-achievement-gap-grow/.

Sadowski, M. 2013. *Portaits of Promise: Voices of Successful Immigrant Students.* Cambridge, MA: Harvard Education Press.

Sato, M. & T. J. Lensmire. 2009. "Poverty and Payne: Supporting Teachers to Work With Children of Poverty." *Phi Delta Kappan* 90 (5): 365–70.

Shor, I. & P. Freire. 1987. *A Pedagogy for Liberation: Dialogues on Transforming Education.* New York: Bergin & Garvey.

Spatig-Amerikaner, A. 2012. *Unequal Education: Federal Loophole Enables Lower Spending on Students of Color.* Education Issues (August 22). Washington, DC: Center for American Progress.

Spring, J. 2013. *Deculturalization and the Struggle for Equality: A Brief History of the Education of Dominated Cultures in the United States*, 7th ed. New York: McGraw-Hill.

Stanton-Salazar, R. D. 2001. *Manufacturing Hope and Despair: The School and Kin Support Networks of U.S.-Mexican Youth.* New York: Teachers College Press.

Strauss, V. 2012. "A 'Value-Added' Travesty for an Award-Winning Teacher." *The Washington Post*, December 3, http://www.washingtonpost.com/blogs/answer-sheet/wp/2012/12/03/a-value-added-travesty-for-an-award-winning-teacher/.

Ullman, C. & J. Hecsh. 2012. "These American Lives: Becoming a Culturally Responsive Teacher and the 'Risks of Empathy.'" *Race Ethnicity and Education* 14 (5): 603–29.

U.S. Department of Education. 2012. "New Data from U.S. Department of Education Highlights Educational Inequities Around Teacher Experience, Discipline, and High School Rigor." Press Release, March 6, Washington, DC. http://www.ed.gov/news/press-releases/new-data-us-department-education-highlights-educational-inequities-around-teacher.

Valenzuela, A. 1999. *Subtractive Schooling: U.S.-Mexican Youth and the Politics of Caring.* Albany: State University of New York Press.

Vasquez, V. 2004. *Negotiating Critical Literacies With Young Children.* New York: Routledge.

Walton, P. H., L. Baca & K. Escamilla. 2002. *A National Study of Teacher Education Preparation for Diverse Student Populations.* Santa Barbara, CA: Center for Research on Education, Diversity, and Excellence.

R. Wei, L. Darling-Hammond & F. Adamson. 2010. *Professional Development in the United States: Trends and Challenges.* Phase 2 of 3. Dallas, TX: National Staff Development Council.

Zemelman, S. & H. Ross. 2009. *13 Steps to Teacher Empowerment: Taking a More Active Role in Your School Community.* Portsmouth, NH: Heinemann.

Zeichner, K. M. 2003. "Pedagogy, Knowledge, and Teacher Preparation." In *Closing the Achievement Gap: A Vision for Changing Beliefs and Practices*, 2nd ed., edited by B. Williams, 99–114. Alexandria, VA: Association for Supervision and Curriculum Development.

Zientek, L. R. 2007. "Preparing High-Quality Teachers: Views from the Classroom." *American Educational Research Journal* 44 (4): 959–1001.

Zinn, H. 2010. *A People's History of the United States.* New York: Harper Perennial Modern Classics.

INDEX

A

AACTE (American Association of Colleges for Teachers Education), 23

Accountability. *See also* Standardization; Testing
 concerns with, 17, 122, 136
 culture of, 1, 89
 and marketization, 5–9, 27
 marketization and, 4
 reasons for, 4
 standardization and, 103–105, 148

Achieve funding, 7

Achievement gap
 narrowing of, 22
 "out of school factors," 10
 race/ethnicity, xiii, 7–10, 15, 27

Acosta, Curtis, 111

ACT, 6

Additive Schooling in Subtractive Times (Bartlett & García), 88

Advisory groups, 150

Advocacy, 106, 107–109, 122, 134–135

African Americans
 barriers for, 9–10
 culture of, 54–55, 102, 108
 poverty and, 12, 73
 teachers as, 15, 17, 19, 34, 41–42

Alcazar, Carmen, 75, 85, 86

Alliance for Excellent Education, 24

American Association of Colleges for Teacher Education (AACTE), 23

American Indians, 9, 17, 53, 69

American Institutes for Research, 29

American Teacher, The, 4

Anyon, Jean, 10–11

Artiles, Alfredo, 13

Asian Americans, 9, 12, 16, 17, 66, 69, 109, 128

Assessments, 28–29, 144. *See also* Testing

Associated Press, 12

Au, Wayne, 6

B

Bad Teacher! How Blaming Teachers Distorts the Bigger Picture (Kumashiro), 27

Ball, Deborah, 19

Bartolomé, Lila, 22

Bechard, Amber
 caring, 148

 challenging the status quo, 133
 culturally responsive, 56–57, 140–141
 identity, 36, 132
 lifelong learning, 61–62, 128–129
 moral responsibility, 47, 51–53, 127
 relationships, 150, 153
 social justice educator, 107
 thriving, 148

Benítez, Griselda
 caring, 149
 challenging the status quo, 132
 honoring families, 143
 personal experiences, 80
 relationships, 85, 86, 89
 social justice educator, 107–108

Berriz, Berta, 149

Bigelow, Bill, 62, 115

Blue Eyes/Brown Eyes (Elliott), 104

Bode, Patty, 12, 141

Bruegmann, Elias, 26

Bullough, Robert, 17, 145

Bush, George W., 5

C

Caroll, Tom, 27

Catcher in the Rye (Salinger), 119

Caucus of Rank and File Educators (CORE), 50

CCSS, 5, 6–7

Center for American Progress, 9

Center for English Learners, 75

Center on Education Policy, 7

Challenge to Care in Schools, The (Nodding), 34

Challenging the status quo, 132–134

Chauncey, Caroline, 14

Chican@ Movement, 111

Children's Defense Fund, 9–11

Christensen, Linda, 62, 115

Chung, Vicki, 14

Civil Rights Project, 9

Cochran-Smith, Marilyn, 21–22

Coggshall, Jane, 27

College Board, 6

Common Core State Standards (CCSS), 5, 6–7

Community circles, 85–86, 132, 143, 149, 151

"Community teachers," 24

Condition of Education, The (Aud), 16

Cook, Kim, 28

Corcoran, Sean, 28

CORE (Caucus of Rank and File Educators), 50
Cowhey, Mary, 115–116
Critical discourse, 116–117
Cultural competence, 137
Culturally responsive teachers, 40–44, 53,
    56–58, 137–141

D
Darling-Hammond, Linda, 8, 10–11, 15, 23–24,
    29
Davis, Jacqueline, 41
*Declaration of Professional Conscience for
    Teachers, A* (Goodman), 4
Delpit, Lisa, 43, 96, 139
Dialogue, 67, 117–118, 119
Diversity
    Blue Eyes/Brown Eyes (Elliott), 104
    CCSS, 7
    demographics of, 15–17
    mentor effectiveness, 26
    premature assimilation, 78
    professional development for, 20, 23–24,
        29–30
    study groups, 26–27
    teachers and, 23–27, 139
    views on, 42–44, 53, 56–58, 113
Domhoff, G. William, 118
Dreamkeepers, The (Ladson-Billings), 53
Dunn, Bill, v, 142–143

E
Ebonics, 54
Elliott, Jane, 104
Elster, Aaron, 52–53
Emergent bilinguals, 76–77
Empathy, instilling values of, 48–53, 126
Engaged pedagogy, 139
Environment
    cultural, 97–98, 100
    foster humanity, 35, 99
    learning, 21, 106, 133, 140
    negative, 59
    school condition, 11–14
Escalante, Jaime, 79
Ethics, 22, 26–28, 53–58, 127–128
Ethnic Studies Program, 112–113
*Everyone at the Table: Engaging Teachers
    in Evaluation Reform* (Public Agenda and
    American Institutes for Research), 29
Expectations gap, 12, 17

F
FairTest, 6, 8, 28, 158
Fajardo, Angela
    identity, 131
    personal experiences, 75, 79–80
    relationships, 86, 88, 89–90
Fecho, Bob, 110
Federico Brummer, María
    advocacy, 135
    challenging the status quo, 132
    culturally responsive, 53
    identity, 36
    love of students, 126
    program lawsuit, 121
    social justice educator, 110–113, 117
    student relationships, 120
Fences, 119
Fenwick, Leslie, 99
Fleming, Jennifer, 82, 88
Forzani, Francesca, 19
Fraser, James, 142
Freire, Paulo, 21, 74, 107, 113, 118,
    145
Fryer, Roland, 136

G
Garet, Michael, 25
Gates Foundation, 7
Gelzinis, Karen, v
Gibson, Margaret, 78
Giroux, Henry, 4, 61
Glass, Ronald, 139
Golden Apple Award, 130
Goodman, Joshua, 5
Goodman, Kenneth, 4
Gorski, Paul, 11
Guerrero, María
    advocacy, 134
    challenging the status quo, 133
    personal experiences, 80, 81
    relationships, 85, 87, 89, 150
    social justice educator, 127–128
Gunderson, John
    advocacy, 134
    challenging the status quo, 133
    identity, 35
    life of service, 98
    love of students, 126
    moral responsibility, 48
    self-reflection for diversity, 139

student dreams, 92, 95–97
student relationships, 99–100, 103–104
teaching expectations, 155–156
thriving, 147–148

H
Haberman, Martin, 22–23
Harris, Yolanda
    identity, 131
    life of service, 98
    student dreams, 92
    student relationships, 99, 101,
        102–103
Hawley, Willis, 111
Hecsh, J., 126
Heenan, Adam
    caring, 149
    challenging the status quo, 132
    culturally responsive pedagogies, 57–58
    Golden Apple Award, 130
    lifelong learning, 130
    moral responsibility, 47, 49–51
    serving community, 127
    social justice educator, 107–108
    thriving, 148
Hill, Heather, 25
Holocaust, 52–53
Horne, Tom, 113
How Standardized Testing Damages Education
    (National Center for Fair and Open Testing), 7

I
Identity, 33–44, 110, 130–132
Ideologies, 12–13
Irizarry, Jason, 137–138
Irvine, Jacqueline, 8, 99, 142

J
Jackson, C. Kirabo, 26
Jefferson, Thomas, 52
Jim Crow laws, 9
Joyner, Tom, 55

K
Kleinfeld, Judith, 141
Kohli, Rita, 131
Konstantopoulos, Spyros, 14
Kozol, Jonathan, 66, 127
Krashen, Stephen, 10, 142
Kumashiro, Kevin, 27

L
Ladson-Billings, Gloria, 53, 137
Lama, Dalai, 52
Lasagna, Molly, 27
Latino/Hispanic, 7–8, 15–16, 53. *See also*
    Mexican Americans
Lavadenz, Magaly, xiv, 75
Law suits, 112, 113, 121
Laws, Jim Crow, 9
Le, Annie, 133
Leana, Carrie, 26
Learning. *See also* Professional development
    environment, 21, 106, 133, 140
    lifelong, 61–62, 128–129
Learning Point Associates, 14
Lensmire, Timothy, 11
Loewen, James, 115
López, Alicia
    identity, 131
    lifelong learning, 62, 66–73, 128
    relationships, 153
    serving community, 127
    thriving, 147
Loyola Marymount University
    Alcazar, Carmen, 85–87
    Benítez, Griselda, 80, 85, 86, 89
    Fajardo, Angela, 79–80, 86, 88, 89–90
    Fleming, Jennifer, 82, 88
    general, xiv, 135, 143
    Guerrero, María, 80, 81, 85, 87, 89
    Meza Buenrostro, Maricela, 78–79, 82, 90
    Olmedo, Gabriela, 84–85, 86
    Ornelas, Leticia, 80–82, 84, 86
    Pérez, Angeles, 82
    Shibata, Katie, 83, 90

M
Maimon, Gillian, xv
Marketization, 4, 5–9, 27
Media teachers, 30
Mentoring
    students, 36, 99, 112, 131
    teachers, 25–26, 36, 61, 99, 153
MetLife studies, 14, 15, 20, 26
Mexican American Studies, 111, 113, 117,
    132, 135
Mexican Americans, 9, 34, 37, 111, 120
Meza Buenrostro, Maricela
    challenging the status quo, 132
    culturally responsive, 140

identity, 131
personal experiences, 75, 78
relationships, 82
thriving, 90
Michie, Greg, 8, 155
Microaggressions, 131
Mir, Asiya, 111
Moll, Luis, 27
Morrell, Ernest, 34–35
Multicultural perspectives, 51, 56
Murrell, Peter, 24

N
Nam, Hyung
challenging the status quo, 133
lifelong learning, 62, 127
relationships, 150
social justice educator, 106, 113–115,
121–122, 128
thriving, 146–147, 154
using dialogue, 118–119
Nation at Risk, A (National Commission of
Excellence in Education), 3
National Board for Professional Teaching
Standards, 29
National Center for Education Evaluation, 26
National Center for Education Statistics, 7, 16
National Center for Fair and Open Testing
(FairTest), 6, 8, 28, 158
National Council for the Social Studies,
143–144
National Council of Teachers of English, 27
National Endowment for the Humanities, 30,
61–62, 116, 129
National Foundation for Educational Research,
108
National Governors Association, 7
National Writing Project, 29, 69–70, 73
Native Americans, 9, 17, 53, 69
NCLB (No Child Left Behind), 5, 8
Newkirk, Thomas, 6
Nguyen, John
advocacy, 108, 134
challenging the status quo, 133–134
identity, 36, 131–132
lifelong learning, 62, 63–66, 128, 130,
143
professional development, 30
relationships, 153

self-reflection, 150
thriving, 73, 154
No Child Left Behind (NCLB), 5, 8
Noddings, Nel, 34

O
Obama, Barack, 5, 12
Office for Civil Rights, 19, 113
Olmedo, Gabriela, 75, 84–85, 134, 135
Opportunity gaps, 8–9
Organization for Economic Development and
Cooperation, 11
Ornelas, Leticia, 75, 80–82, 84, 86
Other People's Children (Delpit), 96, 139
Ott, Amber, 27
"Out-of-school factors," 10

P
Palmer, Parker, 35, 78
Paris, Django, 138
Payne, Ruby, 11
Pedagogy
culturally relevance of, 137–141
culturally responsiveness of, 53–58
engaged, 139
of poverty, 22–23
social justice, 117–119
"Pedagogy of poverty," 22–23
Pedagogy of the Oppressed (Freire), 113
People's History of the United States, A (Zinn),
115
Pérez, Angeles
advocacy, 134
caring, 45
challenging the status quo, 132–133
honoring families, 143
identity, 34, 35, 36–40, 131
love of students, 126
relationships, 82
thriving, 148
Perspectives
multicultural, 51, 56
social justice, 20–23, 49, 107, 133,
154
Perspectives for a Diverse America (Teaching
Tolerance), 7
Peterson, Bob, 62
Philadelphia Writing Project, 62, 110, 129,
141

Pincus, Marcia, 110
Politics and social justice, 21–22
Portes, Alejandro, 78
Poverty
  achievement gap, 9
  breakdown, 16
  "out of school factors," 10
  pedagogy of, 22–23
  statistics, 10–11
"Premature assimilation," 78
Professional development. *See also* Learning
  on diversity, 20, 23–24, 29–30
  mentoring, 24–26
  National Endowment for the Humanities, 116
  National Writing Project, 70
  on poverty, 11
  from professional organizations, 69–71
  in-service, 5, 26–27, 61
  teacher satisfaction, 14
Public Agenda, 14, 29
Public Education Network, 26
Puntel, Christina, 62

Q
Quartz, Karen Hunter, 24, 31

R
Race to the Top (RttT), 5, 6–7
Race/ethnicity, xiii, 7–10, 15, 27. *See also* Diversity
"Racialization of ability," 13
Ramírez Acevedo, María
  identity, 35
  life of service, 97–98
  relationships, 153
  student dreams, 92, 94–95
  student relationships, 99–100, 102
  thriving, xiv, 147
Ravitch, Diane, 6–7
Raza Cities Team, 111
Ready, Douglas, 15
Responsibility, instilling values of, 48–53
Rethinking Globalization (Bigelow and Peterson), 62
Rethinking Schools, 62, 114, 115, 154
Richardson, Joan, 3
Rigor, through CCSS, 5, 7
Roberts, Mari Ann, 34

Rolón Carmen, 137
Rolón-Dow, Rosalie, 34
Ross, Harry, 150
Rothstein, Richard, 28
RttT, 5, 6–7
Rumbaut, Rubén, 78

S
SASS (Schools and Staffing Survey), 26
Sato, Mistilina, 11
Savage Inequalities (Kozol), 66, 127
School environment, 11–14
Schools and Staffing Survey (SASS), 26
Segregation, 9, 88
Shibata, Katie, 75, 83, 90, 128
Shor, Ira, 118
Social justice
  components of, 21, 106
  and curriculum, 115–117
  defined, 21
  dialogue, 117–118
  educator, 106–108, 109–117, 121–122, 127–128, 133–144
  examples of, 107–119
  pedagogy of, 117–119
  perspectives, 20–23, 49, 107, 133, 154
  and relationships, 119–122
Social reformers, 24
Societal barriers, 9–11
Sociocultural consciousness, 126
Solórzano, Daniel, 131
Southern Poverty Law Center (SPLC), 7
Special education, 12–13
Standardization, xv, 4, 47, 103–105, 148. *See also* Accountability; Testing
Student achievement
  learning environment, 21
  teacher collaboration and, 26
  teacher influence on, 13–14
  teacher preparation and, 23–27
  through CCSS, 5
Students
  dehumanization, 22
  dreams, 92, 94–97
  emergent bilingual, 76–77
  identities, 130–132
  mentoring, 36, 99, 112, 131
  moral responsibility, 48
  relationships, 34, 98–104, 120

and teacher caring, 34–36, 44–46
and teacher expectations of, 15
Study groups, 26–27

T
Teach for America, 10, 25, 107
Teacher stories
  Alcazar, Carmen, 85–87
  Bechard, Amber, 51–53, 56–57
  Benítez, Griselda, 80, 85, 86, 89
  Fajardo, Angela, 79–80, 86, 88, 89–90
  Federico Brummer, María, 109
  Fleming, Jennifer, 82, 88
  Guerrero, María, 80, 81, 85, 87
  Gunderson, John, 95–97
  Harris, Yolanda, 92–94
  Heenan, Adam, 49–51, 57–58
  López, Alicia, 66–73
  Meza Buenrostro, Maricela, 78–79, 82, 90
  Nam, Hyung, 109, 113–115
  Nguyen, John, 63–66
  Olmedo, Gabriela, 84–85, 86
  Ornelas, Leticia, 80–82, 84, 86
  Pérez, Angeles, 36–40, 82
  Ramírez Acevedo, María, 35, 94–95, 97-98, 100
  Shibata, Katie, 83, 90
  Tisdale, Carmen, 48–49, 53–55
  Wallace, Roger, 40–44
  Winikur, Geoffrey, 109–110
Teachers. *See also* Teacher stories
  advocacy, 106–109, 122, 134–135
  and caring, 34–36, 44–46, 148–149
  challenging the status quo, 132–134
  collaboration, 26–27
  and community, 24, 127
  culturally responsive, 40–44, 53, 56–58, 137–141
  culture of hope and happiness for, 145–146
  diversity of, 17, 23–27, 139
  effectiveness, 6
  ethical choices, 22, 26–28, 53–58, 127–128
  evaluations, 27–29
  expectations, 155–156
  honoring families, 142–143
  identity, 33–44, 110, 130–132
  incentives, 136
  influence of, 13
  learn about your students, 150
  life of service, 97–98

life-long learners, 60–63, 66–73, 127–130, 143
love of students, 126–127
mentoring of, 25–26, 36, 61, 99, 153
mentoring students, 36, 99, 112, 131
as moral endeavor, 127–128
moral responsibility of, 47–53, 127
multicultural, 20
nontraditional pathways for, 25
preparation, 3, 23–27, 61, 63, 110, 129, 153
qualifications, 15
quality, 27–29
relationships, 82, 85–90, 99–100, 103–104, 150, 153
retention, 27
satisfaction, 14–15
self-reflection, 139–140, 150
social justice, 106–117, 121–122, 127–128, 138–144
as social reformers, 24
socio-cultural consciousness, 126
student expectations, 15
student relationships with, 34, 98–104, 119–120
thriving, xiv, 48, 73, 146–148, 154
value language and culture, 140–141
visit the community, 151–152
voice, 108
Teaching
  advocacy in, 122
  as a craft, 60
  critical discourse, 116–117
  diversity, 20, 27
  social justice, 115–122
Teaching for a Living, 14
Teaching Tolerance (TT), 7
Teaching What Really Happened: How to Avoid the Tyranny of Textbooks and Get Students Excited About Doing History (Loewen), 115
Testing. *See also* Accountability; Assessments; Standardization
  affects of high stakes, 7, 89, 91
  marketization, 4
  standardization, 10, 29, 78, 114, 126
  teacher evaluations through, 6, 27–28
Things Fall Apart, 119
Things They Carried, The, 119
Thriving, xiv, 48, 73, 89, 146–148, 154
Tisdale, Carmen

advocacy, 134–135
and community, 53–55
culturally responsive pedagogies, 61
honoring families, 143
identity, 131
inspiring students, 127
love of students, 126
moral responsibility, 48–49
relationships, 152–153
social justice educator, 107
student expectations, 142
thriving, 147

U
UCLA Teacher Education Program, 24
Ullman, C., 126
U.S. Census Bureau, 9–11, 77
U.S. Department of Justice, 111

V
Valenzuela, Angela, 34, 120
Value-added assessments, 29
Vasquez, Vivian, 116

W
"Walking sets of deficiencies," xv
Wallace, Roger
    advocacy, 135
    caring, 45
    culturally responsive, 40–44
    identity, 33, 34
    learn about your students, 152

lifelong learning, 128
love of students, 126, 127
self-reflection for diversity, 140
thriving, 148
Warm demanders, 141–142
We Don't Need Another Hero (Michie), 155
Wei, Ruth Chung, 23, 25, 26
Western Massachusetts Writing Project (WMWP),
    69
Who Rules America? (Domhoff), 118
Winikur, Geoffrey
    books used by, 119
    culturally responsive, 53
    curriculum integrity, 121
    identity, 132
    learn about your students, 150
    lifelong learning, 62, 128–129
    multicultural curriculum, 128
    professional development, 29–30
    relationships, 152
    social justice educator, 109–110, 116
    student expectations, 141–142
    student relationships, 120
    thriving, 146, 148
    warm demander, 141–142
Wong, Pia, 139
Wright, David, 15

Z
Zeichner, Kenneth, 22
Zemelman, Steven, 150
Zinn, Howard, 115